THE BAILIWICK OF JERSEY

THE QUEEN'S CHANNEL ISLANDS

The Bailiwick of Jersey
The Bailiwick of Guernsey

THE KING'S ENGLAND

Edited by Arthur Mee

In 41 Volumes

ENCHANTED LAND (INTRODUCTORY VOLUME)

THE QUEEN'S CHANNEL ISLANDS

THE BAILIWICK OF JERSEY

By
G. R. BALLEINE, M.A.

Fully revised and edited by
JOAN STEVENS, F.S.A.

Illustrated with new photographs by
A. F. KERSTING

Map by
Charles Stevens

HODDER AND STOUGHTON

Printed in Great Britain
for Hodder and Stoughton Limited,
St. Paul's House, Warwick Lane, London, E.C.4,
by Richard Clay (The Chaucer Press), Ltd.,
Bungay, Suffolk

INTRODUCTION
TO THE REVISED EDITION

THIS book was written by the late Rev. G. R. Balleine. He first wrote it in 1951, and there was a reprint in 1962. Such was its success that the publishers have decided on a revised edition, in order to incorporate changes which have taken place in the intervening years.

It has been an honour for me to undertake this work, for I remember the late Mr Balleine as a friend and as a teacher. He turned the long weary years of the German Occupation to good account, and to the great benefit of posterity, by compiling *A History of the Island of Jersey* and *A Biographical Dictionary of Jersey*, soon to be followed by *The Bailiwick of Jersey* in this present series. All who wish to know about Jersey, be they visitors, residents, students, or research workers, owe him a debt of gratitude for these scholarly works. I know that he would have been the first to welcome well founded corrections, and to hail with delight the results of research which has continued since his death. Nothing would have pleased him more than to know that work had not ceased, and that constant additions were being made to our knowledge of the history of the Island he loved.

Some inconsistencies may be noticed in place names, in indexing, and in choice of either French or English terms and phrases. These, though not intentional as such, underline the bi-lingualism of Jersey, and its historical and cultural position as a link between England and Normandy.

As Mr Balleine said in his original preface, the writer of such a book as this cannot, and should not, pretend to knowledge of all the subjects covered. So, like him, I have consulted friends and officials on many points, and though it is not possible to name them all, special mention may be made of the following:

Mr A. H. Ewen (Neolithic archaeology); Mr R. Falle, F.R.S.A. (The Public Library); Mr Richard Falle (legal matters); Mr R. Lemprière (theatre); Mr R. Long (entomology); Mr F. Le Ruez (agriculture); Mrs F. Le Sueur (botany and ornithology); Dr C. McBurney, F.S.A. (Palaeolithic archaeology); Dr A. E. Mourant,

F.R.S. (geology and archaeology); Mr A. B. Porter and Mr P. Ahier (many points of interest).

To them all, I am most grateful for their co-operation.

Joan Stevens,
La Grange,
St Mary,
Jersey.

1969

LIST OF ILLUSTRATIONS

ILLUSTRATIONS

THE BAILIWICK OF
JERSEY

INTRODUCING JERSEY

A HUNDRED miles south of Portland Bill, in the great bay of northern France that separates Normandy from Brittany, lies the oldest part of the Queen's dominions, a small group of rocky islands, of which the southernmost is Jersey. Speaking unscientifically, this may be described as an oblong block of granite, roughly nine miles by five, tilted to catch every ray of the southern sun. A geologist would no doubt point out that much that looks like granite to the untutored eye is, strictly speaking, syenite or diorite or rhyolite, and that in any case part of the east of the Island is conglomerate and part of the west is shale, but the impression left on the visitor is that wherever he goes he meets granite, sometimes red, sometimes blue, sometimes grey, sometimes orange—granite cliffs, granite castles, granite churches, granite farms, granite piers and pavements. The splendidly rugged precipices of the north coast, honeycombed with innumerable caves, are from 250 to 460 feet high, and from them the land slopes gently down till it reaches sea-level on the sandy beaches of the south. Tiny streams, running south have cut the interior into deep and winding valleys. Thanks to the Gulf Stream, the Island enjoys exceptionally mild winters. The rainfall is high (an average of 44″ annually), tides are exceptionally high and low at the full moon, and particularly at the equinox, and sunshine records equal, and often top, those of any part of the British Isles. Sub-tropical trees like the palm and the eucalyptus flourish; the camellias are often a blaze of crimson at Christmas, while the banks of mesembryanthemum in summer positively make one blink. Magnolia and mimosa can be found in many gardens, and the so-called Jersey lily (*Amaryllis belladonna*) springs up through the gravel and cheers the heart in autumn. Wild flowers abound. On the bleakest cliffs the spring daffodils, or Lent lilies (*Narcissus pseudo narcissus*) push up their heads through the dead bracken, and in every inland valley, though they grace none of the other Channel Islands. Almost every type of common flower grows luxuriantly, together with many plants rarely found in England. In early summer the granite walls are draped with a tiny daisy, the Mexican Fleabane

I

(*Conyza candensis*) which is not indigenous, but flourishes with us, as does the Tree Lupin (*Lupinus arboreus*), introduced from California, which grows on great areas of sand dune, with its bushes of silver grey, covered with sweet smelling spikes of pale yellow lupin flowers. The Jersey Orchid (*Orchis laxiflora*) or Loose-flowered Orchid, while being common on the Continent, appears only in Jersey among the British Isles.

Of the present inhabitants about half live in the town of St Helier. There are two townlets, St Aubin and Gorey, which owed their origin to artificial causes that have now passed away, as well as a fast growing centre on the high land above St Brelade's Bay, where widespread development has taken place since the war. But typical Jerseymen have always lived on scattered farms with their own fields around them, farms that have never clustered in groups, but are sprinkled fairly evenly over the whole countryside, and small clusters with such names as Ville ès Normans and Ville ès Philippes, indicating where a family group built their houses. One surprising feature of the Island is the size of its population. Whereas Ireland has 111 persons to the square mile, France 192, and the Isle of Man 220, Jersey has well over a thousand permanent residents to the square mile, to say nothing of nearly half a million visitors who flock over in the summer. Yet there is still plenty of elbow-room.

It was not always its present shape or size. Once it formed part of the mainland, a mere bulge on the coast of France; but with the rise or fall in the amount of water in the Channel, it has several times been separated, rejoined, and separated again. Raised beaches, that is areas of sea worn pebbles can be seen on its cliffs 30 feet, 60 feet, and 130 feet above the present high-water level. So for three different long periods, while waves rolled those stones about till their edges disappeared, all the lower-lying parts of the Island must have been fathoms-deep under the sea. On the other hand low tides reveal in St Ouen's Bay and elsewhere stumps of a great oak forest that once stretched out towards Guernsey. When those trees grew acorns, Jersey must have been more than twice its present size. But all these changes took place long before history began.

There is a widespread belief that Jersey was called Cæsarea in early times, based on a route list, issued by Rome to guide

officials on their journeys, which makes the ship after leaving
Vecta (the Isle of Wight) and before reaching Uxantis (Ushant)
pass three islands, Riduna, Sarnia, and Cæsarea, which may be,
though this is disputed by many authorities, Alderney, Guernsey,
and Jersey. After the Barbarian Invasion of the Dark Ages, however,
the Island had a new name, which monkish chroniclers of the 6th
century Latinised as Angia or Agna or Andium. The name Jersey
(which early documents usually spelt with a G) appears for the first
time in a charter of 1025 after the coming of the Normans. The
final syllable "ey" is the Norse word for "island", which occurs
again in Guerns-ey, Aldern-ey, Chaus-ey, Angles-ey, Shepp-ey,
and a score of other islands. The meaning of "Gers-" is more
doubtful. It may perhaps come from the old Frisian "*gers*", which
means "grass", in which case Gers-ey would mean "Grassy Isle".
Or, since Geirr was a Norwegian personal name, this may have
been the name of the Viking who seized the Island, which would
then be known as Geirres ey.

Many races have coalesced to form its population. The first
inhabitants, the pre-Neanderthal and cave men, evidence of whom
has survived in the two caves called La Cotte, one in St Brelade
and one in St Ouen, left no descendants, but from at least 6000
B.C. the Island has been continuously inhabited, since traces of
Mesolithic hunters occur here and there. First came groups of a
small, dark, pre-Celtic, agricultural race, called, perhaps wrongly,
"Iberian". They were the people who covered the island with
enormous stone tombs for their dead, most of which were long ago
broken up for building material; but seven impressive specimens
survive, including La Hougue Bie, which is said to be the finest in
Western Europe. They were followed by fair-haired Gauls. Then
for five hundred years, Jersey formed part of the Roman Empire.
Roman coins, which were used throughout the whole western world
for commerce, are sometimes dug up in the Island, but there are
no remains of Roman forts, Roman roads, or Roman villas, which
suggests that few, if any, Romans settled here. When Rome fell, the
Franks became the new masters of the Island; but they too, were
content to rule without colonising. About A.D. 525, however, some
of St Samson's Christian Britons, squeezed out of Cornwall and
Devon by crowds of refugees who were pouring in to escape the

3

Anglo-Saxon invaders, landed here, while the main body passed on and settled round St Malo. For the next two centuries intercourse with Brittany must have been very close. Whatever may be the truth about the Belgian hermit, St Helier, most of the work of converting the island to Christianity was done by Celtic missionary monks, who may have come from the monastery which St Magloire established in Sark. Strangely few traces, however, remain of this connection with Brittany. The coming of the Vikings seems to have stamped it out. None of the Island's present place names are of Celtic origin, except possibly Pontac, and none of the churches except St Brelade's is dedicated to a Celtic Saint.

The people who left the deepest mark on the island were the Northmen or Normans. Scandinavian pirates, coming from Norway, Sweden, or Denmark, after more than a century of murderous raids in which they spared no one and nothing in their search for loot, conquered the slice of northern France, which then became known as Normandy, and in 933 added the Channel Islands to their Duchy. They did not exterminate their Gaulish and "Iberian" predecessors, though many of these must have lost their lives in the century of devastation. But large numbers of Normans evidently settled in the Island, for the typical Jerseyman today, in his sturdy independence, his self-reliance, his shrewdness at a bargain, his tremendous industry, his reticence, his thrift, is almost the exact counterpart of the Norman across the water. It is often claimed that Jerseymen sailed with Duke William in the invasion of 1066, but there is no proof of this. Men with family names which occur in Jersey appear in Duke William's army, notably Malet, Giffard, and de Carteret, but this in no way proves they were domiciled in Jersey.

The old Norman-French which the Conqueror spoke still survives in the country districts. If a Jerseyman says *vaîsîn* for *voisin* or *tchéthue* for *charrue*, so did William. One sample will be sufficient. Bishop Jeune of Peterborough was a Jerseyman. On a visit to the Island he wished to show a friend that he had not forgotten his native tongue. Meeting two little girls, one of whom had something rolled up in her apron, he asked her what she was carrying. *"Tches-un-cakjai,"* she replied. When the Bishop looked puzzled, her com-

A Jersey cow (*A. G. Le Moeur*)

A cider crusher

Bouley Bay, looking east

The lavoir at St Cyr

La Corbière Lighthouse

Elizabeth Castle

The Queen Elizabeth Gate
at the Castle, built in 1600

panion explained, *"Tches-un-cakoula."* The Bishop had to own himself beaten. In modern French the sentences would run, *C'est un chat que j'ai* (It's a cat I have); *C'est un chat qu'elle a* (It's a cat she has). Till quite recently French, but not Jersey-French, was the official language of the Island and was used in all public notices, in the Courts and the States and the Churches. But the great invasion of English residents, which began in Victorian times, together with the influence of English-trained teachers in the schools and the far-reaching effects of radio and television, has made English the dominant language. It was a sign of the end when, in 1900, the use of English was made optional in the States, and one by one all the Churches have dropped their French services. But the older Jersey folk are tri-lingual, speaking either language with equal facility, and sometimes a mixture of the two. On market day one can overhear such phrases as *"Il a bousseté san tyre"* or *"J'soumes okay; et té?"* and even *"Le Docteur m'a dit que je* better remain in bed" clearly quoting what the doctor had said in the language in which it had been said. The local language was given a tremendous boost by the German Occupation during the last war, when it was the perfect medium of conversation, and incomprehensible to the occupying forces. Shortly afterwards an organisation, L'Assembliée d'Jèrriais, was formed to preserve it, and recently a magnificent *Dictionnaire Jersiais-Français,* by F. Le Maistre, was published. Although the terms are translated into French, the English counterparts are frequently given. The preservation of the language is thus ensured for all time.

The Laws of Jersey are somewhat different from those of England, mainly in matters concerning wills, intestacy, and real property. Any English solicitor would be at sea if he tried to intervene in a Jersey lawsuit; for the Normans fixed their legal system so firmly on the Island that Jersey law today is still based on the *Grand Coutumier de Normandie.* For example, if someone starts to cut down one of your trees, you have only to raise the *Clameur de Haro,* to shout aloud in the presence of witnesses, *"Haro! haro! haro! à l'aide mon Prince. On me fait tort* (Haro! haro! haro! Help me, my Prince! I am being wronged)", and the aggressor is bound under heavy penalties to desist until the rights and wrongs of the case have been investigated by the Court, a custom that has much to be said in its favour, for otherwise the tree would be down before the Court could intervene. Although seldom used, and applicable only to harm being done to your real property, this is a dramatic ritual of great antiquity, which offers immediate redress. By invoking not only the Duke, founder of the Norman state, but also the fount of justice, the injured person asserts his identity as a member of that Norman society. If properly raised, that is with justification, the defendant must pay the fine imposed by the Court, as well as ceasing the injury he was committing. But if raised wrongly, *à tort*, the party who thus unjustifiably invokes this solemn procedure is himself fined. The *Clameur de Haro* was last raised both *à tort* (wrongly) and *à bon droit* (rightly) in 1968. A good deal has been done, starting with the 1880 reforms of the then Bailiff, Sir R. P. Marett, to simplify and modernise the old legal system, specially in regard to the tenure, inheritance, and conveyance of real property, but always on independent lines, though with an increasing tendency to uniformity with England.

The Feudal System is a Norman legacy that the Island even yet has not quite shaken off. Although the Islands came under the official jurisdiction of William Longsword in the middle of the 10th century, we do not know how much direct effect this had. But by the time of William the Conqueror, land was being divided up, the Duke keeping much for himself, and this became known as Fief du Roi, and is still so known. The rest of the land he granted to favourites and to great religious houses, and the Island was parcelled out into these fiefs, varying greatly in size and importance. All had the right to hold seigneurial courts, and did so. Not all had manor houses. If visitors hope to find the Island full of exciting old manor-houses with secret passages, haunted chambers, dungeons, and minstrel galleries, they will be disappointed. Prosperous seigneurs of later years naturally valued comfort more than mediaeval quaintness, and modernised their houses. Rozel was entirely rebuilt in 1770, and further altered in 1820. Samarès can show little that is old but the crypt of its manorial chapel and its colombier. Trinity was greatly altered in 1910, though much of the 17th century house remains. Even at St Ouen where a good deal of the ancient work survives, the restoration was so enthusiastically drastic that it is extremely difficult to disentangle the old from the new. At St Ouen,

6

however, and at Rozel the pre-reformation manorial chapels still stand; and several even of the lesser manors preserve their colombiers, great towers with nesting-holes for hundreds of pigeons, which ensured for the seigneur a constant supply of pigeon pie. Permission to build one of these was a highly prized privilege, but they were naturally unpopular with the neighbouring farmers whose crops the birds devoured. So a colombier lifted the manor that possessed it high up on the list of precedence. Down to the 18th century tenants had to cut the seigneur's hay, cart his wood and wine, and perform innumerable other duties, including the cleaning out of the colombier. Most of these dues have long disappeared, but one outrageous one survived until 1966. If a man died without direct heirs of his body, i.e., if his property was inherited by a nephew or a niece, the seigneur seized the income of the estate for a year and a day, an act reminiscent of the days of the robber barons! However the Assize d'Héritage continues; it is a sitting of the heritage division of the Royal Court, at which the seigneurs of certain fiefs attend, and answer when the name of their fief is called, signifying their loyalty to the sovereign.

To return, however, to our history. When William of Normandy conquered England in 1066, he did not annex Jersey to his new domain. It remained part of the old duchy. It still paid its taxes to Normandy. Its Assize judges came from Rouen; it used money coined in the Rouen mint. Everything went on as before. No Jerseymen ever considered that they belonged to England. If they thought about the matter at all, they would have said that England belonged to them. But, when John, a century and a half later, lost continental Normandy, Jersey found itself cut adrift from its accustomed anchorage. It was too remote to be absorbed into any English county. Its laws, its language, its system of land tenure, its money, its weights and measures, were all entirely different from those in use in England. So it was allowed gradually to evolve a constitution of its own.

Two ancient institutions were already in existence. The first was the parish assembly, which had probably evolved from prehistoric times. The men of each parish met regularly to transact parish business under the chairmanship of their elected constable. He, with his elected centeniers who were originally each responsible for a hundred families, and his elected vingteniers who were responsible for twenty, formed the honorary parish police. And this assembly must, to some extent, have curbed the power of the seigneurs.

Even more important was the body of twelve elected magistrates called Jurats, which, so the island frequently claimed, had existed "from time immemorial". After the separation from Normandy, the government of the little community passed into their hands, subject of course to the control of the Warden, or Gardien des Iles, covering the Bailiwick of Guernsey as well as that of Jersey until the 15th century, who was the King's Representative, and of the Bailiff, who in those early days was the Warden's lieutenant. At their weekly meetings, in what came to be called the Royal Court, they not only tried criminals and settled disputes; they also issued ordinances that had to be obeyed. In the 15th century they began sometimes to summon the rectors and constables, as the men who knew best what was being said in each parish, *pour conseiller la Justice* (to advise the Court); and from these conferences of Jurats, Rectors, and Constables there sprang eventually a second body known as the States, which in time became the rival of the Court, and eventually, after many conflicts and reforms, secured for itself the whole power of law-making. Since the Constitutional Reform of 1948, the Jurats have been relegated to their old duties as Judges; the Rectors have been removed from the Assembly, which now consists of Constables, Senators, and Deputies; and the States have taken over all the functions of a local democratic parliament, though of course its Acts do not become law until they have received the sanction of the King, or Queen, in Council.

For more than seven centuries Jersey has enjoyed Home Rule. Successive monarchs have confirmed by charter its complete autonomy. The most surprising example of this is its famous Privilege of Neutrality. In 1483 a Pope persuaded England and France to agree that, whenever they were at war, the Channel Islands should be regarded as neutral territory; and this arrangement remained in force till 1689. When Elizabeth confirmed the privileges of Jersey in 1562, she wrote: "One of these is that in time of war friends and foes can without impediment frequent these islands to escape storms or for purposes of commerce, and depart without molestation, and remain in safety so long as the island remains in sight." She also added that no Jerseyman should be cited by any form of legal process to appear in an English court. Professor Le Patourel in his book, *The Medieval Administration of the Channel Islands*, sums up their relation to England as "that of a principality united to another in the person of the Prince only". The possibility of Britain joining the European Common Market has raised grave problems for the Channel Islands, both constitutional and economic, and the situation is under close review at present.

When Vikings first descended on Jersey, they came as pagan plunderers, church-burners, and monk-slayers; but more than a century had passed before they settled in the Island, and by that time they had become Christians and enthusiastic church-builders. The earlier wooden churches had probably gone up in flames during the raids; but they were now gradually replaced by small stone chapels. A question often asked is: When were the twelve old parish churches built? This is impossible to answer. Two, St Mary and St Martin, are mentioned as early as 1042, and eight others are named in an undated charter which William the Conqueror signed in Normandy before he became King of England, and therefore must have been built before 1066; but how long they had been standing before any surviving document happened to mention them no one can even guess. One thing, however, is certain. The churches in which men worshipped in the Conqueror's reign bore very little resemblance to those we see today. They have been in constant use for over 900 years, and almost every generation has altered their shape and size, lengthening the nave, raising the roof, enlarging the chancel, adding a Lady Chapel here, a new aisle there, two transepts, a porch, a spire, putting up galleries and pulling them down, altering the position of doors and windows, adapting everything to the architectural fashions, the taste, and ritual of the day. Speaking generally, it may be said that, though every church contains some 11th century work, the greater part of the present buildings dates from the 14th, 15th, and 16th centuries, and in two cases there were great enlargements in the 19th. One warning is necessary. The dates given in some guide-books (St Brelade's 1111, St Martin's 1116, St Clements's 1117, etc.) are derived from an impudent forgery. They first appeared in a local Almanac for 1792 as *A List of the Churches in Jersey with the Year and Day in which the Building was Begun, drawn from the Livre Noir of Coutances*. This

9

title was impressive. The *Livre Noir* was the official Register of the Diocese of Coutances, of which Jersey formed part, and it was compiled by order of the Bishop in 1251. Any statement found in this should be authoritative. But when examined, it is found to contain the income of every church in the diocese, including the churches in Jersey, and the name of the patron who appointed its Rector, but it says not a word about the date of the foundation of any of them! No one knows who foisted this bogus list on the un-suspecting editor of the Almanac; but in 1898 the Committee of the Société Jersiaise visited Coutances and inspected the *Livre Noir* and all the other old registers, and reported: "We desire to make known that the dates of our churches given in this list are totally devoid of any known authority, and have not been taken from the *Livre Noir*, of which they never formed part." Once every church had a peal of bells, but in 1550 most of these were sold to help pay for new fortifications, only one being left in each belfry.

The spires of Coutances Cathedral can sometimes be seen from the top of Mont Orgueil; so, while Jersey formed part of Normandy, it was natural that the Island should be included in that diocese. And, when the separation from Normandy took place, England shrank from provoking a conflict with the local clergy. For years there was a dangerous pro-French party among the seigneurs. We constantly hear of estates being confiscated, because their owners "adhered to the French King". If the priests threw their influence on that side, it might mean the loss of the Island. To be cut off from the bishop who had ordained them, who spoke their language, who was almost a next-door neighbour, and be placed under some unknown, remote, English-speaking prelate, would have provoked deep resentment. So, till the Reformation, Jersey remained part of the diocese of Coutances.

The character of the Reformation which reached Jersey was Continental, though the actual Edict of 1547 naturally emanated from the English King. It was a reform full of fierce, fighting, anti-Catholic fury. The Pope was Antichrist. Everything connected with the old worship was a device of the Devil for the destruction of souls, and therefore to be stamped out without discrimination. The old faith seems to have put up surprisingly little resistance. The innumerable wayside crosses were hewn down as being idolatrous. The chantry chapels were turned into cottages or allowed to fall into ruins. The parish churches were ruthlessly purged of altars, fonts, statues, wall-paintings, stained glass, anything that might recall "the teaching of the Great Whore", and were transformed into austere, whitewashed Huguenot Temples with every seat facing the pulpit. Most of the rectors were French Protestants in Presbyterian Orders, Huguenots who had taken refuge here during the French religious wars, a convenient arrangement for all concerned, as the Island needed French-speaking Protestant priests, and every church used the prayer book which Calvin had compiled for the French Huguenots. Jersey became as staunchly Calvinist as Scotland.

Was it this Calvinist régime, one wonders, which frowned so severely on all superstition, that banished from the Island its folk-music? We know that on winter nights the popular form of amusement was to gather in one of the old farm kitchens and spend the evening singing; yet hardly one of the songs has survived. Did a time come when nothing was sung but Marot's Metrical Psalms?

Jersey's Calvinism was responsible for another great immigration. When the savage persecution of the Huguenots in France drove thousands of them into exile, large numbers escaped to join their co-religionists in Jersey, and established families that added a valuable new strain to the Island's population; such names as Girard, Gosset, Dallain, de la Place, de la Taste, Hemery and Le Bailly, and many others, are among families who sought refuge here at this period, or, and this is even more striking, a hundred years later, at the time of the Revocation of the Edict of Nantes, which had given a temporary religious freedom in France. But a time came when Calvinism provoked a revolt. It was not a revolt against its theology or against its form of worship. These remained for generations Jersey's ideal of religion at its best. But Calvin had laid down the maxim, "Doctrine without discipline is a body without a backbone"; and the constant attempts of the church courts to discipline the private lives of the people was something which the sturdy independence of Jerseymen would not tolerate. James I, who hated Calvinism as he had known it in Scotland, took advantage of this discontent to force Anglicanism on the island. More than a hundred years before, in 1499, Henry VII had obtained from that most bribable of Popes, Roderigo Borgia, a Bull transferring the Channel Islands to the Diocese of Winchester; but no one had taken the smallest notice of this. For fifty years more the Bishops of Coutances continued to ordain, institute, and collect their episcopal fees. Then came Calvinism, which had no use for any kind of bishop, Anglican or Gallican. But now in 1620 the Presbyterian form of church government was abolished by the King in Council, and the Island Church placed definitely under the control of the Bishop of Winchester. A French translation of the English prayer book was ordered to be used in every church, and a Dean was appointed to see that the new regulations were rigidly obeyed. But even so Jersey retained a certain amount of independence. The canons drawn up for the church in Jersey differ in many respects from those adopted in England. The first Bishop of Winchester to visit the Channel Islands was Bishop Robert Sumner, who came in 1829.

Apart from a brief revival of Presbyterianism under Cromwell, Anglicanism reigned without a rival till the Methodist Movement reached Jersey in 1783. This made many converts, and large Methodist chapels that catch every visitor's eye are a feature of the landscape in all parts of the Island. The Roman Church regained a foothold in Jersey in 1803, when permission was given to the French Royalists, who had fled to escape the Revolution, to open a chapel in Castle Street. Today practically every denomination is represented in St Helier. Connected with the twelve parish churches, dedicated to St Brelade, St Clement, St Helier, St John, St Lawrence, St Martin le Vieux, St Martin de Grouville, St Mary, St Ouen, St Peter, St Saviour, and the Holy Trinity, mention must be made of the perquages. These were sanctuary paths by which a criminal could reach the shore, from his parish church, and they were in use until the Reformation. If the criminal had friends who supplied a boat, he could leave Jersey, but might never return. Some, but not all of these paths have been traced. They always followed a stream but took devious routes, and often arrived at the shore in a different parish from that of their origin. They were granted, as well as some waste lands called *terres vacantes*, by Charles II to Sir Edouard de Carteret in 1663, and he and his descendants gradually sold off this ground, usually to adjoining landowners.

Jersey has always had to face the possibility of invasion. The great Castels de Lecq and Rozel and other promontory forts show that this was true even in prehistoric times, and today the whole

Island is ringed with fortifications representing every period of history. The Keep of Mont Orgueil was probably begun in the year of the separation from Normandy, and reign after reign, century after century, from the days of bows and arrows well into the age of cannon, it was made ever stronger and stronger with fresh walls and towers. This provided an almost impregnable stronghold, where the garrison could stand at bay till reinforcements arrived from England; but it afforded little protection to the rest of the Island. For the next 280 years, till the Privilege of Neutrality brought relief, Jersey lay at the mercy of raiders of many nations. A few quotations from contemporary documents will show what it suffered. In 1214, that picturesque ruffian Eustace the Monk, a renegade Benedictine who had turned pirate but still wore his monastic robes as he led his cut-throats into battle, harried the Channel Islands so thoroughly "that nought was left to burn". In 1336 David Bruce, the young Scottish King whom Edward III had dethroned, avenged himself on Jersey, "inhumanly committing arson, murder, and divers other atrocities". Two years later the French Admiral Béhuchet "invaded the island with a great host and burnt every blade of corn and all the houses". Next year Sir Robert Bertrand, or Bertram, Marshal of France, "arrived with a multitude of Barons and Notables to the number of about 8,000". They failed to take the Castle, but "they burnt many mills and houses and carried off much plunder". A few months later a petition said, "This island hath been destroyed and burnt three times this year." It was probably about this time that Grosnez Castle was built to be a place of refuge for the north-west, when raiders were reported to be landing; while the great entrenched camp of Chastel Sedement in Trinity parish provided a similar hope of safety for the people of the north-east.

In 1372 a Welsh princeling in the pay of the French King "wasted the whole island" with 600 men-at-arms. In the following year no less a man than Bertrand du Guesclin, the famous Constable of France, landed with a large part of the army that had just captured Brest. He saw that it would be very costly to try to storm the Castle, so he set his sappers to work, and they made a great breach in the outer wall; the garrison then agreed to surrender, if not relieved by Michaelmas. Relief arrived in time, but the rest of the Island remained at the mercy of the French, who "by harsh imprisonments, burning, and deaths" compelled it for the next three years to pay a heavy tribute. In 1406 the Admiral of Brittany raided Jersey as a reprisal for the capture of some Breton ships by the English, and "took prisoners and booty and laid the Island under a contribution of great and intolerable sums of money". A few months later a Castilian corsair Pero Niño, and a Breton knight Hector de Pontbriand, after fighting and winning a battle on St Aubin's sands, marched inland with 2,000 men. "Everywhere houses, gardens, crops were soon all ablaze, a piteous sight"; but the raiders were at last bought off with 10,000 golden crowns. In 1461 Mont Orgueil itself was betrayed into the hands of the French and they ruled Jersey, with great severity, for seven years before they were driven out.

In 1483 the Privilege of Neutrality gave the Island a welcome respite; but by 1531 the Government had begun to doubt whether this could be trusted to last for ever. A Commission was appointed to report on the defences of the Island. The result was the adding to Mont Orgueil of the great central Somerset Tower and the building of St Aubin's Fort to protect the ships that anchored in the shelter of the islet there. Elizabeth Castle, as its name implies, had not been built at this period.

The next great spurt in fortification began in 1778, when France made alliance with the revolted American Colonies and an invasion was thought to be imminent. Then it was that Martello Towers were built in the bays, and the States provided guard houses for the militia at many lonely spots round the coast. After de Rullecourt's attempt to capture the island in 1781, Seymour Tower was erected off La Rocque to prevent any other enemy landing at that spot; and during the Napoleonic Wars the fortifications were still further strengthened all round the coasts. La Rocco Tower, Icho Tower, Portelet Tower, and Fort Regent all belong to this period.

When the Germans occupied the Island in World War II, by Hitler's orders they tried to transform it into an impregnable fortress. They called it "the mailed fist of the Western Wall". A walk round the coast today provides an object-lesson in all the latest devices for modern military defence, anti-tank walls, anti-tank traps, cunningly camouflaged guns, fortresses carved out of solid rock, fire-control towers, and enormous underground ammunition tunnels. Even Mont Orgueil and Elizabeth Castle, which had long been considered mere museum pieces, were strengthened with concrete walls and given a part to play in the defence scheme. Their fortifications were so strongly built that they are virtually immovable, and are gradually being regarded as historic monuments in their own right. It is noteworthy that these 20th century defenders decided to fortify exactly the same places as their predecessors had chosen.

Wealthy Englishmen may settle here to evade their country's taxes. The tourism committee may flood the Island with hosts of summer visitors. But the real Jersey remains essentially a land of farmers. Of the total area of 28,000 acres approximately 12,000 are ploughed, 5,000 under grass, and nearly 100 in reservoirs, leaving a balance of 10,000 in houses, gardens, roads, and heathland. These figures show a marked decrease in ploughed land in recent years. Many farms are small, some not more than ten acres, yet worked by the owner and his family they enable him to earn a reasonable livelihood. Two boons assist this process. The warm climate with its mild winters makes every crop ready for market before its English equivalent can reach Covent Garden, though not ahead of some Continental rivals unfortunately, and the seaweed, which is locally called vraic, can, if certain regulations are observed, be reaped in any quantities freely from the rocks, and when used as manure it prevents the soil from becoming exhausted, being particularly beneficial on light (i.e. sandy) soils. Economic pressure is forcing farmers to rely more and more on chemical fertilisers, but it would be a pity if this excellent manure, so lavishly supplied by nature, were overlooked. There are fields where potatoes have been grown continuously for half a century. In modern days two crops have proved amazingly profitable. First came the discovery of the high prices that new potatoes fetch, if they reach the English markets ahead of the home-grown earlies. In the year before the last war, over 75,000 tons of these were sold to England. For a few years after the war, the Colorado beetle, fatal to potatoes, was a serious menace, but this is now under control. Later it was discovered that, as a second crop, tomatoes were even more profitable, though rather more risky, as they are easily damaged by adverse weather, and are somewhat subject to disease. And in recent years cultivators have started growing these under glass, resulting in fresh tomatoes being available almost all the year round. One curiosity, now seen less and less frequently is the Jersey cabbage (the *Chou Cavalier*), whose stalks grow 10 or even 15 feet high. The heads are used as food for pigs and poultry, and the stalks once found a ready sale when varnished as walking-sticks for visitors, but the demand for these has fallen off lately. Cereals and root crops are decreasing, but a post-war crop, which has had a great measure of success, is the broccoli, grown in great quantity and ready for cutting from October till February. Flowers are also grown widely now. They are mainly all types of daffodil, iris, and anemone, and, later, gladioli. The masses of gold and blue when they are being picked are lovely to behold, and an anemone field in full bloom is like a stained glass window with the sun shining through it. Another recent crop being grown extensively in the east of the Island is lettuce, which can reach mainland markets in fresh condition by air freight.

But the real local champion is the Jersey cow. As a cream-producer she is unsurpassed among all the cows of the world, and she is so patriotic that her children all degenerate, if born in a foreign land, and the strain has constantly to be renewed by fresh importations from the Island. Some hundreds of animals are exported annually, some for handsome prices, and this industry, having decreased since the war, is now showing signs of improvement. In 1967 there were nearly 10,000 cattle in the Island, including 5,500 milking cows. The Jersey Milk Marketing Board is a flourishing concern, and as well as supplying islanders and visitors, it manufactures various milk products for export, and in 1967 produced 18,000 pints of fresh cream, and 1,676,000 tins of cream, for export. A new venture is sending to less fortunate countries Long Life milk, which remains good for many months. Visitors used to be surprised to notice that in Jersey cows were tethered and that in chilly weather each of them wore a coat of some kind, often only a sack, if the true fine boned Island type was desired. The cattle shows, parochial and insular, are an important part of agricultural life, and attract breeders and buyers from all over the world. Here the very best Jersey cattle can be seen and admired at the spring, summer, and autumn shows, and provide a most beautiful sight. There are no foxes in Jersey, but there is a flourishing Drag Hunt and Chase Club which provides a brave sight during the winter, with a surprisingly large number of enthusiastic riders. In recent years electric fences have been increasingly introduced, and in that case both tethers and coat have been dispensed with. Some herds are now de-horned, but the custom is by no means universal. Jersey's once celebrated breed of horned sheep, some with four horns, some with six, has long been extinct.

Douets à laver, or lavoirs, which are communal washing places, may still be seen. Some belong to a particular family, and some are shared by a group of neighbours. These are where women used to gather to wash their clothes and exchange the latest gossip. One at St John has a stone on which are cut the initials of the families who were alone allowed to use it: *Noms des Personnes ci dessous mentionnés qui ont droit au Douet et qui l'ont fait réédifié dans l'année 1813*. No one, however, is ever seen at work in these pools today, except occasionally some Breton women who have come over for the potato season.

Farmhouses have walls of enormous thickness, and some of the older ones are built as a quadrangle enclosing a large courtyard. Three sides of this are formed by the stables, cowsheds, and outhouses, with perhaps a dower-house for the farmer's mother. The fourth is the dwelling-house for the family, often with a tourelle which contains the stone spiral stairs leading to the upper story, bulging from the wall on the north. Doors and windows open into the inner court, which is entered, in many cases, through a spectacular arched entrance, with the large arch for vehicles and the smaller one for pedestrians. The front door is often within a round arch too, the typical Jersey arch, built before 1700, being composed of nine stones, not much more than six foot high, and with chamfered edges and decorated chamfer stops. The window lintels may be elaborately carved. The initials of husband and wife, often with a date recording the building, alteration, or inheritance of the house, are frequently carved on keystone or lintel of the entrance door. In the 18th century it became the fashion to link these initials by a motif of inter-twined hearts. The lettering could be incised or raised and sometimes included heraldry. At night, when the massive doors were barred, the farm stood secure from all intruders.

Two details in the farm architecture attract attention. In days when every roof was thatch, projecting dripstones prevented water from seeping down the side of the chimney; but you will be told that these are witches' stones, provided for a passing witch to rest upon, so that she may think kindly of you and not bewitch your house. Did they, perhaps, serve a dual purpose? More mysterious are the ecclesiastical-looking recesses in the walls of many farm kitchens. Again the story goes that these bénitiers, as they are called, were made to hold holy water. Every altar in the Middle Ages had a piscina beside it, at which the priest washed his hands before celebrating Mass, singing, "I will wash my hands in innocency, O Lord, and so will I go to Thine altar". Bénitiers and piscinae are exactly alike. When the Island was full of chantry chapels that had fallen into ruins, local people building houses, perhaps on the site of a former chapel, naturally used any ready cut stone they found available, but the use to which these former piscinae were put remains a matter of speculation. Unexpected bits of church tracery can be found in the walls of Jersey stables.

But Jersey never kept all its eggs in one basket. Besides its farms it always had supplementary industries; and these it changed with great versatility, whenever something more gainful became possible. First came fishing, in the Middle Ages an important source of income. Large quantities of salted conger were then exported to the Continent; but today, apart from lobster-trapping and the netting of certain gullies, real professional, deep-water fishing has dwindled almost to nothing, and the fish market in the town is largely supplied from Billingsgate. The conger and the ormer are local specialities, the latter procured off the rocks at very low tide, producing a dish of great delicacy.

Next came knitting. Though this seems to have been invented in Scotland, in some inexplicable way remote little Jersey managed to secure the lion's share of this new trade. So much was this the case that the word "jersey" actually came to mean "knitting". In 1587 Harrison's *England* spoke of "coloured stockings of silk jersey", and in the same year an account of Mary, Queen of Scots' execution said that she wore stockings "with silver about the clocks and white jersey under them". And today a knitted sweater is still called "a jersey", the original one being navy blue, and made to a certain pattern, specifically for fishermen. The sister Island produced a "guernsey" which is very similar. Modern machine-made copies can be obtained in the shops, and they are a most useful and comfortable form of sweater. This work became so profitable that even men took to it, and the States grew worried lest the land should go out of cultivation, and threatened imprisonment on bread and water to anyone caught knitting during harvest or the vraicing season. In 1624 a petition asked for larger supplies of wool from England because "more than a thousand souls have no other means to get their living but by knitting stockings"; and in 1682 Poingdestre's *Cæsarea* said: "There are many houses where man, wife, and children, beginning at the age of five, have no other employment, and may be said to make everyone a pair of stockings every week, which must come to more than 10,000 pairs weekly."

Another peril to agriculture was cider-making. As early as 1682 Poingdestre had complained: "The whole Island is in danger of becoming a continual orchard." And in 1832 a Report stated that a quarter of the land was given up to apples, and that many farms in the eastern parishes grew nothing else. In 1839, 268,199 gallons of cider were exported to England. In 1800 almost 20 per cent of all enclosed land was in cider orchards, particularly in the east of the Island, and St Saviour's parish alone had 36 per cent in apples. Everywhere the old cider crushers can be seen, though not in use as such; but they have become very popular as garden ornaments or fish ponds. The apple orchards themselves are fast disappearing, and with them many varieties of apple. Fortunately these, and the pears which also used to be widely cultivated, have been catalogued by the local philologist, Mr F. Le Maistre.

Jerseymen, being true islanders, always took eagerly to the sea. They were some of the first to exploit the Newfoundland fisheries, and for long almost monopolised the job of providing the Catholic world with salt cod for fast days. But whenever war broke out, they turned gaily to a far more exciting and more profitable occupation. Every shipowner mounted a few swivel-guns and applied for Letters of Marque, which made his boat an auxiliary vessel of the Navy. He was then entitled as a privateer to prowl about the Channel, and, whenever he could capture an enemy ship, to keep it and its cargo as a prize. During the Seven Years' War Jersey privateers brought in prizes to the value of £60,000. In the War of American Independence, at one time more than 150 French prizes were anchored in St Aubin's Bay. But in the Napoleonic Wars this proved less successful. The French were more heavily armed and more skilfully convoyed, and in two years Jersey lost two-thirds of its shipping. But the lucky third went on making large profits, and some of Jersey's wealthiest families laid the foundation of their fortunes in this fashion. From this some fine houses built during the 19th century are known as Cod Houses, or, more elegantly in French, *Maisons de Terreneuve*.

After the war the shipping trade quickly recovered. In the 1860s Jersey shipowners had 450 vessels, and, till the advent of steam at last drove sailing-ships out of action, at times the harbour was so tightly packed with schooners, brigs, and brigantines that it was possible to walk across their decks from one pier to the other. Their regular voyage was to take a mixed cargo to the great fishing stations at the mouth of the St Lawrence, then to carry a shipload of cod to Spain or South America, and to return to Jersey with goods from those countries. Most of these ships were home-built, and the southern bays were lined with busy shipyards turning out new vessels, some of which, one must confess, were provided with artfully concealed false bottoms for smuggling. Only a few Jersey sea-captains seem actually to have become smugglers, landing contraband in lonely creeks in Cornwall or South Wales; but the large part that the Island played in this illegal trade was that of providing the professional smugglers with their cargoes. At dead of night an English cutter would sail into some quiet bay, where the watchers employed by the British Customs would not be likely to notice it, and Jersey confederates would be waiting on the sands with kegs of spirits and bales of tobacco ready to be embarked. Similar arrangements were made with French smugglers at the Ecréhous. This shady business reached its peak in the early years of the 19th century.

Jersey's roads at the beginning of the 19th century were some of the worst in Europe. They were nothing but miry lanes, too narrow for carts to pass, which wound to and fro in bewildering fashion to avoid encroaching on this or that farmer's field. "The roads are very bad," wrote Lyle in 1808, "and sunk so low that they act as drains to the adjoining land, and in winter are nearly impassable." But General Don, whose statue towers over the Parade, altered all this. He was Lieutenant-Governor during the Napoleonic Wars, and for purely military reasons, so that his troops and guns could move quickly to and fro, he cut 18 broad military roads, down which artillery could gallop, with many connecting cross-roads, and in this way made access to every corner of the Island easy. The old winding lanes did not go out of use, but have been repaired, and are still available for delightful drives and walks, with the result that little Jersey has today the almost incredible number of 550 miles of first- and second-class roads and probably quite as many lanes.

In 1870 a railway was opened between St Helier and St Aubin, which was extended later to the Corbière, and in 1872 another company laid a line from the town to Gorey. For 60 years both companies did useful and profitable business; but the coming of the motor-bus killed them. Today a bus service covers the whole Island. Had these gallant little railways been able to survive, they would have provided a great tourist attraction now.

The 19th century brought startling changes to the life of Jersey. The chief was the English invasion. Up to Waterloo there had been very few English residents; but in 1824 a regular steamship service began to offer easy access to the Island just at a time when leisured Englishmen were moaning at the high taxation made necessary to pay for the long Napoleonic Wars. News spread of a beautiful island with a delightful climate, where rents were low and living cheap and, wonder of wonders, taxes were unknown. This was literally true. Thanks to the way every islander had been trained to do honorary work for his country—the judges were honorary, the police were honorary, the militia was honorary too—the States were able to meet all expenses out of the harbour dues, the taverners' licences, and the duty on wines and spirits. A great exodus began from England into Jersey. By 1840 there were said to be 15,000 English residents, a large number of them half-pay officers and their families. One result was a rapid spread in the knowledge of English. Shopkeepers had to learn English to serve their customers. Servants soon picked up English when working for English families. English newspapers were started. By the end of the century, in the town at any rate, English had almost ousted French as the language of everyday intercourse. In 1834 the old currency of livres tournois, that had been in use for centuries, was changed to the English one of pounds, shillings, and pence.

Another result of this steady influx of residents from across the

21

Channel was the enormous growth of St Helier. Terrace after terrace, crescent after crescent, in the style of the Regency crescents in Bath, sprang up to house the new-comers. Additional churches and chapels were built, till the tiny town that had once extended no farther inland than King Street became the bustling, populous place that we know today.

Throughout the 19th century the tourist industry had been becoming an ever-increasing source of profit. By the eve of World War I the number of summer visitors had risen to over 70,000. Between the two wars this number doubled. But in World War II this was brought to a sudden stop by the German Occupation. When France surrendered and the Germans held all the Normandy coast, Britain found that it was impossible to defend the Channel Islands. The troops were withdrawn, and ships were sent to evacuate all civilians who wished to leave. About 10,000 fled, but 41,000 remained in Jersey. On July 1, 1940, a German plane dropped an ultimatum ordering every house to fly a white flag: "If these signs of peaceful surrender are not observed by 7 a.m., heavy bombardment will take place."

That afternoon troops arrived by air, and for the next five years Jersey was under Nazi rule. The story of the Occupation has been told by several pens. Here we are only concerned with its permanent results, and these were surprisingly small. But it should not be forgotten that, though the islanders did not suffer the bombing of Britain, nor, with a few exceptions, the cruelty of the concentration camps, they were, through those five years, cold, hungry, fearful of their fate, out of touch with their relatives and friends who had left, and to a large extent, ignorant of true war news. Ironically the last year, after the D-day landing, was the time of greatest distress, when no communication, and therefore no supplies, could be had from France, and many people may owe their lives to the wonderful Red Cross parcels which arrived from time to time during the last bitter period. Lord Coutanche's skill, as Bailiff, in steering Jersey through this time of trial, should never be forgotten. But for him, the fate of the Island and its inhabitants might have been very different. Within a month of the Liberation, on May 9, 1945, the people of Jersey were honoured and overjoyed to have an impromptu visit from their Majesties, and this put new heart into them. Most of the evacuees returned as soon as the war was over. With a sigh of relief the Island slipped back into its old ways, except that the great upheaval brought to a head a reform agitation that had been simmering for years, and changes described in a previous paragraph were made in the States and the Court. Ever since then, and increasingly in the last decade, there has been a steady stream of new residents, attracted by our quiet life, gentler climate, and comparative freedom from governmental control. They are the 20th century version of political refugees. Inevitably their coming has enormously enhanced land and house values. Though in some cases one may lament the over-restoration which has changed the character of an old farm or cottage, in other instances a venerable house has been saved from falling into ruins. Also the large scale modernisation of houses has in many instances disclosed features such as granite fireplaces, which had been covered over and forgotten for a century or more.

With marvellous rapidity the Island recovered its prosperity. In 1947 over seven million 12-pound packages of tomatoes were sent to England. In 1948 more than 2,000 cattle were exported, and of these one bull alone was sold for £2,500. The number of tourists in 1967 was over 725,000, of whom the majority arrived by air.

Considering how small Jersey is, how few until recent years the number of its inhabitants, and how remote it has always been from the main current of events, it is remarkable how many of its people have made some stir in the world. In the 12th century there was Wace, the Anglo-Norman poet, who said: *"En l'isle de Gersui fu nez,"* adding, with dramatic impact, *"A Caen fui petit porter."* In the 14th century Roger Walden, perhaps a form of the local name Vaudin, the rector of St Helier, became Archbishop of Canterbury. In the 16th century the two Westons, born in Rozel Manor, secured high positions under Henry VIII, one as judge of the Star Chamber and Under-Treasurer of England, his brother as Prior of the Knights Hospitallers. In the 17th century Aaron Guerdain, Cromwell's Master of the Mint, who took the king's head off the coins, Nicholas Lemprière, who as commissioner for the sale of crown property "brake the King's crown", and Philippe de Carteret, Cromwell's Judge-Advocate, were all Jerseymen; while on the Royalist side Sir George Carteret, after the Restoration, became

Treasurer of the Navy; and on nobody's side but his own that extraordinary impostor Jacques de la Cloche, whose identity has never been established, was persuading the Jesuits that he was the eldest son of King Charles. The 18th century produced celebrities of many types—Lord Carteret, the Whig statesman, and Martel, the brandy merchant. Monamy, though apparently not born in the Island, is accepted as a Jerseyman, and became England's first marine painter; he worked very much in the style of the van der Veldes and his works deservedly now fetch very high prices; Mary Manley, the first lady noveliste; Philippe de Carteret, who sailed round the world in the little *Swallow* and added nearly fifty Pacific islands to the British realm; Joyce, the leader of the mutiny at Spithead; Lemprière, who compiled the famous *Classical Dictionary*; and Cabot, founder of that super-aristocratic family in Boston, of whom it was sarcastically said:

> *The Lowells speak only to Cabots,*
> *The Cabots speak only to God.*

In the 19th century we meet François Jeune, Master of Pembroke College, Oxford, the University Reformer who later became Bishop of Peterborough, and his son, Lord St Helier, Judge in the Probate, Divorce, and Admiralty Division; Sir John Millais, President of the Royal Academy, again accepted as a Jerseyman, though born in England. And, too, Philippe Jean, the famous miniaturist, and William Mesny who became a Chinese General and a Mandarin of the First Class; Dr R. R. Marett, the anthropologist, and Lillie Langtry, the world-famous beauty. For the 20th century it would be invidious to mention names of the living, but among many distinguished islanders were the late Baron du Parcq, Lord of Appeal in Ordinary, C. T. Le Quesne, Q.C., Lieutenant Bailiff, and the late Sir Seymour Hicks the actor. Ivy St Helier the actress, Frederick Lonsdale the playwright, and Elinor Glyn the novelist, were born in the Island. The late Edmund Blampied, superb draughtsman of the Jersey scene, who painted and drew in many media, but perhaps excelled as an etcher, has preserved for all time the life of the farm and the sea shore, and, of great historical importance, life during the German Occupation.

Everywhere on public buildings, official notices, and the copper coinage one sees the three weird beasts, which heraldry experts call leopards. For some obscure reason, which had nothing to do (as is sometimes alleged) with Normandy or Aquitaine, Richard I adopted these fearsome creatures as his armorial bearings. They first appear on the Great Seal of 1198, and ever since they have remained the arms of the Kings of England. They still prowl ferociously across what is popularly known as the royal standard. How, then, did Jersey obtain the use of them? Before 1279 all documents needing the King's seal had to be sent to Westminster; but in that year Edward I, having heard that many had been lost "at times through shipwreck, at times through robberies and other hazards of the roads," sent the Bailiffs a replica of his seal (*quoddam sigillum nostrum*) with permission to use it. About 1302, since it was awkward for two islands to share the same seal, each Bailiff was supplied with a separate one. The original seal bore the inscription in Latin: "Seal of the Bailiwick of the Islands for the King." The later Jersey one said more briefly: "Seal of the Bailiwick of the Isle of Jersey." The constant use of this seal for more than 500 years naturally gave the impression that this was the seal of the Bailiwick, and the custom became firmly established of speaking of the three leopards as "the arms of Jersey". This was, of course, historically incorrect; but in 1907 Edward VII graciously regularised the practice. The Secretary of State wrote that he "had submitted to His Majesty for decision the question of the continued use by the Island of the Arms at present claimed, and His Majesty has been pleased to sanction their continued use".

On festive occasions in Jersey almost every flagstaff, public and private, flies a white flag with a red saltire, i.e. the St Andrew's Cross. The origin of this is obscure. Major Rybot, who has investigated the subject, says that the earliest association of this flag with Jersey that he has been able to trace is in Bowles's *Universal Display of the Naval Flags of all Nations*, published in 1783, in which a picture of it is headed JERSEY. But Bowles was only reproducing pictures from a collection of Dutch charts, either one by Carel Allard published in 1705, or one by Van Kuelen published about 1720. In Allard's book the flag was labelled IERSE; but Van Kuelen put IERSE at the top and IRLANDOIS at the bottom, evidently thinking that this was the flag of Ireland. Someone obviously blundered; but was it the Englishman or the Dutchman? Was the

Dutchman wrong when he assumed that the mysterious word IERSE meant Ireland, since in Dutch the word for "Irish" is "Iers"? Or was it the Englishman who misread the word IERSE as JERSEY? Till someone discovers a picture that is older than 1783, which shows a Jersey ship or building flying the red saltire, the question must be left unsettled. But, since Jersey has used this flag unchallenged for 150 years, we may surely claim that by the Law of Prescription it is now the Island's flag.

Bonne Nuit. A favourite beauty-spot. A small bay about half-way along the north coast of the Island surrounded by hills over 400 feet high. We first meet its curious name when, about 1150, Guillaume de Vauville gave the Chapel of Ste Marie in St John's parish to the Abbey of St Saveur le Vicomte, and the King, when confirming this gift, called it the Chapel of Bonne Nuit (*de Bono Nocte*). Guillaume's son Richard gave 12 quarters of wheat rentes to support the monks in this priory and land on Frémont to provide them with firing, and, when selling another field, he described it as "alongside the Chapel *de Mala Nocte*". In three old maps (1689, 1710, and 1786) the sea outside is called Maurepos (Ill Repose). So the chapel could be named either after the bay or after the outside sea.

The priory is mentioned from time to time in the Island records. Every Midsummer Day the prior was bound to give a dinner to the Bailiff, the Vicomte, and the King's Receiver. In 1309 Dionysius, the prior, was fined 20 livres for threatening that, if the Assize judges tried to stop offenders against Church Law being sent for trial before the Bishop's Court in Coutances, the Bishop would send 80 men-at-arms to seize the judges and throw them into his prison. In 1413 Henry V determined to stop English money being sent to his enemies in France; so he suppressed all alien priories. The Bonne Nuit monks then had to return to their Normandy abbey, and their priory and chapel gradually fell into ruins. The site has been entirely forgotten. Henry VI transferred its revenue to Eton College, which he founded.

In the middle of the bay can be seen a rock which was known as *Le Cheval Guillaume*, and on Midsummer Day (which is St John the Baptist's Day, and Bonne Nuit is in St John's parish) crowds from all parts of the island used to flock to the bay to be rowed round the rock to avert ill-luck during the coming year. Perhaps this was the reason why the prior had to feed the Court officials on that day. Did they come to make this pilgrimage? The custom was probably pre-Christian. In Orkney and Shetland the idea still survives that certain rocks must be visited every Midsummer Day.

In 1792, when that dynamic person Philippe Dumaresq, founder of the *Gazette*, Jersey's first newspaper, came to live in St John, he tried to brighten things up. "For years," he said in his paper, "an old custom has drawn on St John's Day a very large concourse of people to enjoy the insipid amusement of being rowed in a boat round a rock. That done, there was nothing to do but to drink gin and cider." He resolved to establish a two days' fair like those so popular in France. He erected 50 tents for the sale of clothes, cakes, butter, stockings, gloves, hats, handkerchiefs, ribbons, and lace. He organised an open-air market for cattle, horses, and pigs. He engaged comedians and tight-rope dancers from France. He roasted an ox whole; and ended with a firework display. This lasted for five years; but then the States suppressed it as "contrary to good morals".

Bonne Nuit might easily have afforded a possible landing-place for an enemy; so the States were constantly strengthening its defences; first a boulevard for two cannons in 1736, then a guardhouse, then a powder magazine, then a fort, named La Crête, a beautiful piece of military architecture, then barracks; but no attack was ever made at this point. The Bay, however, in the 19th century became a rendezvous for smugglers. Here, for example, is the confession of the master of the *Eliza* in 1836: "Instead of proceeding to St Germain, for which we had cleared, we went to Bonne Nuit, and took in 2½ tons of tobacco, spirits in casks, segars, and snuff, which I agreed to take to Wales at the rate of £50 per ton. We proceeded to Fishguard, where we arrived on the fifth day, and, running in about eleven that evening, assisted in conveying the goods to a store close by. We then went to St Germain, took in 32 sheep, and returned to Jersey." The pier was built in 1872.

Bouley Bay. A large bay in Trinity parish, five miles north of St Helier, two miles wide and more than a mile in depth. A popular place for picnics. The hills on the east are over 400 feet high. The name comes from *bouleau*, a birch-tree. Many placenames are derived from trees. Eight French villages are called Boulay or Le Bouley. In England we have Bircham, Birchden, Birchanger, Birchengrove, Birchington, etc. The bay is in some ways the ideal spot for a harbour. There is good anchorage, and at least 6 fathoms of water close to the shore. The first time its name is mentioned (in the *Extente* of 1274) it is called *Portus de Boley*, the Port of Bouley. Dumaresq wrote in 1685: "Here has been a design to build a mole, which might be made to secure great ships from all winds or weathers, the materials being at hand." But the steepness of the hills would have made it difficult to transport the cargoes, nor could a town of any size have been built on them. In 1828, however, the States constructed a small pier for the oyster fishermen and for defence, and the initials of the contractor, F. de la Mare, can be seen incised in the harbour wall.

More than one military expedition has landed here. In 1549 the French seized Sark, and then landed in the bay; but the Militia met them, and after a fierce fight, at an area called Le Jardin d'Olivet, they were routed and retired to St Malo. During the Civil War in 1643 Parliamentary ships put ashore sailors to capture all the prominent Royalists who had not taken refuge in the castles. After the Riot of 1769 Colonel Bentinck disembarked his Highlanders here and marched into the town to restore order.

Such a danger-spot obviously had to be guarded. When the first three cannon arrived in Jersey, apart from those in the castle, one was placed in the bay; and from that day forward the States were constantly discussing further defences. Two bulwarks were made, and a guard-house and two magazines. A beacon was erected to give the alarm signal. Then L'Etaquerel Fort was built on the east of the bay and on the west a two-gun battery was erected above the present pier. This is called the Lisscester battery, and a demi-culverin had been installed there in 1596, hence the name, after the Elizabethan Earl of Leicester. In 1835 a lower battery was built at L'Etaquerel, and the one on the west was replaced by a larger five-gun battery.

More than once in the 19th century the Admiralty toyed with the idea of establishing here a great naval station. Several times surveys were made and soundings taken; but nothing came of it. Except when the Jersey Motor Cycle and Light Car Club invades it for a hill-climb, Bouley Bay remains one of the loneliest spots in the Island. So it is not surprising that it was thought to be haunted. An enormous black dog with saucer eyes was believed to prowl up and down the cliffs at night; but nothing serious was ever laid to its charge. The worst ever said about it was that its appearances presaged a storm.

Corbière, La. The name name La Corbière can be found wherever French is spoken. There are two Corbières in Guernsey, a Banc des Corbières in the Bay of Mont St Michel, a Pointe Corbière on the Breton coast, the wild Corbière Mountains between the Pyrenees and the Mediterranean, a town called Corbière in Central France, and a Canton called Corbières in Switzerland. We are told that the word comes from *corbeau*, a crow, rook, or raven and, if we ask why our forefathers specially noted the haunts of crows, the most probably answer is that the crow was considered a bird of ill omen. Certainly Jersey's Corbière has proved a death-trap to many a ship.

The name first occurs in our records in the Assize Roll of 1309, when questions were asked about a tub washed ashore "from a wreck at the Corbière". The *Chroniques* tell how in 1414 "a great Spanish ship was lost on the Corbière, and the sands of St Ouen Bay were strewn with casks of wine", and the hall of the manor, for the seigneur had the right to all wreckage, could hardly contain the puncheons that were stored there. On St Catherine's Day, 1495, five Spanish caravels were driven on these rocks, and the sand-storm which destroyed the fertility of Les Quennevais was attributed by tradition to God's wrath at the cruelty shown to their crews. And so the dismal tale went on throughout the ages. At last, in 1873, a lighthouse was built by the States. Imrie Bell, the engineer, chose an isolated rock 500 yards from the shore. On this he placed a concrete platform 9 feet high, and a tower 35 feet high on the top of that, the first lighthouse in the British Isles to be built of concrete. The light, which is now electric, can be seen for 18 miles.

The rush of the tide round these rocks is extremely dangerous. At the entrance to the causeway is a memorial stone to "Peter Edwin Larbalestier, assistant keeper at the lighthouse, who on the 28th of May 1946 gave his life in attempting to rescue a visitor cut off by the incoming tide. Take heed, all ye that pass by!"

The headland is studded with concrete fortifications that the Germans left behind. Near their tall fire-control tower is a tiny cove known as La Rosière (this may mean a place where reeds grow, from the old French *ros* a reed, or it may refer to wild roses, of a creeping variety, which grow in the vicinity). There are caves there which, it is firmly believed, used to be used by smugglers. It was here that, in September 1859, the mail steamer *Express* was wrecked, with some loss of life. A large area of headland has been generously given to the Island by the Le Quesne family, to be preserved for ever as an open space. A deep quarry, long derelict, is to be used to house a sea-water desalination plant, but it is hoped that this project will be discreetly planned, and not interfere with such a splendid open, unspoilt area.

The other object of interest on this wind-swept point is the Table des Marthes (the table on which children played *marthes*, i.e. knucklebones). It lies at the spot where in railway days the Corbière station stood. This great block of red granite, 12½ feet long, 6½ feet wide, and 2½ feet thick, is undoubtedly the cap-stone of a prehistoric tomb. As late as a hundred years ago contracts signed on this table were regarded as especially binding.

Ecréhous, Les. A chain of rocky islets north-east of Jersey, about half-way between Rozel and the French coast, of which the largest are Maître Ile, 300 yards long and 150 yards broad, Marmoutier, considerably smaller, and Blanche Ile, smaller still. *Hou* is a common contraction for the Old Norse *holm*, an islet. We get it elsewhere in the Channel Islands in Jethou, Lihou, Brechou, and Coquelihou. The origin of *Ecre-* is less certain. One possibility is the Old Norse *sker*, a rock. The Vikings might well have named it Skerholm, the Rocky Island. This would become in French Le Scerhou, and then L'Escréhou, which is the usual spelling before 1607. The name Marmoutier is puzzling. It apparently means "the monastery by the sea", for *moutier* is old French for "monastery". But, as we shall see, the priory was not on Marmoutier but on Maître Ile. Perhaps once it was possible, at low tide, to walk from one island to the other; so they were regarded as one, and shared a common name.

Palaeolithic flint implements show that these islets were inhabited in prehistoric times, when they were probably part of the mainland; but they first appear in history in 1203, when Pierre de Préaux, Warden of the Channel Islands, granted to the Cistercian Abbey of Val Richer, near Lisieux, "for the salvation of the soul of the illustrious King John, who gave me the Isles, and of my own soul and those of all my ancestors, the isle of Escréhou, that a church may be built there in honour of God and the Blessed Mary, and the Divine Mysteries celebrated therein daily". The ruins of this little chapel can still be seen on Maître Ile. He endowed it with rentes in St Martin, Trinity, Grouville, and St Saviour and St Clement.

At the Assize of 1309 the prior testified that he lived on the islet with one fellow-monk and a servant, that they said Mass daily, and kept a lamp burning all night "that mariners might avoid the dangerous reef contiguous to the Chapel", an act of real utility, for in those pre-compass days all ships hugged the shore, and much of the shipping up and down the Channel passed between Jersey and the Cotentin. When the alien priories were suppressed in 1413, the monks returned to Val Richer; their house and chapel gradually fell into ruins, but their well remains.

Jerseymen have always made use of these islets for fishing and cutting vraic (i.e. seaweed) for manure. At the Assize of 1309 it was reported that 24 men of St Martin had been drowned while returning from the Eskerho with vraic, and under the contemporary law of deodand the boat that had caused the accident was sentenced to be confiscated for murder. In due time a number of huts were built on the rocks, especially when the value of vraic ashes as a fertiliser was realised, for it was easier to burn vraic on the spot than to carry it home. But at the end of the 17th century a new industry developed. Les Ecréhous became notorious as a smuggling centre. In 1690, while the war with Louis XIV was raging, the Privy Council complained: "The inhabitants are sending ammunition to St Malo. The trade is carried on in the Ecréhou, encouraged by the fact that lead is in Jersey but two pence a pound, whereas in St Malo it is sold for 2s. 6d. a pound." The following year another report said: "The French come to the Ecréhou and make great fires, which is the signal for boats to come from Jersey. The Lieutenant-Governor grants passes for these boats. When a Trinity Centenier stopped a boat going to the Ecréhou, he was ordered by the Court to beg pardon of the Lieutenant-Governor on his knees. On information that a quantity of lead was going to the Ecréhou the Constable of Grouville stopped it. For this he was called a dog and a rogue by the Lieutenant-Governor and his commission as a Major taken from him." The quibble apparently was that, since Les Ecréhous were part of Jersey, there was nothing illegal in taking goods there, and no Nosey Parker need inquire what happened to them afterwards.

During the ferociously contested elections of the 18th century, when Charlots and Magots, the nicknames of the two contending political parties, were struggling for the mastery, each found these islets a convenient dumping ground for voters kidnapped on election day so that they could not vote.

Towards the end of the 19th century Frenchmen began to cast covetous eyes on Les Ecréhous and to suggest that they were either no-man's-land or even a dependency of France. But in 1883 Earl Granville, the Foreign Minister, wrote firmly to the French ambassador: "These islets have always been treated as a dependency of Jersey; the soil belongs entirely to Jerseymen, and the islets for administrative purposes form part of the parish of St Martin." Yet the French still hankered after them, asserting that they once formed part of the parish of Portbail. But in 1953 the dispute was submitted to the Hague Tribunal. In this case, which equally concerned Les Minquiers, the reef to the south of Jersey (q.v.), a most distinguished part was played by the then Attorney General, later Bailiff of Jersey, the late Cecil Harrison, C.M.G. After a most lengthy hearing the sovereignty of both groups of islets was decided in favour of the United Kingdom. The case was in fact of greater importance in international law than the size of the islands concerned might suggest.

In 1848 a Jersey fisherman, Philip Pinel, built himself a cottage on La Blanche Ile, in which he lived for nearly fifty years, catching lobsters and burning seaweed to ashes, and doing quite a flourishing export trade to Jersey. He was humorously named the King of Les Ecréhous and when Queen Victoria visited Jersey in 1859, the two monarchs exchanged gifts. He sent her a three-tiered basket that he had woven out of dried seaweed, filled with different kinds of fish, and she in return presented him with a blue coat.

On Marmoutier today there are a dozen houses of considerable age, and in good condition, the largest being the Jersey Customs House with its three leopards on the wall. A new two-storied house has been built on Blanche Ile. And on the Maître Ile one house has been built, with a fresh water well, but for most of the year it is left to the sea-birds, who nest there in great numbers.

Elizabeth Castle. About half a mile out to sea from St Helier lies an islet 60 yards broad and about 500 yards long, which can be reached at low tide by a causeway of shingle across the sands. For 400 years this contained a priory, and for the last 350 years a castle.

The Normans were great church-builders, and at some date,

33

probably a little before 1150, Guillaume Fitzhamon, a knight who held land at St Maurice, near Carteret, decided to found an abbey for canons of the Augustinian Order. He had evidently been reading the sensational *Passion of St Helier* (*see* article HERMITAGE), for he chose as his site the islet near the rock on which the hermit was said to have lived, and dedicated his new foundation "to the honour of the Blessed Elerius". He built a fine Romanesque church (of which pictures survive) and the usual monastic buildings, and then began to collect endowments from his friends. He had been for years a close companion of Prince Henry, the future Henry II, and, when the latter became King, he conferred on the abbey the town mill and the marsh, the rich meadow-land on which the town was beginning to spring up. Later he added 21 acres from the crown estates at Crapedoit, the name of one of the three fiscal areas into which the Island was divided at that time; Crapedoit probably comprised the four western parishes. Other benefactors followed suit and a prosperous future seemed assured.

But soon after Fitzhamon had settled his monks in their new home, the Empress Matilda, the King's mother, was caught in a storm in the Channel, and vowed to found a monastery if she came safe to land. She kept her promise by building the Abbey of Our Lady of the Vow at Cherbourg, and she too gave this to the Augustinian Order and appointed the Abbot Robert of St Helier to superintend the building operations. At first Cherbourg seems to have been considered a daughter abbey of St Helier; but after Robert's death trouble arose. The jealousy was partly financial. A document at the time complains that it was unseemly for a knight's foundation to be three times as rich as that of the Queen-Mother. There were also difficulties of discipline. The Augustinians at this time were split into two factions. St Helier sided with the Party of Artois and Cherbourg with the Party of Paris. This led to such ungodly bickering that in 1179 the Archbishop of Rouen amalgamated the two abbeys, "that they may be one flock under one shepherd", and reduced St Helier to the rank of a priory, in which Cherbourg pledged itself to keep five canons in residence. Its life as an abbey had lasted only about 30 years.

For the next 200 years the tiny band of monks on their lonely islet must have led uneventful lives. They sang their daily Offices in the great abbey church. They collected the rents due to Cherbourg from local tenants. But in the 15th century things began to happen. One evening in 1406 raiders landed on the islet, 1,000 men-at-arms with a number of light armed troops and archers, under Hector de Pontbriand, a Breton knight, and Pero Niño, a Castilian corsair. Next morning, as the tide fell, they advanced across the sands, where 3,000 Jerseymen under the King's Receiver had mustered to repel them. "Then you could see," wrote Niño's standard-bearer, "helm severed from breastplate, and arm-plates and greaves hacked off. Some grappled with daggers drawn. Blood flowed in torrents. Such steadfast courage did both sides show that all would have been slain had not Niño observed a white flag with St George's Cross, which, though many a standard had been battered down, still remained upright. So he called to Pontbriand: 'While yon flag flies, they will never own themselves beaten. Let us go and capture it.' With 50 men-at-arms they wheeled out of the mêlée to where the banner stood. The colour-party were doughty knights and the fight was hard; but in the first assault the Receiver was slain. I saw him lying at my feet. Then the Jerseymen began to fly; but the French were so fatigued that they could not pursue." The defenders then withdrew with their families and cattle inside the great earthwork at Trinity known as Chastel Sedement. When Niño's captains reconnoitred this they realised that its capture would be costly. They heard too of Gorey and Grosnez Castles, and they knew that the English fleet was at sea. They may have made a final stand at the top of Grouville Hill, at the spot known as La Croix de la Bataille, now owned by the National Trust for Jersey. So they agreed to withdraw on payment of a ransom of 10,000 golden crowns, and, loading their ships with booty, they sailed away.

Soon after this the empty buildings of the priory were filled to overflowing. The Abbey of the Vow was burnt to the ground, and the monks migrated to their daughter house on the islet, bringing with them the Abbot and some of the monks of St Sauveur le Vicomte, whose abbey had also been destroyed. But they had hardly settled in when a new blow fell. Under Henry V the Hundred Years' War flared up into new vigour, and the King's first step was to stop English money passing into enemy hands through the dues which alien priories were sending to parent houses in France. In 1413 Parliament ordered all the property of foreign ecclesiastics to be handed to the Crown. This meant the suppression of the other Jersey priories; but Governors hesitated what to do about the priory on the islet, which was no longer sending money abroad as its parent house was destroyed. "The Kings of England," wrote the Abbot later, "sent Lords who wished to expel us. To obtain permission to stay, we agreed to make an annual payment of 40 livres. The Isles were then given to the Duke of Bedford, who remitted these 40 livres; but the Duke of Gloucester, who succeeded him, took away a great part of our income and forced us to pay 84 livres. When the Isles were given to the Earl of Warwick, he did us divers wrongs, but notwithstanding we remained in our Priory; but King Henry VI restored our revenue to us." The names of these Governors show that the Cherbourg monks must have occupied the priory for more than 50 years. When the French captured Jersey in 1461, the monks were again in trouble. They complained to the French King that those who governed the Island in his name had seized their property and forced them to beg for a living.

By 1464, however, the Abbey of the Vow was rebuilt, and the islet was left once more with only its five monks. As the Reformation drew nearer, the priory began to go downhill rapidly. Its endowments were used to provide incomes for people who never came near Jersey. John Carvanell, chaplain to the Scottish Queen, who was Henry VIII's sister, was made prior of the islet in 1517, though he continued to live in Scotland; and in 1536 the unspeakable Thomas Cromwell, Henry's most disreputable agent in the destruction of the monasteries, obtained a written promise from the King that he should succeed Carvanell. But by 1540 the last English abbey had been suppressed, and before this St Helier's priory had ceased to exist. The great church, however, remained standing for another hundred years, and is shown in two of Wenceslaus Hollar's etchings in 1651.

A new use was now found for the islet. By Henry VIII's reign the invention of cannon had revolutionised the art of siegecraft, and Mont Orgueil had become vulnerable. Moreover, the town of St Helier, which was the most important place in the Island, was entirely at the mercy of raiders. So in 1550 the Privy Council ordered the States to "make a bulwark" on the islet, and authorised the Governor to provide the necessary funds by selling the bells of the parish churches, leaving only one for each church. But the States were busy building St Aubin's Fort, and for forty years nothing was done. In 1590, however, the work began in earnest. Paul Ivy, a military engineer who had just completed the forts at Falmouth and two castles in Ireland, was put in charge. The Queen contributed £500, and every house had to provide four days' labour, and two Jurats were appointed to see that everyone worked from six to six. The work was finished about 1600, when Sir Walter Ralegh became Governor, and he was the first to live in the new Governor's House. Life-size waxworks have now made the Castle look inhabited. In one room Ivy is showing his plans to Ralegh, and in another Charles II is seen giving the first grant of lands to be called New Jersey, to Sir George Carteret. Ralegh, with the fulsome flattery of the period wrote that he had presumed to christen the Castle Fort Isabella Bellissima, Elizabeth the Most Beautiful. This pretentious Latin name never came into general use; but an Act of the States in 1603 calls it *le château Elizabeth*. It was not yet, however, the size that it is today. Ivy only fortified the high rock on the south-west corner of the islet, leaving all the rest to the abbey ruins and the rabbits.

The first big extension was in Charles I's reign, when Sir Philippe de Carteret trebled its size by enclosing the ground that contained the monastic buildings. This work took ten years (1626–36). "The slothfulness of the workmen," he wrote, "doth impose on me intolerable trouble." Nevertheless, it was well done, and when the Civil War broke out in 1643, it stood the test. Some Jerseymen supported Parliament, but Sir Philippe remained loyal to the King and withdrew behind the Castle walls, which were besieged by the Parliamentary Lieutenant-Governor Major Lydcott. The walls, however, proved impregnable and, as the Castle could be revictualled from the sea, the garrison could not be starved out. The militiamen lost heart and drifted away to their farms, and Captain George Carteret, Sir Philippe's nephew, recovered the Island for the King.

Meanwhile, in England the royal cause was losing ground. The 15-year-old Prince of Wales, the future Charles II, retreated from Cornwall to the Scillies, and in April 1646 he took refuge in Elizabeth Castle, Jersey being the only place in his father's domain where he could feel secure. His arrival caused tremendous enthusiasm

37

locally. Chevalier, our local diarist, gives a picture of the boy at dinner in the Governor's House: "As he took his seat, a kneeling Squire presented a silver dish in which he washed his hands. On his right stood a Doctor of Divinity ready to recite the grace. The dishes, with which the board was loaded, were placed before him one by one, and, when he had chosen, the Gentleman-Carver tasted a portion and laid it on the Prince's plate. His drink was brought by a page about his own age, who tasted the goblet, and offered it kneeling on one knee, holding another cup under his chin lest a drop should be spilt on his clothes." Fortunately for Carteret's purse the visit lasted only ten weeks. Then the Prince and his 300 retainers left to join his mother in Paris.

Carteret now began to strengthen the Castle by building a fort at the opposite, the northern, end of the islet. This was finished in 1647 and named Fort Charles. In 1649 Charles returned, no longer as Prince but as King. Parliament had now abolished monarchy as "unnecessary, burdensome, and dangerous", and Jersey was almost the only corner of his kingdom that he could visit safely. This time he remained for 20 weeks, most of which were spent by his Council angrily debating whether he should try to regain his throne via Ireland or via Scotland. But Elizabeth Castle now saw a strange ceremony. It was widely believed that a King's touch could cure scrofula, a skin complaint, and Charles was persuaded to prove his kingship by showing that he had this power. Eleven persons, certified as scrofulous, were brought to the abbey church, a corner of which had been fitted up as an Anglican chapel. The King touched them on the breast saying, "May God heal thee" —"and," says Chevalier, "all were cured."

Charles eventually chose Scotland; but his invasion of England with the Scots was overwhelmingly crushed at the Battle of Worcester, and Cromwell then had time to attend to Jersey. In 1651 a Parliamentary army, under the command of Admiral Blake, exhausted the local forces by decoys, and eventually landed in St Ouen's Bay, and Carteret withdrew behind his Castle walls. He boasted that he was provisioned for three years; but a bomb from one of the big mortars, which the invaders installed at the foot of the Town Hill, landed on the abbey, crashed through the roof and floor into the crypt below, where Carteret's powder was stored, and caused an explosion which wrecked the church and all the adjoining

Grève de Lecq

Le Castel de Lecq

In St Helier's Harbour

The main arch at Grosnez Castle

The Hermitage Chapel at Elizabeth Castle

La Hougue Bie: Interior of the Chapel of Notre Dame de la Clarté

La Hougue Bie: Twin Chapels on the summit of the Neolithic mound

buildings and destroyed two-thirds of Carteret's provisions. A granite cross now shows where the abbey stood. The soldiers clamoured for surrender, and even the brave Carteret recognised that he must give in. The garrison marched out with the honours of war, receiving generous terms and for the next nine years Cromwell's nominees lived in the Governor's House.

The Castle then had a quiet time for more than a century. It did not assume its present form till after the Restoration, when the whole islet was enclosed with walls and Fort Charles and the older buildings were linked together. Twice during the 18th century unpopular Lieutenant-Bailiffs and Jurats had to take refuge behind those walls to escape the wrath of the people; but the guns were not fired again in anger till de Rullecourt's raid in 1781. When the French caught Corbet, the Lieutenant-Governor, in bed, and bluffed him into signing an order to all his troops to surrender, Captain Mulcaster, who was in command at the Castle, kept his guns firing to give the alarm, and, when de Rullecourt rode out with Corbet to insist on the order being obeyed, a cannon-ball took off the leg of one of the French officers and forced them to retire. Within a few hours the Battle of Jersey had decided their fate.

The modern history of the Castle can be briefly summarised. The breakwater, which today joins the islet to the Hermitage and runs out 660 yards to sea, was part of a new harbour scheme of 1872. Another arm should have come out to meet it from La Collette; but three years running this was smashed to pieces by south-westerly gales, and the project had to be abandoned. In 1922 the War Office handed over the Castle to the States as a historical monument no longer of any military value. The Governor's House, which had seen such stirring events, was in a poor state of repair, and had for some time been used as a garrison chapel. It was excellently restored. Nothing has survived of La Maison du Chancelier, the house in which Clarendon lived, and in which he wrote part at least of his *Great Rebellion*. But when the Germans came, they had other views. With large gangs of Russian slave-labour, they made a modern fortress, fitted it up with guns and searchlights and all the latest appliances, and placed in it a garrison of 100 men. After the Liberation it was again handed back to the States.

39

First Tower. When the American colonies revolted against England and France made a military alliance with them in 1778, Jersey, to improve its defences, built round towers in its bays of a type common in Mediterranean countries, but differing in shape from the so-called martello towers on the Sussex coast. These later came to be called martello towers from a famous defence made by one of them on Cape Mortella in Corsica. They were numbered, and the First, which stood on the sand-hills a mile west of the town, has given its name to the new suburb which has sprung up round it.

But something is there older than the suburb or the tower. Ships needing ballast used to send carts to these dunes for sand, and one day in 1865, while sand was being removed, some great stones were uncovered, which archaeologists recognised as part of a prehistoric tomb. They were not, however, finally unearthed till 1883; but today they can be seen in the park, which Jurat Gervaise Le Gros gave to the district in 1911. They proved to be two tombs of entirely different types, a long narrow passage-grave and a dolmen in the strict sense of the word (i.e. a large flat stone laid horizontally on upright ones), surrounded by a stone circle. It is impossible to say which is the older, but later immigrants, finding the first tomb there, regarded this as a sacred spot and built theirs alongside it. Then came a third wave of invaders, known as the Beaker Folk from a peculiar type of beakers that they used. They invaded Northern France and Britain about 1800 B.C., and fragments of their beakers have been found in the passage-grave. But they were not megalith-builders; so this simply means that they used an older tomb that they found already in existence.

Bellozanne Valley, which comes down to the sea at First Tower, gets its name from another bit of ancient history. In 1198 a Norman knight named Hugh of Gornay founded a monastery near Gournay in Normandy, and called it Bellozanne Abbey. He must have been a good beggar, for he got a subscription from that blasphemous little scoffer, John, Count of Mortain, who later became King of England. His subscription consisted of 20 liv ées, (2 librates = 1 carucate or about 100 English acres), of land in Jersey, and that remained the property of the abbey till the reign of Henry V; so the valley was called Bellozanne Valley and the hill behind it Mont à l'Abbé.

In a corner of the park stands the fine modern church of St

Andrew, a church with an unusual history. It began life in 1850 in Castle Street, close to St Helier's harbour, as a seamen's mission. The harbour was then full of ships and the mission flourished, and in 1854 a permanent church, dedicated to St Andrew the fisherman, was built on the Esplanade. But Jersey shipping gradually disappeared, and many of the houses in St Andrew's parish were turned into stores. Meanwhile, near First Tower, new streets were spreading by leaps and bounds, for which All Saints' parish, within whose boundaries they lay, had provided a wooden mission church. It was decided to close the old St Andrew's and transfer its name, its vicar, and its endowments to a new church to be built in First Tower Park. The chancel and the first bay of the nave were consecrated in 1927; in 1930 the second portion of the nave was added.

Nor among the sights of First Tower must we forget the Dogs' Cemetery, where you can buy a grave, with a tombstone, for your dog or cat. Recently, a complete modern sewerage works has been installed in Bellozanne Valley.

Fort Regent. The town of St Helier was built at the foot of a little hill called *le Mont de la Ville* or the Town Hill. Till the beginning of the 19th century this was a breezy, furze-covered common; "a lovely walk," wrote Falle in 1734, "with most extended prospect on all sides." Durell, who had known the common before it was sold to the Crown, adds, "On a clear day could be seen rising above the distant horizon the towers of the Cathedral of Coutances and a wide extent of the coast of France. Though bleak and exposed in rough weather, it was much resorted to for recreation at other times. On Sundays and holidays it was the best frequented walk in the neighbourhood of the town." In 1619 the residents in the Vingtaine de la Ville, which included the whole town as it then existed, built a shelter there for their sheep and paid a shepherd to watch them. But in 1674 Philippe Dumaresq, as seigneur of La Fosse which had been absorbed into the fief of Samarès, claimed the exclusive right to hunt rabbits on the hill. This the vingtaine strenuously resisted, and after lawsuits before the Royal Court and the Privy Council, Dumaresq "for the sake of peace" agreed to hand over to the vingtaine whatever rights he had.

But for a long time the military authorities had coveted this hill.

41

As early as 1550 an order had come from the King: "Because on occasion of foreign invasion we be informed you have no place of strength to retire unto, we require you to convey your Town unto the Hill above the same, which we be informed may with little charge be made strong and defensible." But the townsfolk could not be persuaded to abandon their old homes, nor was there then any water on the mount. In 1591, however, when Spain was preparing a second Armada, the vingtaine agreed to sell part of the hill to the Crown for a fortification, "owing to the danger that daily threatens utter ruin to this isle"; but nothing was done. De Rullecourt's raid in 1781 brought the matter up again, and once more the vingtaine consented to sell the common for a citadel. A wall of turfs was thrown up round the top of the hill and some guns mounted, and the rough dunes inside were levelled to form a drill-ground for the town militia. While this was being done in 1785, a remarkable prehistoric burial-place was unearthed. It consisted of a covered passage 15 feet long, leading to a ring of thirty upright stones against which were built five large cells, each roofed with a cap-stone. General Conway, the Governor, grew quite excited about this, and had models of it made to scale, one of which is in the Museum and another in the Public Library. But militia drill was considered more important than pre-history; so, since Conway showed such interest in this tomb, the vingtaine presented it to him, and he removed it and set it up in his Berkshire park, where it stands today.

This was apparently not the only megalith that had stood on the hill. Conway wrote: "The present Temple remained entirely covered with earth till the summer of 1785, having the appearance of a large barrow, which I had constantly seen, when I was in the Island." But earlier writers had described stones that were clearly visible. Philip Morant, in a paper read before the Society of Antiquaries, had said in 1761: "On the Town Hill stands a stone 14 feet long and 7½ broad and above 3 feet thick, which is supported by five others. South-east of it was a circle of stones, of which only one, 6 feet high, is still standing, the rest having been broken up to make a neighbouring wall." It is easier to believe that the breaking-up process had continued, until this tomb had disappeared, than that in 24 years it had been so completely buried that all memory of it had been lost. Moreover, the two descriptions do not tally.

There is reason to believe that many other prehistoric remains have disappeared like this.

Within the earthwork had been made a powder-magazine holding 5,000 barrels of powder. June 24, 1804, was the King's birthday. At noon the royal standard had been hoisted and a royal salute fired. That evening panic-stricken soldiers rushing down the hill shouted to Lys, the officer in charge of the signal post, that the magazine was on fire. A careless gunner had put back there a smouldering fuse, which had set the other fuses alight. Lys called Touzel, a carpenter, and Penteney, a private, and the three men burst open the door, threw out the fuses, and extinguished the fire. They were only just in time, for chests full of powder were found to be badly charred. The States gave each a gold medal and a monetary reward, stating: "We feel it our duty to pay this tribute of gratitude to these intrepid men, who, realizing that the explosion would certainly demolish part of the town and destroy many inhabitants, decided without hesitation to risk almost certain death in the heroic hope of saving their fellow-citizens." The Museum owns Touzel's medal.

In November that year, after much haggling, the Crown acquired the hill from the vingtaine by an Act of the Court, which ordered the registration of the findings of a jury of 24 men (*Ressort de Grande Vue*) in respect of the area and value of the site ceded. The price agreed on was £11,280. This produces an income of about £600 a year, which still provides funds for many town improvements. The present fort, which covers four acres, was planned by Major-General Humphrey, and incorporated all the latest devices for defence. The labour of the Island was mobilised. Each parish agreed to supply carts and men on a separate day. The slopes of the hill were blasted away, leaving only stark precipices, such as can be seen at the back of the houses in Hill Street. The 12th century Chapelle des Pas was blown up, lest it should provide cover for an attacker. A well 233 feet deep was sunk. The total cost was £375,203, on which the British taxpayer is still paying about £10,000 a year interest. The foundation-stone was laid in 1806, and the work was finished in 1814. It was named Fort Regent after the Prince of Wales, the future George IV, who was acting as regent during his father's madness. This great fortress had never fired a gun in anger till the Germans marched in after the surrender of the Island in 1940. Then their ack-ack guns frequently roared against

43

British aircraft. The whole area is soon to be converted into a recreational centre, with lifts to take people up from the town level. It is hoped that this will provide enjoyment for everyone, on a site of unsurpassed magnificence of scenery, but most particularly for visitors who find themselves somewhat forlorn during wet weather.

At present work is starting on a tunnel roadway, piercing the fort from Green Street to the harbour area, and it is hoped that this will greatly ease traffic congestion.

Gorey. A townlet that has grown up at the foot of Mont Orgueil. The oldest documents spell the name Gorric (1180), Gorryk (1274), or Gourroic (1331). Gorroic was the eastern of the three Ministeria, which were fiscal divisions, into which the Island was divided in Norman times, the other two being Groceio in the centre and Crapedoit in the west. Since there are a Gouarec and a Gueric in Brittany, it is possible that the name had a Breton origin. Long before Mont Orgueil was built, in the days when Roman officials came to the Island to collect tribute, and later when de Carterets, and other landowners, crossed over to visit their insular estates, the hook caused by the Castle Hill made this the obvious landing-place for boats coming from France. In the *Extente* of 1274 it is called *Portus Gorryk*, the Port of Gorey; but not till 1826 were ships given a better protection than a roughly built jetty. In 1593 a report stated that the castle stood near neither road nor harbour. In 1617 Commissioners declared: "The harbour is not good." In 1685 Dumaresq wrote: "At the foot of the castle is the most ancient harbour in the Island. There is an old, decayed pier, where such small boats as use the neighbouring coast of Normandy resort." By the beginning of the 19th century this had decayed to such a point that it had entirely disappeared. J. T. Serres' painting of the castle in 1802 and Tobias Young's in 1815 show no trace of it.

The castle and the port made Gorey a place of some importance, and in the 17th century a village began to grow up there. By 1669 it had evidently attained a fair size, for, when a cavalry regiment arrived from England, part of it was quartered here, and the inhabitants were ordered to provide beds and stabling. But it was the oyster fishery that made Gorey what it is today. There had always been an oyster-bed not far from the shore. Even prehistoric man liked oysters, for oyster shells have been found in La Hougue Bie.

44

Throughout the Middle Ages Jersey fishermen had visited that bed unchallenged; but in 1606 the Governor claimed it as Crown property. The Court, however, decided that by ancient custom every islander had the right to dredge there. For centuries this bed had been used only by local fishermen; but early in the 19th century news of it reached the ears of fishing companies in England. Then the village began to grow apace. A report in 1830 said: "Messrs. Alston and Co., Messrs. Martin and Co., and six or seven other firms at Sittingbourne, Faversham and other places in Kent employ upward of 250 boats, each manned with six men." There were besides boats from Colchester, Portsmouth, Shoreham, and Southampton. At least 2,000 men must have been engaged in this work, and hundreds of women and girls were kept busy grading and packing the oysters before they were exported to England; 305,000 bushels were sent in 1834. To house this new population rows of cottages were run up, and the present pier was built to shelter the oyster fleet. Oysters were so cheap in Jersey that they were served free at all hotel meals.

These new-comers were by no means law-abiding citizens, and they soon began to poach on the French oyster-beds off Chausey. The French had never protested against occasional visits of Jerseymen. There were oysters enough and to spare. But when foreign commercial companies began to send large fleets, they were quickly told, "Trespassers will be prosecuted!" In spite of warnings from Whitehall that they could not expect protection, the poaching went on, and it culminated in a fight. In 1828 the *Sunday Times* reported: "An unpleasant affair has taken place between English fishers and French vessels-of-war, many lives being lost. About 300 English vessels are engaged in oyster-fishing on the coast of Jersey, and have been repeatedly warned not to approach within a certain distance of the French shore. These warnings have been disregarded, and two French vessels-of-war captured an English boat. On news of this reaching Jersey, all the fishing smacks proceeded to the French coast, boarded the vessels-of-war, retook the English boat, and brought her back in triumph to Jersey. But several boatmen lost their lives, and a number were taken prisoner."

Later these reckless fellows got at loggerheads with the island authorities. To help them, the States laid down new beds in Grouville Bay, but these had to be carefully preserved till they were

45

ripe for dredging. In 1838, however, 120 boats raided the forbidden
beds, and when the Constable of St Martin followed, the men
snapped their fingers at him. Next day he arrested the ringleaders.
Four days later, however, a fresh raid was made; so the Constable
appealed for help to the Lieutenant-Governor, who marched out
at the head of the regiment and the town militia. A couple of
cannon-balls brought the boats back to port, and 96 more captains
were arrested. The unfortunate Lieutenant-Governor, Major-
General Archibald Campbell, died soon afterwards, his death being
attributed to having caught cold in this incident.

The arrival of these unruly strangers proved a perplexing problem
for a country parish like St Martin. The French services in the
parish church were unintelligible to the new-comers; so the rector
borrowed a room in the castle, and held English services there.
These were sufficiently successful to encourage him to build a
church, which was opened in 1833 and consecrated two years later;
but Gorey did not become an independent church parish till 1900.

The oyster industry was killed by over-dredging. By 1864 the
number of boats had dwindled to 23. But its place was taken by
seven ship-building yards that were set up along the shore. They
too died in time with the passing of the wooden ships, and today a
sea-wall and promenade occupy this site.

Gorey is five miles from St Helier; but in the 18th century it
was much more, for one had to wind one's way through many
meandering lanes. The first direct road was made by General Don
in 1806, and the States were so pleased with it that they decreed
that it should be called for all time the Route Don. In 1873 the
village was brought still nearer to the town by the opening of the
Jersey Eastern Railway, which ran its trains till 1929, when it was
put out of action by the coming of the motor-bus.

Gorey Castle. *See* MONT ORGUEIL.

Grève de Lecq. A small bay on the north coast partly in St
Ouen's and partly in St Mary's parish, the mill stream of the Moulin
de Lecq dividing the parishes. *Grève* is the French word for a
sandy shore. In Jersey we have Grève au Lançon and Grève
d'Azette, in Sark La Grande Grève and La Grève de la Ville, in
Guernsey La Belle Grève. The meaning of Lecq is uncertain. In
1215 it was spelt La Wik, which makes it tempting to derive it from

Old Norse *Vic*, a bay; but the name seems to have extended over a wider area than the bay. The district known as Lecq is some way to the west. The Chapelle de Lecq was a mile inland. The older name for the Paternoster Rocks, four miles out to sea, is Les Pierres de Lecq. It seems doubtful whether so small a bay could have spread its name so far.

On the east of the bay is the Castel de Lecq, a mound 270 feet high, artificially contrived upon native granite, which bears obvious traces of ancient entrenchments. Until proper excavations have been made, it is impossible to date these; but they probably belong to the Late Iron Age, when many similar promontory forts were made in Cornwall and Brittany, and along our north coast. Some experts think this one is later, even perhaps mediaeval. They may, however, have remained in use as late as the 15th century, for Diaz da Gomez, who accompanied Pero Niño in his raid of 1406, says that there were then "five fortified castles" in the island. Three of of these would be Mont Orgueil, Grosnez, and Chastel Sedement. It is difficult to guess what the others could have been, unless they were the Castel de Lecq and the similar Castel at Rozel. A remarkable cave runs right through the eastern headland. It is a tunnel 60 feet long, 15 feet wide, and 20 feet high, and emerges into the little creek on the other side of the hill, named Le Val Rouget.

The Assize of 1309 mentions a shipwreck "at the Port of Laic", when a Jean Patier was accused of removing wreckage belonging to the king; but usually this was a quiet little cove, where nothing exciting happened, merely used by small boats sailing to Guernsey and Sark. When Dumouriez in 1779 drew up his detailed plans for the capture of Jersey, he arranged that half the expeditionary force should land at Grève de Lecq. The bay had to be defended. That year a guard-house was built. Then a martello tower in 1780. By 1783 a redoubt had been placed on the eastern hill. A report in 1804 mentioned "two twelve-pounders on the west flank and three twelve-pounders on the east, 600 yards apart and about 100 feet above high-water mark; a battery of three-pounders, the foot of which is washed by spring tides; about 150 yards in rear of this is a Tower." The barracks were a later addition, and in 1817 Plees writes, "of late years some very neat barracks, for the accommodation of 250 men, have been erected". The pier was not built till 1872, and thirteen years later it was partially destroyed by a storm.

How old the water-mill may be is unknown. In a map of 1783 it is marked "Fuller's Mill", but there is no doubt that it is centuries older than that.

Meanwhile, in the Rue de la Capelle at the top of the hill was another building that figures often in mediaeval records. In 1168 Robert de Torigni, the most famous of the abbots of the great monastery of Mont St Michel in Normandy, visited his kinsman Philippe de Carteret at St Ouen's Manor, and Philippe presented to the abbey "the Chapel of St Mary, beside which I have prepared a suitable house". When fifty years later his grandson transferred "29 perches of land to the west of this house to the monks who there serve God", he described the chapel as the Chapel of St Mary de la Wik. It was only a small priory; towards the end of its life it seems to have had only two resident monks, who collected the dues owed to the parent abbey, but the prior was a person of some importance in the Island. The chapel had its own perquage leading down to the bay, being apparently the only chapel in the Island to enjoy this privilege, which elsewhere was reserved for the parish churches. But when Henry V in 1413 suppressed all alien priories, the prior and his monks had to depart for Normandy, and henceforth its endowments were collected for the Crown. In an *Extente* as late as 1749 the item appears: "Wheats due for the Chappell de Laicq."

Leland's map in 1540 mentions "Ruined Chapel of Ste Marie de Lec"; and in that year it appears for the last time in history. On Shrove Tuesday a surreptitious wedding took place among the ruins. Edward de Carteret, the 22-year-old Vicomte, was married by a priest to the widow of old Michel Sarre, the richest man in the Island, who had died only a fortnight before. Soon after this de Carteret was arrested for the murder of Sarre. It was alleged that he had broken into Sarre's bedroom, where he and his wife were in bed, savagely beaten him, and thrown him into an empty room and fastened the door with a cord, where he left him to die of his injuries, while he spent the rest of the night with the wife. The case dragged on from Court to Court, and eventually came before the Star Chamber; but the verdict is not recorded.

Grosnez. The name may, of course, simply mean "the Big Nose". But *nes* was Old Norse for "headland", and the Vikings gave this name to many of the promontories they passed. In England are Skegness, Sheerness, Shoeburyness, Dungeness, etc.; in Northern France Gris Nez, Blanc Nez, Nez de Jobourg, etc., as well as the Gros Nez, near Flamanville. So Jersey's Rougenez, Nez du Guet, etc., probably have the same origin. Grotness, in Shetland, is derived from Old Norse *grjot*, a rock, and this may have been the original name of our Grosnez, Grotnes, the Rocky Point, which Jersey later gallicised into its present spelling. Grosnez forms the north-west corner of Jersey. From it can be seen on a clear day all the other Channel Islands, including Alderney. The most prominent thing on the point is a gaunt ruined castle. A space of almost an acre was once enclosed by a roughly circular wall. On three sides—west, north, and east—it was protected by precipitous cliffs; so there the wall was lower; but on the landward side it is even today 16 feet high and once was higher. The gatehouse had a portcullis and battlemented roof, and on either side two projecting bastions with arrow-slits, through which archers could shoot down anyone who approached the gate. In front of this was a broad ditch cut through the solid rock, which was not easy to cross unless the drawbridge was down. Inside the walls can be traced the foundations of groups of small houses or shelters. A collection of carved corbels from the castle is preserved at the Museum.

This castle has little history. In Leland's map of the Channel Islands, published about 1540, it is marked as *Grosnes Castrum dirutum* (Grosnez Castle, destroyed). In 1607 the Attorney-General challenged the right of the seigneur of St Ouen to hold his feudal court there, on the ground that all castles belong to the king; but the Commissioners ruled that, as it was "but a heap of rubbysh and stones," the seigneur might be left in possession. But no record tells when the castle was built or why it was destroyed.

Four facts about it seem certain: (i) the ruins show that it was built in the bow-and-arrow age; (ii) its corbels suggest that it must have had a machicoulis gallery with holes in the floor for dropping stones on the heads of enemies below; if so, it cannot be much earlier than the 14th century, when this form of defence first became common in northern Europe; (iii) it can never have been meant to stand a siege, for it had no well; (iv) the way its stones were thrown into the ditch shows that it was deliberately destroyed and did not crumble through age.

49

The 14th century was the period of the Hundred Years' War, when the French were making constant tip-and-run raids on the Island. The castle was probably a refuge to which St Ouen farmers hurried their wives and cattle whenever the church bells gave warning that the French had landed. Then they could man the walls and hold the enemy at bay, knowing that they would not settle down to a long, systematic siege.

But when we ask who destroyed the castle, we can only guess. In the account of du Guesclin's raid in 1373 the Duke of Bourbon's standard-bearer reports: "We arrived in Jersey, where there are two castles. The Duke and his men set themselves in array against one and the Constable and his men against the other." We know that du Guesclin attacked Mont Orgueil. What can the other castle have been if it were not Grosnez? "Next morning they attacked, and the Duke captured his castle, the first to enter being Barberié, the Duke's carver. The Duke then joined the Constable, who had not yet taken the other castle."

Place-names sometimes preserve facts that history has forgotten. A gully on the north-west of the castle is called *Le Creux aux Français*. Does this imply that the Duke, instead of a frontal attack, led his men round to the back of the castle and stormed it at its weakest point? We cannot say. But its capture by the Duke of Bourbon is one possible date for its destruction. Before rejoining du Guesclin, he may have made certain that Grosnez could give no further trouble. Or was it destroyed in the French Occupation of 1461–68, during the Wars of the Roses? The de Carterets favoured the White Rose; so when the Red Rose won, their castle may have been dismantled. And this may explain why the Jersey chronicler never mentions Grosnez. Writing in the reign of Elizabeth, who was proud of her Lancastrian blood, he would not wish to call attention to the fact that his heroes, the de Carterets, had been on the other side. The flight of steps to the right of the arch was put there by the Société Jersiaise to prevent visitors from damaging the moat by climbing over it.

In recent years a lighthouse has been built half-way down the cliff to guide ships coming from the Race of Alderney round the dangerous Paternoster Reef. It is worth descending to the platform of this lighthouse for the sake of the view along the coast.

Grouville Church. This church, whose full name is "the Church of St Martin de Grouville", is less ancient than the other St Martin. The latter is called in ancient charters St Martin le Viel, St Martin the Old. Nevertheless, St Martin of Grouville is of quite respectable antiquity. It was already a parish church before the Battle of Hastings, for it was one of eight Jersey churches which Duke William robbed of half their tithes to endow the Abbey of Montvilliers. In early days it apparently belonged to the Bisson family, for on the day his wife was buried in 1149 Godfrey du Bisson gave the church to the Abbey of Lessay.

In most Jersey churches the oldest part is the chancel; but in Grouville the original church was the nave, as can be seen by looking at the walls, which are built of rough stones from the beach. Everything else has been added later, the chancel and tower probably in the 14th century, the chapels on either side of the chancel in the 15th. One guide-book dismisses this church as "containing nothing of interest", but it has more relics of mediaeval days than most Jersey churches. First, there is the curious font with its double bowl. In the Middle Ages the water in a font was only changed at intervals, and there grew up a scruple against letting drippings from a child's head fall back into the hallowed water. To avoid this, some French fonts in the 15th century were made with a small bowl inside to catch the water that had been used. The history of this font is peculiar. Chevalier, the diarist of the Civil War, describes how two Royalist divines discovered in 1650 two fonts in a farmyard being used as pig-troughs. These proved to be those of the town church and the old abbey church, which had been thrown out at the Reformation. One, we are told, had a bowl inside carved out of the same block of granite. They were brought to the town churchyard, but the Calvinist congregation refused to allow them to be placed inside the church. Then we lose sight of them, till an oil-painting of about 1830 shows what is obviously the Grouville font lying derelict in the grounds of La Hougue Bie. The owner of the grounds had evidently bought it, meaning to place it in his chapel. Later, when the grounds became a pleasure park attached to a public-house, the proprietor put it in the chapel as one of his curios. But a small chapel such as this would not have a font, and when La Société Jersiaise bought La Hougue Bie, it presented the font to Grouville Church, in whose parish La Hougue Bie stands. The plinth on which it is mounted is modern, and the rim of the actual bowl was damaged and had to be restored.

In the chancel and north chapel of Grouville can be seen the piscinas, where the priest used to wash his hands ceremonially before the Communion. The south chapel has, beside the spot where the altar used to stand, a mysterious low recess with a carved head inside. This is a puzzle for antiquaries. It does not look like a piscina. It may have been an ambry or cupboard to contain the Communion vessels; but, if so, it is curiously low. Some have suggested that it was an oven for baking the wafers; such ovens are found in a few English churches, but never, I think, inside the sanctuary. And none of these theories explains the presence of the carved head with a hole in the middle of its forehead. Was any Saint martyred by having his forehead pierced with a nail? St Damian is a possible identification, but if so, why should his head have been placed in this dark recess, where no one, before the invention of electric torches, was ever likely to see it? Before the raising of the floor level by two feet in the restoration of 1838 this recess would have been at a more reasonable height, and some form of ambry seems the most likely explanation. This chapel also retains traces of ancient paintings on the wall, too dim, however, to enable the subject to be identified. And there is an ancient holy water stoup, and this, like the font, has been brought in from outside, but may have come from the parish church in the first place. It is elaborately carved, with intricate designs including a monogram which appears to be S.M. and could represent St Martin. It would appear to be 14th or 15th century in date.

When the Battle of Jersey was being fought in the town in 1781, the Company of the 83rd Regiment that was stationed at Grouville was attacking the rearguard that the French had left at La Rocque. Seven grenadiers were killed in this little action, and a large granite slab now stands in the corner of the churchyard, "erected to the memory of these brave men by the principal inhabitants of the parish."

Grouville Parish. The southernmost of the two parishes that form the east of the Island. The old form of its name seems to have been Grosville; so in pre-Norman days, when people still talked Late Latin and *villa* meant "a farm with the land attached to it", someone must have possessed here a specially large estate.

Other articles deal with GOREY, part of which is in Grouville Parish, GROUVILLE CHURCH, LA HOUGUE BIE, LA ROCQUE, and SEYMOUR TOWER. This only leaves a few minor points to be mentioned. In addition to the church, there were three mediaeval chapels in the parish—Ste Marguerite on the hill above the church, which was turned into a barn at the Reformation and not pulled down till the 19th century; Notre Dame close to the church, which became a tavern; and the manorial chapel at La Malletière. The sites of some of the wayside crosses are also still remembered: La Croix Câtelain, La Croix ès Renauds, La Croix ès Chiens, and La Croix de la Bataille, the last a memorial of a skirmish with the French on one of their many raids.

In 1957 a considerable hoard of Armorican (i.e. from Brittany) coins was found at Le Catillon, in this parish; they have been closely dated between 52–50 B.C. and are of great antiquarian importance.

Of the manors, La Malletière, the original home of the Mallets, is mentioned in 1331. Of the existing buildings, the newer half bears the date 1635, but the other part, with its fine circular stone stairs, is considerably older. There was a manorial chapel there, of which the dedication may have been to Ste Suzanne.

Land in Jersey is so valuable that inland field-paths are rare, but Grouville has a delightful one in Queen's Valley down which runs a stream which once turned three water-mills. The parish also possesses the oldest windmill in the Island. Its history can be traced continuously from 1331, and though it has now lost its sails, its tower is preserved by the Admiralty as a landmark to guide ships into safe anchorage.

The best-known feature of the parish, however, is its Common, the 160 vergées of dry, sandy heath that border the sea. This has been used for many purposes. In the 18th century it was heavily fortified. When France was the enemy, this bay was considered a danger-spot, and Le Couteur's sketch in 1804 shows six martello towers and two square redoubts, Fort Henry (or Fort Conway) and Fort William. It was also the favourite spot for duels. In 1799 two officers of the garrison who had quarelled in their cups fought here with pistols, and at the sixth exchange of shots one of them, the surgeon of the regiment, fell dead.

In 1843 the horse-races, which had previously been held on St

Aubin's sands and then at Grève d'Azette, were moved to the Common, and became for sixty years the annual carnival of the Island. Ouless's picture of the scene in 1849, which hangs in the Museum, shows a much more spectacular fête than anything that the Island has devised since.

But it was golf that made this Common famous. In 1878, when golf.had hardly been heard of south of the Tweed, a band of enthusiasts got permission to map out greens and tees. The Grouville Golf Club grew into the Jersey Golf Club, and then into the Royal Jersey Golf Club, and here some of the world's best players received their early training: Harry Vardon, for example, who five times won the British Open Championship; Ted Ray, who held both the British and American open titles, and Aubrey Boomer, who was five times Champion of France.

In 1859 an unusual compliment was paid to Grouville Bay. A communication was received by the Bailiff from the Secretary of State, announcing that Queen Victoria, who had recently visited the Island, desired that it should in future be called the Royal Bay of Grouville.

Grouville became the chief tomato-growing parish.

Harbour. One amazing thing about Jersey is that it had no harbour until modern times. As early as 1275 Edward I had ordered Guernsey to "build a stone wall between our Castle and our Town of St Peter Port", and this was expanded into a proper harbour in 1570; but Jersey, apart from a few rough moles for fishing-boats, like those at St Brelade and Gorey, gave no artificial shelter to its shipping, till the pier at St Aubin's Fort was begun in 1670, and even then progress was so slow that it was not finished till 1700. When Dumaresq wrote in 1685, St Helier was still harbourless. "Under the churchyard," he said, "is a shelter for boats, which with the help of the brook that comes down there might with no great charges be made fit to secure greater vessels; that would be a great conveniency to the commerce of the Town, with is at great charges to bring its merchandise by land from St Aubin's."

When in 1700 the States at last decided to give St Helier a harbour, they laid their plans on a very modest scale. On either side of the small projection on which the house called La Folie now stands, there was a tiny cove (one was called later the *Havre des Français*, the other the *Havre des Anglais*). A start was made to build a hooked pier south of the *Havre des Français*, which would partially shelter both these coves from south-westerly gales. The first stone was laid in 1700; but taxes were unknown in Jersey; the only funds available were the import duties, and these produced so little that the work had to stop. In 1720 the States issued paper money to the value of 50,000 livres tournois (a few thousand pounds in modern money); merchants lent considerable sums free of interest; and in 1751 George II gave £200. But even when finished this little harbour had many drawbacks. It could only be entered at high tide. The water inside was always rough when a gale was blowing, and no road led to it. Carts crossed the sands at low tide and drew up alongside the ships to receive their cargo.

In 1788 it was decided that something better must be provided; so the States invited to the Island, Smeaton, the famous engineer who built the Eddystone Lighthouse. Local sea-captains, however, criticised his plans so severely that the States devised a scheme of their own. They built what was later called the Old North Pier, and prolonged the South Pier till it almost met it. This work, again through lack of cash, took 25 years. Meanwhile, the merchants at their own expense built the *Quai des Marchands* (now Commercial Buildings) on the land facing the pier. The result was the Inner Harbour.

But this still had the defect that it could be entered only at high tide. When the Duke of Gloucester, the King's nephew, came to Jersey in 1817, he had to land on the rocks outside, and slipping on the seaweed he fell and scrambled ashore on all fours to where the States and Militia were drawn up to greet him, a royal entry that certainly lacked dignity. The Newfoundland Fisheries were now booming, and the number of Jersey ships was increasing by leaps and bounds. The new harbour grew hopelessly congested. So the States decided to treble its size by building the outer harbour. The foundation-stone of the new South Pier was laid with great ceremony in 1841, and a large oil-painting of the event hangs in the Museum. The work was finished in 1846. One of the first persons to step ashore on it was the young Queen Victoria, and it was then and there named the Victoria Pier. The new North Pier was begun in 1846 and finished in 1853; and this was called the Albert Pier after the Prince Consort.

But still the number of ships increased, and the old fault remained, that ships arriving when the tide was out had to wait in the roads until there was enough water inside to float them. When Queen Victoria landed, the Prince Consort asked, "Why do you Jerseymen always build your harbours on dry land?" Innumerable plans were now debated for harbour improvement. The boldest was the proposal to build a sea-wall from the end of St Aubin's Pier to the tip of the Fort Pier and then right across the Bay to the Albert Pier. It was claimed that this would add 3,000 vergées to the Island, which by the aid of the town sewage could soon be transformed into rich agricultural land, and would also provide a fine supplementary harbour at St Aubin. Another idea was a great breakwater along the Castle Bridge, extending beyond the Hermitage to a point where the largest ships could unload. One group pressed for an entirely new harbour at Noirmont, where the water is always deep; while a fourth suggestion was a new harbour behind the Victoria Pier.

When the States invited engineers to submit definite plans, 42 were sent in, and the Committee selected that of Sir John Coode. This seemed a wise choice, for he was the best-known harbour engineer of the century, and had constructed harbours in many parts of the world. He proposed a great breakwater stretching out from Elizabeth Castle, and this part of his work still stands, with another pier three-quarters of a mile long reaching out from La Collette to meet it. The model that he submitted is in the Museum. But he underestimated the force of the waves that come thundering in from the Atlantic during south-westerly gales. In December 1874 a great breach was made in the La Collette Pier. This was repaired, but the following winter another large section collapsed. When a third winter came and again the great wall was pounded into ruins, the States gave up the struggle, though it had cost them £160,000; and contented themselves with the harbour they possessed, deepening it by dredging. Further dredging has been done since so that the mailboats can enter harbour at any tide. In recent years a new electricity power station has been built, with a tall chimney which now dominates the harbour entrance.

The beautiful bay of St Aubin was the scene of an exciting event when the royal yacht *Britannia* cast anchor in the roads bringing Her Majesty Queen Elizabeth II and the Duke of Edinburgh on a visit on July 25th, 1957.

Havre des Pas. Today this is a seaside suburb, consisting largely of hotels and boarding-houses. But till the 18th century the houses of the town ended at Snow Hill, and between them and the sea there was nothing but open fields and sand-dunes. One solitary building stood in this district, the Chapel of Notre Dame des Pas. Marks are sometimes found in rock which look like human footprints, and wherever they exist, they are always attributed to some supernatural cause. One in Ceylon is claimed by Buddhists as a footprint of the Buddha, by Hindus as a footprint of Siva, by Moslems as a footprint of Adam, and by native Christians as a footprint of St Thomas. Four religions send long processions of pilgrims to worship on that spot. Every Roman Catholic country shows footsteps of the Virgin Mary. And Havre des Pas boasted of two of these on a rock off Green Street, where some rather unprepossessing blocks of married quarters, for the troops stationed at the Fort, used to stand. They have now been replaced with blocks of States sponsored flats, of pleasing architectural appearance; the tenants in the upper levels of these tall structures have a superb view, and this must rank among the nicest housing estates one knows. A vague tradition said that the Virgin Mary had appeared to someone on that spot. An alternative explanation is that it means Our Lady of Peace, that is "pace" in place of "pas".

A Chapelle des Pas was built there, which is mentioned in 1200 in a charter granted by King John when he was Duke of Mortain. By the 15th century this had a fraternity attached to it, with its own cemetery around the walls of the chapel. At the Reformation, like other private chapels, it was confiscated by the Crown. During the Civil War Sir George Carteret quartered Irish soldiers in it, who made themselves an intolerable nuisance by plundering the whole neighbourhood. It later became a dwelling-house; and in the early days of the Methodist movement it once more was used as a chapel. But its remoteness encouraged hooligans to disturb the services, and it was soon abandoned. In 1814 it was blown up by the military authorities, lest it should provide cover for an enemy attacking the Fort. The only relic of the chapel is a stone, now in the Museum, which was dug up on the site. It had evidently been part of a statue of a saint, for the folds of the robe are clearly marked upon it.

This chapel explains the last half of the name of the district. But how could such a rocky coast ever have been called a *havre*, an anchorage? Rocks are the seaman's enemy, but they can also be his friend. To get under the lee of a ridge of rocks affords shelter from a storm, and there was a narrow channel between two reefs, through boats could pass into calm water behind the Pointe des Pas. In 1643, when Carteret recovered Jersey for the King, most of the Parliamentary leaders slipped out of Havre des Pas by night in a little frigate and escaped to England. In Colonel Legge's *Accompt of Jersey 1679*, he says, "The haven is from the Town of St Hilary Three quarters of a mile not commanded by the ridge and very good materials upon the place." Between 1678 and 1697 there were various schemes for building a proper harbour there, "but," wrote Dumaresq in 1685, "its entrance is so narrow and full of rocks that it discourages bestowing any charges on it."

In 1682 Poingdestre tells of an industry that has long vanished. The sand-dunes swarmed with tiny field-mice, which he calls *musquines*, whose excrement sent out a strong smell of musk. Boys used to collect this in baskets and sell it to the perfumers.

In the 18th century four shipyards occupied the foreshore. As late as 1867 the firm of Vautier had on its slips a ship of 1,000 tons and a schooner of 100. Then came the building boom. The shipyards were swept away and replaced by big hotels. The sand-dunes and market gardens were covered with streets and houses. The bathing pool was opened in 1895, and Havre des Pas became an important centre of Jersey's tourist industry. Much later, the attractive La Collette Gardens were laid out, with their terraces of semi-tropical plants and shrubs.

Hermitage. Three hundred yards south of the Island on which Elizabeth Castle now stands is a high rock. Before the new breakwater was built this was a separate islet, cut off from the Castle by a gully through which the waves rushed with such force that it was called Hell's Gate. Here a hermit called Helier is said to have lived in the 6th century. This is by no means impossible. The hermit movement was then at its height, and islands round the Breton coast were dotted with hermits' caves. But St Helier himself is a very shadowy figure. Our knowledge of him comes from a Latin book called *The Passion of St Helier*, written at least 400 years after its hero's death, for it speaks of "Normandy", which did not receive this name till after the Normans had settled there. In this, stories borrowed from legends of dozens of other saints are fitted together as in a jigsaw puzzle to form a thriller full of murders, pirate raids, and miracles.

With memories of the Book of Samuel, it tells how a childless couple in Belgium begged a saintly hermit to pray that they might have a son, promising, if his prayers were answered, to dedicate the boy to God; so when Helier was born he was entrusted to the old hermit to train. Quite twenty per cent of the Celtic saints were brought up by hermits; so this was the obvious way for the story to begin. He tended the hermit's garden; but the hares came and ate his cabbages; so he drew a line with his finger on the earth, and gave all on one side to the intruders, and not one of them ever crossed the boundary again. But the same story had already been told of St Antony and St Godric. A hunter broke through the hedge to kill one of the hares, but a branch pierced his eye and would have blinded him had not Helier restored his sight. Dozens of saints saved hares from hunters, who were injured when they tried to hurt them, but, when penitent, were healed. A woman with an issue of blood, which no physician could cure, ate some of Helier's greens, and was at once healed, a story obviously suggested by an incident in the Gospels. A lad went to sleep with his mouth open, and an adder slipped down his throat. St Helier made the sign of the Cross, and the reptile crept out, much ashamed. Precisely the same incident occurs in *The Miracles of St Hilary*. It is not certain, but more than likely, that our local saint was Helibertus rather than Hilerius. But there is much confusion about the name, which has continued throughout the centuries. Of his existence and influence there can be no doubt, and place names being as significant historically as they undoubtedly are, it is not without good reason that our town has, from the earliest recorded times, borne his name.

Helier's father now desired to recover his son; so he sent two of his henchmen, who cut off the hermit's head; but the boy escaped and went to Therouanne, south of Calais. Here, in a corner of a ruined church, he made a private torture chamber, in which he prayed day and night standing on jagged stones in icy water. This, if we can believe their legends, was a favourite form of discipline with many of the Celtic saints. St Cuthbert used to do it in the North Sea, and the porpoises swam ashore to thaw his toes with their breath. The people now began to honour Helier as a saint, especially after he had raised from the dead the child of one of their nobles; so, as overmuch admiration is bad for the soul, an angel bade him go to Nanteuil in Normandy. On the way (like Elisha) he cleansed a spring by sprinkling it with salt. At Nanteuil he found St Marculf, who after three months' training sent him to Jersey (Gersuth) to be a hermit. On landing he healed a cripple with twisted legs, and traces of this miracle, it is said, can still be seen on the rocks. The man's name was Anquetil, the earliest record of a local family name.

He chose as his home a cave in a crag cut off at high tide. When three years later Marculf visited him, he wept to see how worn he was with fasting. During Marculf's visit 30 pirate ships from the Orkneys threatened the Island; but the saints prayed, and the pirates began to fight among themselves so fiercely that not one returned home to tell the tale. Exactly the same story is told of St Magloire in Sark. Twelve years passed. Then barbarian pirates, probably of Saxon origin, arrived again, and discovered Helier's cave through the clouds of birds that surrounded it. St Fructueux's hiding-place was revealed in the same way. The pirates cut off Helier's head, and the bloodstain is still on the rock. Indelible bloodstains are pointed out on dozens of scenes of martyrdom. But Helier picked up his head in his hands and walked with it towards the shore, a startling feat which is attributed to 86 other martyrs, including St Denis of Paris and the British St Alban. Helier's "pedagogue", whoever he may have been, laid the corpse in a boat, and fell asleep for sorrow. When he awoke, the tide had carried the boat to Holland, where Willibrod, the Bishop, buried it in a noble mausoleum. This miraculous voyage is one of a large group of similar stories. The world-famous pilgrimage to Santiago was based on a belief that, when Herod beheaded St James, his disciples placed his body in a boat. "Then they fell asleep, and, when they awoke next morning, they found themselves in Spain" (*Acta Sanctorum*).

To doubt these stories is not to sneer at the teaching of the Roman Catholic Church. Catholic writers like Father Delahaye warn us that hagiology is not history. *The Catholic Encylopaedia*, in its article on legends of the saints, says: "The stories were embellished by the people according to their primitive theological conceptions, and the legend became to a large extent fiction." The Bollandists, the

Roman Catholic fathers who specialise on legends of the saints, describe *The Passion of St Helier* as a *légende peu sûre*, a legend on which little reliance can be placed. St Helier's name has never been placed on the Roman *Martyrology*, the official list of martyrs recognised by the Roman Catholic Church. This book was obviously written for edification, not as sober history; but it had a fair circulation. So, while realising that much of the story of St Helier is legend, which has grown up around his name through the centuries, let us continue to revere our patron saint with humility and thankfulness.

In the 12th century the small oratory, now called the Hermitage, was built on the rock, and became a place of pilgrimage. When the breakwater was built in 1872, the first plan was to destroy the whole islet, and it was suggested that the little chapel might be rebuilt on Westmount; but the engineers relented and only half the rock was blasted away, and the chapel was spared. Dean Falle in 1923 revived the pilgrimage to the chapel, and processions of churchfolk march across the sands for a service at the Hermitage on St Helier's Day (July 16).

Hospital. In 1741 a wealthy widow died in St Aubin, Mrs Marie Bartlet. She had no children, so she had resolved to use her money to provide a home for the homeless. But, though she was a successful business woman, a prosperous importer of coal and wine and spirits, she could not spell, and had no skill in will-drafting: "i give," she wrote, "to the Poore of the ilande fifeteay thousent livers turnois, taigne thousent to build them a House, and forty thousent to beay a Reivenu to mantaigne the Poore that shall be pouite in the House, wiche shall be poore widows and fatherlaise childrane and enchant piple of the ilande; and shale alwaise be quipe foule; and shale the saide House be built in St. tobin's; and everything be ordered as my Excers hear after named and the Staites of the ilande shall judge fiting." Clearly she intended to found a poor house, not a hospital in the modern sense of the word. It took three years to get the will registered. First one cousin tried to overthrow it "by reason of the wrong spelling thereof". Then two other cousins made the same attempt. Next came the difficulty that no suitable site could be bought in St Aubin. So the seigneur of Mélèches offered some land on the sand-hills west of St Helier. This meant that the States had to appeal to the Privy Council for

61

leave to ignore the "St. tobin's" clause. Then they fell out with the executors, and another lawsuit ensued, and yet another before Mrs Bartlet's London agent would hand over her English securities. It was not till 1765 that the foundation-stone was laid, and the first inmates were not admitted till 1772. But military eyes were envying this fine building. In 1779 General Conway requisitioned it for his troops. At the time of the Battle of Jersey, Highlanders were quartered there, and in 1783 their gunpowder exploded and destroyed two-thirds of the structure. After much pressure the Government consented to make good the damage, but the promised £2,000 did not arrive till 1788, and it was not till 1793 that the "fatherlaise childrane and enchant piple" re-entered their rebuilt home. In 1799, however, they were again evicted to make room for Russian troops, who were waiting for the Baltic ice to melt before they could return home; and it was not till 1801 that the States again secured possession of their poor house. A new wing and the present chapel were added in 1844. A great fire in 1859 reduced most of the building to ruins, and it had to be rebuilt at a cost of £9,000.

Meanwhile, the work of the hospital had been gradually changing its character. Originally a poor house pure and simple, a doctor was only called in from outside when one of the inmates was ill; but in 1835 the committee added a doctor to their staff. But a hospital in the English sense of the word was clearly needed in the Island. Accidents and sick cases in ever-increasing numbers began to be brought to Gloucester Street. For many years the hospital tried to cope with the two types of work side by side. There were often as many as three hundred paupers within the walls, together with numbers of poor-law children and lunatics, while more and more beds were being needed for the sick and injured. Obviously the two tasks had to be separated. In 1863 the older girls were removed to the Orphans' Home at Grouville, and four years later the boys were transferred to the Jersey Home for Boys, Gorey. In 1870 the Lunatic Asylum, now St Saviour's Hospital, was opened to receive the mentally deranged. In 1934 all infectious cases were moved to the Overdale Isolation Hospital.

The Germans commandeered half the hospital for their troops; but after the Liberation the new Public Health Committee carried out far-reaching reforms. The old ladies of the poor-law department were installed in a pleasant country house near Beaumont, and the old men were duly accommodated elsewhere. A hundred beds were added to the wards by building for the nurses a comfortable hostel next door. All maternity cases were transferred to a separate branch in St Saviour's Road. And the hospital itself was thoroughly modernised and provided with equipment of the latest type. The staff of doctors and nurses was increased. Today in organisation and work it compares favourably with the best English provincial hospitals.

Hougue Bie, La. For two or three thousand years La Hougue Bie was merely a mysterious mound, a mound much older than its name. The latter dates only from the Viking raids of the 10th century. "*Haugr*" is early Norse for "a mound", and when French became the language of the Islands, this was softened to *Hougue*. Jersey abounds in Hougues: La Hougue Boëte, La Hougue Mauger, La Hougue de Forêt, Belle Hougue Point, Les Hougues de Millais, etc. Guernsey has even more. Wherever Vikings saw a conspicuous mound they called it a Haugr or Hougue. The origin of the Bie is more doubtful. It may be a contraction for Hambie, for a legend connected this mound with the Castle of Hambye in Normandy.

Folk-lore is full of serpent-slaying heroes. Some were saints. Cerisy Abbey stood where St Vigor was said to have killed a serpent. St Lô, Bishop of Coutances, delivered his diocese from another. More often the slayers were knights. And one of these legends became linked with La Hougue Bie. It was said that a serpent in the marsh of St Lawrence wrought great havoc in the Island, till the seigneur of Hambye came from Normandy and cut off its head. But his servant murdered the seigneur, and returned, boasting that he had slain the monster after it had killed his master, and that his lord's dying wish had been that his widow should marry his avenger —"which for love of her husband she did". But the varlet talked in his sleep, and the lady learnt the truth and had him hanged. She then, so the legend declared, raised the great mound over her husband's grave, and built on the top a little chapel, where Masses could be said for his soul. This romance may have caused the mound to be known as La Hougue Hambye, which could easily be pruned to La Hougue Bie.

One grain of truth may perhaps lie behind this story. Hambye was the ancestral home of the powerful Paynel family, one branch

63

of which held land in Jersey. So La Hougue Bie may have been on Paynel property, and the older of the two little chapels on the top may have been built by some lady of Hambye. This tiny sanctuary, only 20 feet long, was dedicated to Notre Dame de la Clarté, our Lady of the Dawn, a dedication found in several parts of Brittany. But by the 16th century it was falling into ruins. In 1509, however, Richard Mabon became Dean of Jersey. He owned the property on which La Hougue Bie stood, and, as a thankoffering for his safe return from a pilgrimage to Jerusalem, he restored the old chapel, rededicating it to Our Lady of Loretto, the Assumption, and St Michael. Against the east wall he added a second small chantry, which became known as Jerusalem, in which Masses could be said for the souls of his own family. Some of the paintings that he placed on the walls can still be dimly discerned, and appear to represent the Annunciation. In the crypt beneath he made "an imitation of the Holy Sepulchre at Jerusalem, so far as he could remember it", i.e. of the rock-hewn tomb in the Church of the Holy Sepulchre, and pilgrims passed before it, entering by one door and leaving by another.

The eve of the Reformation witnessed a revival of pilgrimage, but our only knowledge of what went on in Mabon's chapels comes from hard-shelled Calvinists, to whom every Catholic priest was a rogue. Writing 40 years after Mabon's death, the author of *Les Chroniques* said: "This Priest was an idolater and great maker of images, who persuaded poor people to believe a pack of lies and rascalities to induce them to bring him offerings." Another writer of the same school declared: "He placed an image of Notre Dame in an oven-like recess, and the people passed down a covered arcade to make offerings to the idol, whereby this impostor gained great booty. The head of the image rested on one arm, while it held out the other to receive gifts, which Mabon did not fail to collect for his own pocket. The hand had a hole, through which the coins fell on a spring, which caused the arm to move as though thanking the donor, whereby the superstitious were still further seduced." This simple mechanical device may have encouraged offerings, but few in the sceptical 16th century can have regarded it as a miracle. His accuser goes on to assert that, when offerings began to fall off, "this insatiable Priest proclaimed a miracle. He hid in the wick of candles a very thin wire, which he fastened to the roof of the Chapel. The

smoke from the flame made the wire invisible, and the candles
seemed to float in mid air, and people believed that they were held
up by the virtues of Our Lady." But slanders like these were the
stock-in-trade of the baser type of Reformers.

Only four years after Mabon's death the Reformation ruined all
his plans. In 1547 every chantry chapel was confiscated by the
Crown, and Mabon's were sold to a Thomas Tanner. They changed
hands frequently in the next two centuries; but in 1759 the property
was bought by James Dauvergne, Adjutant in the Household
Cavalry. Though his duties kept him most of the year in London, he
spent a small fortune on his new possession. The grounds, which
had been completely bare, were laid out with blue hydrangeas and
trees. He made the winding path to the summit of the mount; but
when he came to the chapels, he proved himself a veritable vandal.
He threw the two into one by pulling down the dividing wall. He
paved the floor with blue and white marble, and coated the walls
with marble-like stucco. He replaced the narrow Norman west
window by a large, sham Gothic one filled with gaudy glass. He
turned one of the altar alcoves into a fireplace. And then he
smothered the chapels with a great brick tower, a kitchen, a library,
and two round rooms, and then a flat roof, from which one could
see almost all the Island. It is a marvel that the weight of this did
not bring the whole building down. For years he collected curios
for his chapel, the most interesting being a double font, now in
Grouville Church (q.v.), which had been thrown out of the town
church during the Calvinist régime. A diary of 1818 says, ". . . La
Hougbie now belonging to General Gordon. The spot is very
elevated on which stands this beautiful tower, and is encompassed
all around with all kinds of deciduous and evergreens. From the
bottom of the declivity to the top you ascend gradually through a
winding path of about three feet broad, till you reach the top from
whence the prospect around is charming. . . . The old Castle (i.e.
Mont Orgueil) is very visible from thence. There are five rooms in
the tower beautifully and elegantly done up with fine sophas and
chairs." In 1792 he transferred the property to his nephew, Captain
Philippe Dauvergne, R.N.

Philippe had been adopted by the Duke of the midget principality
of Bouillon; so he became known as the Prince de Bouillon, and
the tower as the Prince's Tower. As he commanded a small flotilla

for the protection of the islands, he used the tower to keep watch on the enemy's fleet. On his death the property was sold. In 1830 a visitor wrote: "The building is untenantable through dampness. A year ago some tons of lead were stripped from the roof and rolled up like a sheet by the wind."

In 1835 a tavern was built in the grounds with a dance-hall, skittle alley, and all the fun of the fair, and one guide-book declared, "The cell of superstition has become the Temple of Taste!" But fashions change. Customers fell off. Methuen's *Little Guide* described the tower in 1910 as "a damp neglected place with little interest". But in 1919 it was bought by the Société Jersiaise, who thereby showed wisdom and foresight. Nothing could be done till a lease expired; but in 1924 the restoration of the chapels was begun. Dauvergne's tower was entirely demolished. The dividing wall between the chapels was rebuilt. They were roofed with old tiles, and a small belfry replaced one that had been struck by lightning. Doors and windows were as far as possible replaced as in Mabon's day, and a mediaeval piscina, of extremely simple design, was discovered in the wall. Later an ancient altar-stone with five consecration crosses, which had been used as a gun platform at Mont Orgueil, was brought to Notre Dame de la Clarté as an altar. In 1931 the chapel was "reconciled" by the Bishop of Winchester. Recently the floor, previously of earth, was paved with granite setts, for convenience and cleanliness.

But all this time the mystery of the mound remained unsolved. It was obviously no natural formation. Why should men have toiled to throw up such an enormous erection, which is 40 feet high? In 1682 Poingdestre suggested that it was a look-out to keep watch for pirates "that the inhabitants, discovering their ships from afar, might have time to hide." But by the 18th century archaeologists had discovered that artificial mounds often covered prehistoric graves. In 1837 Durell had written: "It is a pity that the Hougue Bie has never been dug into." In 1924 the Société began to dig, and after ten days a great stone was uncovered. Those present have described the tremendous and dramatic thrill of excitement they felt when this discovery was made. Further investigation disclosed what proved to be one of the finest Neolithic tombs in Europe. This must have been the grave of a very great chief. Seventy huge stones had been selected, most of which, as they are seaworn, were evidently lying on the shore. The moving of these gigantic blocks, some weighing 30 tons, in days before the invention of wheels, must have been a stupendous task. Hundreds of labourers must have toiled, with the aid of rollers, to drag them up the hill, where even today the modern road is known as Rue Crèvecœur or Heartbreak Hill. When they reached the site selected, 53 of the stones were man-oeuvred into sockets in the earth, so that they stood upright, forming a long narrow passage leading to a larger chamber with (to use modern ecclesiastical terms) a side chapel on the north and south. Beyond, on the west, was a smaller room, which might be called the chancel and beyond that, like the Lady Chapel in a cathedral, a square cell. All was then buried under a mound of tightly packed earth, so that the cap-stones could be levered up, and placed as a roof on the whole; and, when that was done, the gaps between the stones were filled with dry-walling, and the tomb was ready for use. When it was opened, the Société found scattered bones of eight persons, of whom at least two were women; so, if we like to give play to a romantic imagination, we may picture the Chief's favourite wives being sent with him to the Spirit World with some slaves to wait on them. The tomb was then buried beneath the present enormous mound. This is only a baby compared with Silbury Hill in Wiltshire, which is 125 feet high; but La Hougue Bie is 40 feet, and the rubble of which it is composed weighs at least 18,000 tons. To carry this more than a mile from Queen's Valley, from which most of it seems to have come, can have been no light task. Whether it was done out of reverence for the dead or out of fear of his ghost, no one can say. These chamber-tombs were probably built, between about 2200–1800 B.C., by the pre-Celtic folk who are generally called Iberians, and the size of the work suggests that this was not one of their early efforts.

The Great Chief slept in peace for 3,000 years or more. Then came the Vikings. They knew that prehistoric tombs often con-tained treasure. *Beowulf* describes how one party dug into an English barrow and found "rich ornaments and vessels of gold". In an Icelandic saga the hero opened the barrow of Karr, and, though the skeleton of the dead warrior drew his sword to defend his treasures, the Viking got away with the loot. This probably explains why, when the Société got inside La Hougue Bie, they found nothing but two beads, some fragments of pottery, and the bones already mentioned. The Vikings had been ahead of them.

One find, however, was interesting. Built into the wall of the north "side chapel", in such a way that four-fifths of its marks were invisible, was a stone with twenty "cup marks" on it. These are still one of the unsolved problems of archaeology. They may be the heraldry of primitive man, boundary marks to indicate the territory of a tribe, or the earliest step towards writing, a code conveying a message. The stone walling round it has now been removed to show the whole stone, which must be older than the tomb, for it was used merely as building material.

During the German Occupation La Hougue Bie was fortified with barbed wire, trenches, and machine-guns; a timber observation tower, 26 feet high, was built on the top of the mound, and a large concrete dug-out made in the grounds. This has been turned into an Occupation Museum, showing samples of things left behind by the enemy and other exhibits illustrating their five years in the Island, and this is a most popular feature among visitors to Jersey. An Agricultural Museum of old farm implements has been built in the grounds, painstakingly labelled with their Jersey-French names, thus preserving for all time knowledge which might otherwise have perished.

Icho. An islet, 40 yards by 20, which lies a mile and a quarter out to sea from St Clement's Bay. Flint chippings, fragments of pottery, and human bones prove that in Neolithic times it was inhabited, though then it may have formed part of Jersey. In Popinjay's map of 1563 it is called Le Hyge Hoge, and is represented by a cone like half a pineapple, surmounted by a cross. The cross is even clearer in Mercator's map of 1606. Dumaresq, in his *Survey of Jersey*, 1685, speaks of "Ickhoe, the most eminent of St Clement's rocks, also called Croix de Fer from an iron cross formerly upon it." The name Croix de Fer continued in use long after the cross had disappeared. It is found in a French map of 1649, a Dutch map of 1737, and an English one of 1825. In the general fortification of Jersey that followed the Napoleonic Wars, a tower 28 feet high was built on this rock. This is sometimes occupied by parties for fishing, and to see the brent geese that fly overhead on migration, though shooting them is, of course, illegal.

Longueville Manor: The north courtyard

La Hougue Bie: Interior of the Neolithic tomb

Mont Orgueil Castle: Queen Elizabeth's Gate, built in 1593

Mont Orgueil Castle: seen from the south

Mont Orgueil Castle: The crypt of St George's Chapel

At the Museum:

The gold torque

A 17th century round arch

A bénitier from a farmhouse

La Rocque. The south-east corner of the Island, where the tide recedes two miles, exposing the Banc de Vielet, a wilderness of jagged rocks, through which it would seem madness to try to bring a boat. Nevertheless, there is a narrow channel through the rocks, down which fishing-boats can pass in safety to the shelter of the Plat Rocque Point. In the Middle Ages a fishing hamlet had grown up here, and in 1602 the States had appointed Jean du Parc "Supervisor of the Fishing Harbour of La Rocque". The harbour was purely a natural one without any jetty or pier. The *Extente* of 1607 records: "The King's Tenants in the Vingtaine of La Rocque ought to find two boats at all times of need to pass in message with letters or otherwise to Guernsey on reasonable warning given them from the governor or his Lieutenant."

It was realised that this point ought to be fortified. In 1540 the Royal Court ordered the Parish of Grouville to build a tower there. In 1646, when Prince Charles was in Jersey, his council surveyed the Island, and ordered a fort to be built to hold two or three cannon, and, says Chevalier, "when they began to dig, they found the foundation of the earlier fort". This second fort must have fallen into ruins, for a report in 1778 said: "A Tower and Circular Work should be erected at La Rocque Point, where an old Tower stood." In the critical year 1781, when the French landed here, the only defence was a dilapidated battery with four ancient cannon and a guard-house manned by a militia corporal and eight militiamen.

Baron de Rullecourt, the leader of the raid, had visited Jersey in the guise of a smuggler, and had realised that La Rocque was a place where no one would dream that an enemy would try to land. So he laid his plans skilfully. He would land his troops on a moonless night on the islet of L'Avarizon, more than a mile from the shore. There they would be out of range of the battery's guns. Then, when the tide went out, he could march them up the narrow channel, le Canné de l'Orgeon, where they would be hidden and protected by the rocks on either side.

But, instead of landing on December 26, as he had intended, contrary winds held him back till January 5. Then the difference in the tide upset his plans. The tide was rising, and he had to bring his boats right up the channel. But he had with him Pierre Journeaux, a La Rocque pilot, who had fled from the Island two years before after killing a man with his fist. Though the boats crept up in single file with muffled oars their approach must have been detected, had the militiamen obeyed orders. But it was Old Christmas Day, and (as it was reported at Corbet's court martial) "the Chef de Garde was intoxicated, and neglected to fix his sentinel on the battery, which so perfectly commands the shore that no such noise as the landing of troops could escape the ear of any man who was awake. He sent no tide-patrols, which his orders strictly enjoined. He quitted guard himself before the day, and suffered his men to follow his example in disobedience of the orders which direct the night guards not to quit their posts till relieved an hour after it is light." The result was that, when de Rullecourt's leading boat drew up at the Plat Rocque, which is now embedded in the pier, he found the point deserted, and he marched through the dark lanes to St Helier without any warning being given. (What happened, when he got there, is told in the article on the ROYAL SQUARE.)

But he left a hundred men at La Rocque as rearguard to secure his retreat, if necessary. When the sun rose, they were seen and their 25 boats that were waiting out at sea. Five companies of the 83rd Regiment were stationed in Fort Conway on Grouville Common, and they fell in at once and awaited orders from Corbet, the Lieutenant-Governor. To their amazement the order came to lay down their arms and surrender. The young lieutenant in command was in an awkward position. It seemed impossible to disobey his commanding officer's orders. Then François Le Couteur, rector of St Martin's, arrived burning with patriotic zeal, and bringing with him two field pieces that he had bought out of his own pocket after a previous attempt of the French to land. He urged an immediate attack. "I am a man of property," he said, "and, if you lose your commission, I will see that you shall be fully indemnified." But a note from Major Peirson, who was advancing on the town from the west, settled the matter: "Make haste. Come to our assistance. We are going to engage." They found the French at La Rocque drawn up four deep. As the grenadiers charged with fixed bayonets, seven were killed and eight wounded; but the French broke and fled to hide among the rocks. Le Couteur reported with pride that his guns had driven back the boats that had put out to pick up the runaways, who were all rounded up as prisoners-of-war. Short as the actual engagement was, its importance from the military point of view, and the potential danger it revealed, should not be minimised.

When the raid was over, to prevent a recurrence of the danger, two new martello towers were built, one on La Rocque Point and one close to Plat Rocque, and Seymour Tower out at sea to guard the entrance to the channel.

The little Church of St Peter la Rocque was built in 1851 as a chapel-of-ease to Grouville. The pier dates from 1881.

L'Etac. From the Old Norse *stakkr*, a rock. Wherever Norsemen went we find this word. Shetland is surrounded by Stakks: Grostakk, Gronastakk, Hoostakk, etc. The Stack of Noup is a great rock off the Orkneys. The North and South Stacks are off Holyhead. The Channel Islands abound in Etacs: the North and South Etacs in Grouville Bay, the Gros Etacs off La Rocque, the Gros Etacq and Petit Etacq off Guernsey, etc. The north point of St Ouen's Bay is a high rock called L'Etacquerel. South of this some narrow channels between reefs enabled fishermen to bring their boats into the shelter of this rock; so this uninviting spot became known as le Port de L'Etac. On the north of the rock is another small cove called Le Pulec. Here some peculiarity in the set of the tide piles up seaweed 10 or more feet high, during spring tides, and farmers bring their lorries down to gather up vraic for manure.

The most curious thing about L'Etac is its legend of a lost manor. An old document of uncertain date says: "The Fief of Morville and Robillard, which is part of the Fief of Sts. Germains, belonged to a gentleman named John Wallis. His Manor was on this Fief in the valley of a village called L'Etac and was known as the Manor of La Brecquette. Near it was an oak forest to the east and north. This valley and house for many years have been covered by the sea; howbeit at low tide one can still see the ruins of the manor." There is evidence that this manor of Brecquette is more than a fable. In a lawsuit in 1669 Philippe Mahaut, aged 80, testified on oath that, when he was young, he had seen at low tide some stone walls, which the old men who were with him declared to be the ruins of the Castle of Brecquette. John Wallis was evidently an ancestor of the Geoffrey Wallis, seigneur of St Germains, who was killed at the Battle of Barnet in 1471; the evidence, such as it is, points to an

71

inundation in about 1350. But many place-names in the district preserve memories of the lost manor. There is still a rock called La Brecquette and a Baie de la Brecquette and a stream known as le Douet de la Brecquette; and a Chemin Public de la Brecquette is mentioned in a contract of 1749. The word "brecque" means a gap or opening, for instance a gap in a hedge or bank.

In 1871 three veins of lead were found in rocks at Le Pulec, and attempts were made to form a company to sink a mine, but the venture was not economically viable.

In 1923 a human skull was found here in a prehistoric midden. For some obscure reason English, French, and American papers boosted this as a possible rival to the famous Java skull, but it proved to be quite a normal skull of the Bronze Age.

Longueville Manor. An ancient manor, which has given its name to three vingtaines, one in Grouville and two (Grande Longueville and Petite Longueville) in St Saviour. It was said that the house was once a nunnery, but this belief seems to rest on no firmer foundation than some small crosses cut as chamfer stops on an arch in the dining-room, a form of decoration which appears in about twenty instances in the Island, and probably carved there as a protection against evil spirits. The so-called "Nuns' Walk" in the grounds was only made in 1864 on the old course of the seigneurial water mill, called Le Moulin de Fossard. If nunneries had ever existed in Jersey, they would have been daughter houses of some great Normandy convent. But all religious houses preserved careful records of their possessions. We hear much of the Jersey priories for men attached to the Norman abbeys; but nowhere is there any hint of a nunnery.

In the 13th century the manor belonged to the powerful de Barentin family, who were seigneurs of Rozel; later it passed to the de Carterets; but in 1480 it was bought by John Nichol of Penvose, a Cornishman who had become Gentleman-Porter of Mont Orgueil. His descendants spelt their name Jerseywise as Nicolle, and his great-grandson Hostes Nicolle became Bailiff in 1561. Of him the chronicler tells a Naboth's-vineyard-like story: "There was a poor man, whose house and fields adjoined those of the Bailiff. This land the Bailiff coveted, but knew not how to get it. One day, however, he bade his servants slay two of his finest sheep, and carried them to the poor man's house, who was a butcher by trade. Next day he roused the Constable and his officers, and bade them search the butcher's house, where they found the sheep dead and hanging in a stable, where the Bailiff's servants had put them. The man was at once arrested, and brought into Court, and without any defence condemned to be hanged that day, though he was in no wise guilty. As the hangman put the rope round his neck at the door of the Court, he said to the Bailiff before everyone, 'I summon you to appear within forty days before the just Judge of all to answer for this injustice.' And on the thirty-ninth day that unjust judge fell dead by the wayside, as he was returning from Town." The chronicler is our sole authority for this story; but he wrote only 21 years after the event, so he is likely to have known the facts. The victim's name is said to have been Anthoine, and a field nearby, held for centuries by members of that family, is called Le Pré d'Anthoine.

The manor next passed to the La Cloches for about a century and a half, and Jurat Benjamin La Cloche has left a most important diary covering the years 1617–52, which is full of news and gossip of the times. Then it was sold and resold, till in 1863 it was bought by the Rev W. B. Bateman. He found it in extreme dilapidation, and spent more than £2,000 on a drastic restoration. Till the beginning of the 19th century the grounds had been surrounded by a high wall with an arched gateway and a porter's lodge. The ruins of the manorial chapel, dedicated to St Thomas the Martyr, i.e. Thomas à Becket, had been pulled down only in 1813. The water-mill on the stream through the grounds was still standing when Bateman bought it. The colombier with its 700 nesting-holes is not the original one mentioned in 1299, but was built in 1692, when George La Cloche reported that the old one was in ruins, and obtained permission to erect a new one "in the Garden of St Thomas".

Mr Bateman removed the cowsheds, stables, and pig-sties from the back of the house, and made a lawn there. He filled in the mill-pond and diverted the course of the stream. He added another 30 feet to the tower and he thoroughly modernised the interior of the building. In the dining-room the oak panelling at one end of the room was found by Bateman in position, but all the rest was obtained by buying and breaking up forty old oak chests. The house is now a hotel, and has been considerable enlarged.

Minquiers, Les. Anglicised to "Minkies". In old French *minkier* meant a man who sold fish wholesale; so the name may have been given humorously to a fishing-ground teeming with fish. It is a rocky reef nine miles south of St Helier and thirteen from the French coast. At low tide the area uncovered is larger than that of Jersey; but at high tide only nine peaks remain visible, and of these only one, the Maîtresse Ile, is habitable. Three Neolithic hearths, some flint knives, and a mass of bones of the grey seal show that in pre-historic times this was inhabited by seal-hunters.

Till 1929 no one doubted that the Minquiers belonged to Jersey. Acts of the seigneurial court of Noirmont in 1615 and 1617 show that the Crown claimed all wreckage on this reef. In 1692 the Dame de Samarès disputed this claim, asserting that the rocks formed part of her fief; but she lost her case. The Maîtresse Ile has always been a resort of Jersey fishermen. Towards the end of the 18th century they built 20 granite cottages there, in which they slept during the fishing season. It is said that much of the granite for Fort Regent was quarried from the Maîtresse Ile, till in 1807 the fishermen, fearing that their isle would be entirely destroyed, dropped the quarrymen's tools into deep water, and so stopped the work. Deeds of the transfer of huts and houses are registered in the Jersey Land Registry. The States have a Custom House on the isle. The harbours committee have erected beacons and pay an annual visit. All who sleep on the Maîtresse Ile on census night are included in the population of Jersey. No one ever questioned the fact that this was part of this Bailiwick.

But in 1861 a French cutter was wrecked on the Minquiers, and 51 lives were lost. So the French Government placed a lightship off the reef, which was later replaced by eight light-and-whistle buoys; and neither the States nor the British Admiralty raised any objection as the lightship was outside the three-mile limit. This encouraged some Frenchmen to assume that the rocks belonged to them, and in 1872 St Martin fishermen complained to the States that fishermen from Granville were interfering with their lobster-pots and nets. From time to time for half a century brawls broke out between the rival fishermen, and more than once the British fishery guardship had to intervene.

In 1929, however, Monsieur Leroux, a French banker, brought matters to a head. He obtained from the Land Registry at Coutances a lease of part of the Maîtresse Ile, and began to build himself a house. Strong protests were raised, and after many letters had passed between Whitehall and the Quai d'Orsay, his Government asked him "to consider as suspended the lease which permitted you to build on the Minquiers and to stop the building," adding, however, "The question of the sovereignity of the Minquiers has not ceased to be contested between France and England."

In 1939, however, another Frenchman, Monsieur Marin Marie, took up the cudgels. By the help of a subscription raised among ardent nationalists he ordered at Granville a prefabricated house. On the night of June 10, he and his friends set out in 15 boats, and in 24 hours the house had been erected on Maitresse Ile. Then came the war. The Germans stationed an ack-ack unit on the Island, and to keep themselves warm, they stripped the cottages of every scrap of wood, leaving nothing but bare walls. In 1953 the question of sovereignty was submitted to the Hague Tribunal, which confirmed United Kingdom sovereignty. This is discussed under the **Ecréhous,** the other reef which was similarly concerned.

Mont Orgueil. A magnificent example of mediaeval military architecture, a castle whose fighting life continued through the ages of bows and arrows well into the days of cannon. Every advance in the art of siegecraft had to be met with new methods of defence; so for 400 years new towers, new bastions, new battlements, new weapons were constantly being added, and the massive walls that we see today were produced by a gradual process of evolution through the ages. For example, the old keep dates from the reign of John, the Harliston Tower from the reign of Edward IV, while the mighty Somerset Tower is Elizabethan. Here can be studied side by side 13th, 14th, 15th, and 16th century systems of defence.

Even a civilian can see that this would be a formidable fortress to capture. Imagine that you have stormed the outer gate with considerable loss of life. You then rush down a narrow passage with stones and arrows pouring on you from walls far above your head, only to be held up by a second gate with its portcullis down and its drawbridge up. If you get through that, you find yourself in an open space, still under a heavy hail of missiles from the walls, with a third gateway and portcullis facing you. If you burst through this, you have to climb a long flight of steps with bowmen on right and left shooting down at you, till you reach a fourth gateway and portcullis with a wooden gallery over it and holes in the floor through which the defenders pour boiling pitch and possibly molten lead. You then climb up a narrow gorge with towering walls on either side, from which all sorts of unpleasant things come hurtling on your head, till you reach a fifth gate, where those who survive are confronted with the hardest task of all, the capture of the keep.

When England and Normandy were united, Jersey needed no castle. It lay snugly almost in the middle of the King's dominions. But when John lost Normandy in 1204, Jersey became a frontier outpost within sight of the enemy, and it obviously had to be fortified. Our castle is first mentioned in 1212, when John granted to Philippe d'Aubigny "the custody of Jersey *with our Castle*". So it must have been built by his predecessor, Hasculf de Suligny, for no castle is mentioned in the Exchequer Roll of 1180. Suligny's old keep still stands on the highest point of the rock, though almost hidden by the later Somerset Tower; and from that beginning bit by bit sprang the castle that we see today.

During the Hundred Years' War the French frequently overran the Island. In 1338 Admiral Béhuchet besieged the castle for six months, but failed to take it. Six months later Sir Robert Bertrand, Marshal of France, summoned it to surrender. "But," says the report sent to the King, "we made answer, 'Not while ten men are alive in it.' They sent many times to reconnoitre it by land and sea; but, thanks be to God, they saw every side so well prepared for defence that they retired to their fleet."

In 1373 Bertrand du Guesclin, the foremost soldier of the age, landed in the Island. He lost no lives in trying to force his way through the intricate chain of gates. He set his sappers to work on the opposite, the north-east, wall. "The besieged," we read, "did their duty staunchly, hurling down rocks and casks full of earth, while the crossbowmen poured arrows from every loophole." But the sappers undermined the foundations, propping them up on beams. They then filled the cavity with brushwood, which they lighted, and made their escape. As the props burnt through, a section of the mighty wall crashed down. We do not know the strength of the garrison, but it was hopelessly outnumbered by the 2,000 men-at-arms whom du Guesclin poured in through the breach; so it retired to the keep. Du Guesclin had by-passed all the cunningly planned defences, and, moreover, he had captured the castle well, which meant that the defenders would be forced to give in when the water in their cisterns was exhausted. So the warden of the castle made a pact (a thing quite usual in those days), that if he was not relieved by Michaelmas he would hand over the keys; and, leaving a small covering force, the French sailed away. On September 2 the English fleet arrived, and the castle was saved. Seven years later, however, it was actually captured by the French, and held for two years, till they were driven out by Sir Hugh Calverley.

The next crisis came during the Wars of the Roses. The Red Rose Party was losing ground, and Queen Margaret, its indomitable leader, persuaded her cousin, Pierre de Brézé, who was then Grand Seneschal of Normandy, to seize Jersey to be a refuge for the royal family if the worst came to the worst. One night in 1461 a postern was left open, the guards were plied with drink, and a French force secured the castle without striking a blow. The traitor was probably Guillaume de St Martin, the Lancastrian Attorney-General, perhaps in collusion with Nanfan the keeper. They held it for seven years.

About this time the name Mont Orgueil (Mount Pride) ousted the older name, Gorey Castle. We should have guessed this to be the invention of some poetic Frenchman, were it not that in 1292 a Patent Roll speaks of "Orgoil Castle in Guernsey". If this is a slip for Jersey, it shows that the name is earlier; but, if so, it is odd that it does not appear again for 170 years.

In 1468 the position of Carbonnel, the French commandant, grew difficult. Civil war broke out in France. De Brézé fell in the fighting. For a short time Normandy became an independent duchy; but the French King reconquered it and its duke had to fly. Carbonnel, however, was an enthusiast for a free Normandy; so he now had against him, not only the King of England, but also the King of France. But the castle, lately rearmed with culverins and cannon, was considered impregnable—*un castello inexpugnabile*, the Milanese ambassador called it—and the duke had poured in supplies of food and powder. Yet, when Richard Harliston, whose daughter Margaret is the heroine of Jersey's most famous epic, the Yorkist vice-admiral, blockaded it from the sea, and Jersey rose in revolt and besieged it from the land, after nineteen weeks the garrison had to surrender.

Seventeen years later Harliston himself was besieged. Henry VII had seized the throne, and the Red Rose again ruled the roost. Harliston, staunch old Yorkist, tried to hold the castle for his side; but his was a lost cause, and after some months he had to yield.

By Elizabeth's reign the castle seemed to have outlived its usefulness. The newer types of cannon could bombard it from the opposite hill. The Council wrote in 1593: "We have been credibly informed that the Castle is very ill-seated, and lieth subject to a mighty hill but 400 feet distant, and so overtopt by it, that no man can show his face in defence on this side. We require you to deal with Mr. Paul Ivy, purposely sent into those parts, to consider what were meet to be done." Ivy was an expert who had written books on fortification. By his advice it was decided to spend no more money on Mont Orgueil, and to use all resources for pressing on with the new Elizabeth Castle (q.v.).

When a castle was scrapped as of no further use, the usual course was to "slight" it, i.e. to throw down the walls to put them out of action, the equivalent of the modern "scorched earth" policy. From this fate Mont Orgueil was saved by Sir Walter Ralegh. When he became Governor he wrote: "It is a stately fort of great capacity. It were a pity to cast it down"; and Elizabeth did not insist.

Indeed, the castle's fighting days were not yet over. At the outbreak of the Civil War, while Sir Philippe de Carteret held Elizabeth Castle for the King, Lady de Carteret kept the royal banner flying over Mont Orgueil. The local militia besieged her, but their obsolete cannon could do no more than knock a few chips off the castle, and they had none of the tackle needed for scaling the walls. After three months they grew weary of their task, and began to drift home; and, when Royalist reinforcements from France reached the castle, the power of Parliament crumbled away and the Island was recovered for the King.

Eight years later, however, a Parliamentary army, fresh from its victory at Worcester, landed in St Ouen's Bay, and set up its cannon on Mont St Nicolas, overlooking Mont Orgueil, while Admiral Blake's fleet anchored in St Catherine's Bay. The castle had been strengthened and revictualled for the expected siege; but Worcester had knocked the heart out of the defenders. What was the good of fighting for a King whose cause was lost? "The English

Major", says a contemporary manuscript, "caused the troops to mutiny. They threatened to hand their Captain over to the enemy, if he did not capitulate." The Parliamentary commander offered generous terms, so the garrison marched out after a siege of only four days.

We have thought hitherto of the castle as a fortress; but it had other functions. For nearly 400 years it was the Governor's residence. Here for nine years, till the Civil War, Sir Philippe de Carteret, as King's representative, held his Viceregal court in the spacious apartments added to the old keep. "Roast partridge", wrote a local diarist, "is served in the castle at every meal." Distinguished visitors stayed with him. Once, five Portuguese princesses waiting for a ship to Holland; on another occasion, the Duc de Vendôme, the Queen's half-brother.

The castle was also a state prison for political offenders. One of the first of these was William Prynne, the little Puritan lawyer whose book on the immorality of the stage had been taken as a personal attack on the theatre-loving Queen. He arrived with twice-cropped ears and S. L. (Seditious Libeller) branded on each cheek, and de Carteret's instructions were, "Suffer no man but his keeper to speak to him. Permit him neither pen nor paper, and no book but the Bible." The Castle accounts show £10, probably livres tournois rather than sterling, spent on 103 pounds of iron for "bars for Mr Prynne's windows". Sir Philippe, however, took a fancy to him and got these conditions relaxed, and later treated him almost as a family guest.

When the Royalists recovered the Island, most of the Parliamentary leaders escaped to England, but Dean Bandinel and his son were caught and committed to the castle. Seven months later, when news came of the execution of Archbishop Laud, rumour said that Carteret meant to hang them as a reprisal. So they attempted to escape. "With a gimlet," says Chevalier, "they bored holes through the plank of a door, and by boring them close together they brake that plank. The door led to another room, next to the outer wall, which had a closet, into which, by removing some stones, they crept with difficulty. Here was a narrow window, through which they had hard work to squeeze. Then, by the help of a cord and towels fastened to a kitchen ladle fixed in a crack in the wall, they began to climb down. The wall was high and terrifying to descend, and they chose a night when a fierce gale was blowing, and trees were torn up by their roots. At the foot of the wall was a rugged rock sore difficult to clamber down. The son slid down first; but the rope was too short, and he fell on the rock and lay senseless. When the father was half-way down, the rope snapped, and he crashed on the rock, and broke all his bones." The Dean was discovered next morning, and died a few hours later. The son managed to crawl away, but was found and taken back to the castle, where death delivered him, too, from the gallows.

Cromwell frequently used the castle as a state prison. First came honest John Lilburne, dauntless defender of the common people's rights against King or protector; then Overton, Governor of Hull, one of Cromwell's ablest generals, who had joined the Fifth Monarchy Men, and accused Oliver of "taking the crown from the head of Christ and putting it on his own"; then a large batch of Royalists, among them that nasty knave, the Duke of Buckingham, who was always trying to run with the hare and hunt with the hounds; Sir Thomas Armstrong, caught carrying money out of England to the King; three of the tiny band of Royalist members of the Long Parliament—Sir Thomas Peyton, member for Kent, John Ashburnham, convicted of sending money to the King, and his brother William, who was involved in a plot against Cromwell's life, and John Weston, who had been in the Tower ever since he had been caught planning the release of Charles I before his execution.

After the Restoration, five of the late King's judges, who had escaped the hangman, were sent to Mont Orgueil—Sir Hardress Waller, one of Cromwell's major-generals, James Temple, Gilbert Millington, Henry Smith, and Thomas Wayte, members of the Long Parliament. There came too Colonel Salmon, Governor of Scarborough, Cromwell's Admiralty Commissioner; and General Overton, though no regicide, returned to the cell from which Cromwell's death had released him, because he was too sturdy a republican to be left at liberty.

These were the distinguished prisoners who had cells in the keep. But till 1693 the castle was also the prison for criminals, and it must have been a most unpleasant one. In the *Extente* of 1274, it is reported that one prisoner had lost the use of his legs and another the soles of his feet through being inhumanly chained in the castle. When the Governor cast Bailiff Clement Le Hardy into prison in

1494, the chronicler says, "He died there covered with lice and vermin." These, however, were quite usual prison conditions at this period.

Tenants of the Crown fiefs in the parishes of St Martin, Grouville and St Saviour had, by the terms of their tenure, to shoulder halberds and guard the prisoners on their five-mile march to the town for trial. This duty appertained to the house itself, rather than its occupant, so that when the ownership of a house on these fiefs changed, the halberd should always have been left there. In early days the prisoners were not numerous. There were cheaper ways of getting rid of undesirables, and for any serious crime the penalty was death, while lesser offences were punished by flogging and banishment. For minor transgressions there were the stocks and the pillory. Moreover, there was the right of sanctuary, or, to be more precise, a sanctuary path leading from church to shore, a right thought to be unique to Jersey, and not occuring even in the other Channel Islands. Any culprit who could reach a church before he was caught was safe for several days, and, if his friends could provide a boat, he could walk unarrested down the Perquage, or Sanctuary Path, which ran from every church to the sea, and escape from the Island, a simple way of encouraging criminals to deport themselves. So the squat Busgros Tower in the middle ward was probably big enough for a time to provide all the room that was needed.

But by the 16th century the number of prisoners increased. The right of sanctuary ceased after the Reformation, and the death penalty was inflicted less lavishly. Under the Calvinist régime the civil authorities had to enforce the decrees of the Church Courts. Dancing or skittle-playing on Sunday meant a fortnight in the castle. "Whosoever shall swear by the Name of God, for the fourth offence he shall be imprisoned." The witch movement too brought in wild, fanatical women. In the list of their trials we find: "Committed to the Castle, Fate unknown"; "Died in the Castle before trial"; "Detained twelve months in the Castle on bread and water." And in addition the custom arose of imprisonment for debt. The Gentleman-Porter, who was the man responsible for their safe-keeping, must sometimes have been puzzled where to put all his guests.

The 18th and 19th centuries were for the castle a time of neglect and decay; but in 1907 the Crown transferred it to the States.

A great deal of repair was then intelligently done, the cost of which was largely met by visitors' entrance fees. King George V and Queen Mary came to the castle on the occasion of their visit to the Island on July 12, 1921. The Germans converted it once more into a formidable fortress, strengthening its outworks with concrete, and building a fire-control tower on the top of the keep. But in 1946 the whole building was again handed back to the States, and is now in excellent condition, drawing many thousands of visitors annually. A wax work exhibition shows the death of Major Peirson in 1781, at the Battle of Jersey in the Royal Square. Another exhibit is an effigy of Prynne, with his cheek branded with S.L., sitting in the cell which he in fact occupied. A militia museum is gradually being organised there, showing uniforms and other reminders of Jersey's Royal Militia. The distinction of having the word "Royal" was accorded by William IV in recognition of the militia's part in that battle.

Museum. More than one unsuccessful attempt was made to give Jersey a museum. The first gave its name to Museum Street. In 1836 an advertisement said: "The Museum near the Public Baths is now open. An Exhibition of Egyptian, Grecian, Roman and other Antiquities collected by John Gosset, Esq., during his travels in the East, including a Mummy, together with Fossils, Shells, Specimens of the Arts of the South Sea Islands, China, and America, from private collections, liberally lent for the purpose of ultimately establishing a National Museum." But on the first free day such a mob invaded the building and so much damage was done that the owners of the exhibits demanded them back, and the museum was closed.

Fourteen years later the Royal Gallery of Arts and Sciences was opened in the Square. The Queen and Prince Albert became patrons. The old exhibits were borrowed again, including the mummy. Sir John Millais lent some of his paintings. A large collection of Le Capelain's water-colours was gathered together. But this praiseworthy effort died in its fifth year.

In 1875 the Société Jersiaise, then only two years old, decided to start a museum. This was opened in 1877 in King Street, and when it outgrew those premises, was moved to Morier Lane, in premises where Martin's Bank now is. But in 1893 Jurat Falle presented to the Société a fine 19th century merchant's house in Pier Road, and the Museum was transferred there. At first the committee accepted almost anything that was offered—Etruscan tiles, Brazilian fireflies, lamps from Pompeii, scarabs from Egypt, stuffed serpents, Chinese umbrellas, coins from Afghanistan. But later they wisely decided to confine their museum solely to local objects.

It covers now every side of the Island's story. The Geological Room shows specimens of all the local rocks and minerals; and Jersey presents problems of exceptional interest to petrologists. In the Herbarium, nearly a thousand specimens of native wild plants are arranged, a surprising number for so small an area; of these, 22 are unknown in England and others are extremely rare there. One room is devoted to marine biology, for Jersey is remarkably rich in salt-water fauna. At least a hundred species of sponges are found here—scarlet, orange, green, white, and black, and almost as many anemones. Of special interest are the octopus with its powerful arms, the electric ray which kills its prey with an electric shock, the hideous angler-fish, often called the sea-devil, and the ormer, meaning oreille de mer, or sea-ear, from the shape of its mother-of-pearl shell; its flesh provides one of the greatest local delicacies. Of insects, over two thousand species are mounted and labelled in the cabinets, several of which are not found in Great Britain, and one, a grasshopper, is found nowhere else in the world. Jersey has given its name to the beautiful Jersey Tiger Moth, a conspicious vividly coloured day-flying species.

The bird collection is good, containing specimens of most of the birds which breed in or visit the Island. Golden eagles have been shot here, and once the rarer fish eagle. There is a variety of Dartford Warbler which is very rare in England, but which nests in Jersey's gorse-covered commons. The collection of birds' eggs is thought to be complete. In the British Isles the white toothed shrew occurs only in the Scilly Isles, Sark, and Jersey. It is *Crocdura suavestens*, and not the same as *Crocdura russula* found in Guernsey and Alderney.

Turning now to human inhabitants, even non-archaeologists, if they take the trouble to read the very full explanatory labels, will derive a fairly complete picture of the prehistory of the Island. Here are relics of the two long extinct races of cave-men who inhabited Jersey about 50,000 years ago at the upper level, and more, perhaps 100,000 at the lower level. The teeth of Neanderthal man, *Homo Breladensis*, are among the Museum's most valuable possessions. Other cases show specimens of pottery and implements of the Neolithic or New Stone Age, about 3000–1800 B.C., with models and photographs of some of its chamber-tombs. In the garden also can be seen some tombs of this period, removed from Green Island to save them from being washed away by the tide; and the hollowed stones in the entrance yard are querns in which their women used to grind corn. Another room illustrates the progress made when the use of metals was discovered, i.e. in the Bronze Age, which began about 1600 B.C., and the Early Iron Age, which followed. To the Bronze Age belongs the magnificent gold torque dug up in St Helier in 1888. These rooms deliberately contain only selected, typical specimens. An immense store of other finds is reserved for specialists and students.

About 300 B.C., or a bit later, came the Gauls, and large hoards of their coins have been discovered, crude copies of Greek coins of Philip of Macedon. And after them came the Romans, and, since Jersey formed part of the Roman Empire for 500 years, their coins too are found. The collection of Armorican coins found in various hoards and at different times, is of prime importance to numismatists. A long case in the Historical Room shows specimens of all money that has been used in the Island: Gaulish, Roman, French (for centuries the coins minted at Tours, the livre tournois, the sol tournois and the denier tournois, were the local currency), English ones brought by the English garrisons, Russian ones brought by the Russian troops quartered here in 1799, Jersey's own copper coinage, the fantastic bank-notes that anyone was once allowed to print and circulate, and the paper money used during the German Occupation.

Moving on to historical exhibits, almost every period is well represented. For example, for the Civil Wars there are cannon-balls dropped on the town by Royalist guns from the Castle, the actual Proclamation of Charles II as King that was nailed to the Court door when news arrived, only a fortnight later, of his father's execution. The signing of this proclamation was a very brave act, and no man knew what the future held, nor what repercussions there might be. There is also the Diary of Jean Chevalier, a unique record of events during the Civil War, and from Jersey's point of view, equivalent in interest to Pepys' Diary. There are, too, the pistol-holsters used by Charles in the Island, of sombre hue because he was in mourning, and a copy of the printed Declaration of Loyalty to the Republic of England that everyone had to sign under Cromwell. There is a copy of Copley's famous picture of the Battle of Jersey, and two other completely different prints published at the same time in London. Here are Peirson's watch and a miniature of him by Jean, side by side with de Rullecourt's sword and snuff-box and the proclamation that he issued.

On the ground floor is a reproduction of an old Jersey kitchen and bedroom showing conditions that existed in a country farmhouse up to the beginning of this century. The lintel of the entrance door came from an old house at Beaumont, the kitchen door from one at St Peter, the fireplace from a dismantled farm at St John, the bénitier (the problem of these is discussed in the Foreword) from a ruined house at La Moie. Of the five hundred articles in these two rooms we can only call attention to four. There was no form of illumination at night but the *crasset*, the iron hanging lamp with an inner saucer to hold the oil and a bit of rag as a wick, and an outer one to catch the drippings. The stench must have been as strong as the light was feeble. The *veille*, the box full of dried bracken which formed a primitive sofa, was found on every farm. Here the women used to sit at night and knit by the dim light. The *pouchette*, the hiding-place for valuables, was a tunnel in the wall ending in an earthenware jar, the opening being masked by clothing or kitchen utensils. In this kitchen it is inside the fireplace. Here the gold torque rested securely throughout the German Occupation. The four-poster bed is of French workmanship, a reminder that in olden days the wealthier Jersey families did much of their shopping at St Malo. Next door is a room with old farm implements (more will be found in the Agricultural Museum at La Hougue Bie) and an old Jersey bow-fronted window, from a demolished shop in Colomberie.

At the top of the house is the Ship Room, with relics of the great days of Jersey shipping. Here boys who have been reading sea stories can see the difference between barques and brigs, brigantines and schooners, for the pictures of Jersey ships are arranged according to their rigs. There are examples of Letters of Marque, a form of licence which amounted to legalised piracy. A corner of the room is devoted to the once flourishing ship-building industry. In another room will be found a collection of old Jersey needlework, lace, and costumes.

There is a small exhibit of documents connected with the German Occupation, the actual ultimatum dropped on the town ordering every house to fly a white flag; leaflets dropped by the R.A.F.; proclamation announcing the shooting of a Frenchman, Scornet, at St Ouen; and military maps and photographs left behind by the Germans showing the position of their guns, searchlights, and troops. A much larger collection of articles will be found in the Occupation Museum at La Hougue Bie. The collection of Jersey-made silver is noteworthy, and visitors should particularly notice the Jersey christening bowls, which are peculiar to this Island, and are of great beauty. Of the hundred thousand exhibits or more in the Pier Road Museum, only a few have been mentioned, but enough to show that no one can really understand the Island without spending several hours inside its walls. Its library of 4,000 volumes is available to students who need them for research. It also owns many thousands of ancient documents of all dates from the 14th century, as well as copies of almost all newspapers that have been printed in the Island.

A delightful addition to the Museum is the Barreau Art Gallery "for the exhibition of works of Channel Island artists or works of other artists illustrative of Channel Island scenery or of local interest", presented to the Société in 1924 by Miss E. A. Barreau in memory of her artist nephew, Arthur Hamptonne Barreau. Among Jersey artists, eight may be said to have secured a permanent niche in the Temple of Fame: Monamy, the first British marine painter; Jean, the miniaturist; Le Capelain, who is often called the Jersey Turner; Millais, who became President of the Royal Academy; Poingdestre, who for thirty years was President of the British Academy at Rome; Walter Ouless, R.A., the portrait-painter, F. W. S. Le Maistre, who committed the churning waves and sun-lit rocks of his native isle so faithfully to canvas; Thomas Berteau, exquisite in fine pencil work as well as oils, and Edmund Blampied, who has already been referred to in the Introduction. Some of these men were not actually born in the Island, but all have full cause to be considered Jerseymen. Characteristic work of all these artists will be found in the gallery.

The actual Museum is run by the Société Jersiaise, whose other functions include research, preservation of ancient monuments, and publication of learned works, in addition to their annual report, the Bulletin. There are at present, ambitious plans afoot for the re-organisation of the actual museum and its recent acquisition, the adjoining property, no. 7, Pier Road. This latter is in itself a museum exhibit, having retained, almost intact, its early Georgian staircase and panelled rooms. It is hoped that in the near future the Société's perfectly wonderful collection of exhibits concerning the Island will be able to be shown to greater advantage, as it deserves. Nearly 18,000 visitors saw the Museum in 1967, but the weather is a dominant factor, and a wet summer is a more prosperous one for the Museum.

Noirmont, the Black Mount, called in old charters Niger Mons, is the dark, heather-clad promontory that forms the western wing of St Aubin's Bay. An old weather forecast runs: *Quand Nièrmont met san bonnet, ch'est signe de plyie* ("When Noirmont dons its cap, it is a sign of rain").

The promontory gives its name to an ancient fief and a vingtaine, the only case in the Island where the two coincide. The fief originally belonged to the Crown, being one of those kept by the Duke for himself when the Normans conquered the Island; but before the reign of John some king, perhaps Henry II, had transferred it to the monks of Mont St Michel in exchange for a fief in Alderney. The Assize Roll of 1309 stated: "On the Fief of Noirmont is a certain Chapel of old; the Abbot of Mont St. Michel is bound to provide for the celebration of Divine Service in it on one of the Feasts of St. Michael, and the Rector of the Parish on the other." The site of that chapel is unknown. Mont St Michel also held land at St Clement, and the prior of St Clement had the task of collecting the Noirmont dues, and between him and the tenants there was perpetual friction. In 1413, when all alien abbeys were deprived of their English possessions, Noirmont reverted to the Crown. In 1643, Charles I granted it to Captain George Carteret, the future Royalist leader, as a reward for freeing from the Moors at Sallee 400 Christian slaves, some of whom were Jersey sailors and one a Noirmont tenant. Sir George's great-grandson, Lord Carteret, sold it to Elie Pipon, and the Pipons held it for nearly 200 years. Philippe Pipon built a manor-house on the fief in 1695, which

87

was demolished in 1810, and replaced by the present house in about 1830. In 1880 James Pipon sold it to Girard de Quetteville, from whose family Guy de Gruchy bought it in 1909. Lillie Langtry, the famous beauty, spent her honeymoon in it, and left her name scratched with a diamond on a window-pane.

Working up the east side of the point you come first to Bellecroute Bay, a fine anchorage where ships from plague ports had to remain during their time of quarantine. Then comes Pointe de Boue, which appears with various spellings throughout the years, where in 1646 Sir George Carteret built a little fort with two cannon. Farther south are rocks called Les Cracheurs. In 1865 a petition signed by all the principal shipowners urged the States to build a great harbour here, which would provide deep water at the lowest tides and make any further extension of St Helier's harbour unnecessary. This would have been linked to the town by a railway. If this scheme had been carried out, Noirmont today would be a bustling hive of industry; but after a sharp debate the project was defeated. The Tour de Vinde at the tip of the point was begun in 1810 and finished in 1814 as a defence against Napoleon. During the German Occupation a fire command tower was erected on the top of the cliff controlling all the coast-defence batteries right and left. This was equipped with every conceivable kind of modern apparatus for accurate gunnery, and for the comfort of the troops plenty of luxurious easy chairs were requisitioned from private houses and even a grand piano.

On September 26, 1946, the States approved the purchase of a large part of the promontory as the Island's war memorial. But certain legal difficulties arose about obtaining permission to divide what was an indivisible fief, and official wheels move slowly. These have at last been overcome, and this glorious headland is now public property. La Hougue de Vinde, to the south of the promontory, is probably of Bronze Age date. At the extreme point there is a defensive tower, built in the early 19th century, which now houses a shipping light, fed by acetylene gas.

Pinnacle, The. Reverence offered to holy stones is one of the most primitive and universal forms of religion. Rude blocks of stone around which religious customs have gathered are found in Asia, North Africa, Western Europe, and South America. In parts of India every village has its fetish-stone, in which some divine spirit is supposed to dwell. In Palestine, in Bible days, several of the popular sanctuaries grew up round stones said to have been erected by some ancient worthy—the stone at Bethel by Jacob, the stone at Shechem by Joshua. Archaeologists call these stones "menhirs," from two Breton words, *men* a stone and *hir* long. More than 10,000 have been counted in Tripoli, more than 800 in Brittany. Of the latter, one at Locmariaquer, before it fell, was 67 feet high and must weigh 370 tons, yet this huge block of granite is not of a type that is found in that district, and so must have been dragged from a distance.

When the so-called "Iberians" reached Jersey about 3000 B.C. they erected many menhirs, e.g. the Dame Blanche at Samarès and many others. But they found that nature had provided them with one beside which the Locmariaquer monster was a mere baby. The Pinnacle Rock in the north-west corner of St Ouen is about 200 feet high, and rises sheer from the sea; and, though the soil is barren and the site exposed to the fiercest gales, at five widely divided periods of history men have made settlements at its foot. The careful excavations of Father Burdo, S.J., and Major Godfray revealed deep down in the sand remains of a typical Neolithic settlement with numerous hearths, 700 stone implements, and fragments of round-bottomed pots. On the top of this came relics of an entirely different race, whose flat-bottomed pots were of very inferior ware, but whose arrow-heads of Grand Pressigny flint from Touraine show that they were in touch with traders from abroad. A copper axe proved that this camp belonged to the Copper Age. Above this came a Bronze Age fort protected by two ramparts, its date indicated by a bronze spearhead. And still nearer the present surface, just below the roots of the grass, came a fourth encampment, which an iron wedge, four iron bars, and part of an iron blade identified as belonging to the Iron Age. A Gaulish coin showed that it had been occupied after the Gaulish invasion. From the Neolithic to the Iron Age was fully 2,000 years. Why should four races separated by such long periods of time have chosen such an uninviting spot to live in, though the sea has probably considerably eroded the neck of land with passing time? The only possible answer seems to be the attraction of this awe-inspiring rock.

Nor is this the end of the story. The veneration for menhirs lasted

89

well into the Christian era. As late as A.D. 567 the Council of Tours forbade priests to allow inside their churches "any who offer worship to stones set up on end". So it is not surprising to find at the close of the 2nd century A.D., long after most people had adopted the worship of the Roman gods, that there were still some devotees of the older forms of paganism. All over Normandy little shrines called *fana* were being erected in out-of-the-way places to obscure local deities; and the foundations of one of these were discovered just outside the earthwork at the Pinnacle. A coin which some worshipper had dropped in the sand helps to date this *fanum*. It bears the head of the Emperor Commodus and was minted in A.D. 181. It would probably take some years before it reached the Island; so as late as A.D. 200 we may picture little bands of pilgrims wending their way westward to worship the god of the Pinnacle. No shrine in the Island preserved its sanctity for so many generations. From at least 2000 B.C. till A.D. 200 this tremendous rock was filling men's minds with awe for the Unseen. This is a wonderful place to see wild flowers in the spring, including horse-shoe vetch, the brilliant gold of creeping broom (*Sarothamus scoparius prostratus*), bluebells, and thick clumps of thrift (*Armeria maritima*) making a glorious kaleidoscope of colour. The Jersey thrift (*Armeria arenaria*) grows elsewhere, but not here.

Portelet. A little harbour; two bays in Guernsey bear the same name. A picturesque cove in St Brelade parish, lying just west of Noirmont, once one of the beauty-spots of the Island, now alas, largely spoilt by a sprawling holiday camp. In the centre of the Bay is the Ile au Guerdain, which is an old family name found in the parishes of Trinity and St Brelade, on which stands a martello tower, built by the War Office during the Napoleonic Wars. This is often mistakenly spoken of as Janvrin's Tomb. Philippe Janvrin, captain of the *Esther*, had been dead for 90 years before the tower was built. He was a St Brelade sailor who, in 1721, when he brought his ship back from Nantes, where the plague was raging, was ordered to remain in quarantine in Bellecroute Bay. There he died, and, as his body was not allowed to be brought ashore, he was buried on the Ile au Guerdain within sight of his home. His widow erected a stone over his grave; but this was probably destroyed when the tower was built. On the west of the bay is a raised beach of large water-worn boulders, showing that the waves once reached a higher level than they do now; and the Ile Percée is a rock through which the sea has made a complete tunnel. The western headland was obviously once a prehistoric flint-chipping area, for flint implements are often found in the shallow soil. The rush of the tide as it meets round the islet is very dangerous, and in 1915 eight young Jesuit students were drowned there, an episode which filled the whole populace with horror.

Prison. Till 1679 the only prison was Mont Orgueil, and prisoners had to be marched five miles to the Royal Court for trial. This was so inconvenient that in that year the States obtained permission from the Privy Council to use part of the import duties to build a prison in the town. They chose an extraordinary site. They built it straddling right across the road at the spot now called Charing Cross, a few yards below the point where King Street and Broad Street meet. As the Esplanade was not yet built, this was the only entrance to the town from the west, and all traffic had to pass through a dark tunnel beneath it. Whether this was meant to be a sort of city gate to protect the town from attack, or whether it was merely a copy of old Temple Bar in London, no one knows.

Punishments in those days were still very barbarous. Prisoners were frequently flogged all the way from the court to the prison. In 1787 David Brouard and his wife were found guilty of theft. First the woman was stripped to the waist, and led slowly to the prison, while the hangman flogged her at every step "till the blood ran". Then the husband had to follow the same route; but, when they had nearly reached their destination and respite seemed in sight, the husband was not allowed to take the last few steps: the procession halted, and the hangman continued to wield the scourge "as if he were drunk or mad". "The man's howls and contortions," we are told, "moved all the spectators to pity." And that was not the end. the hangman then took a knife and cut off half the man's ear and nailed it to the prison door.

The old prison remained till 1811 with its heavily barred windows and underground cells, a grim warning to evil-doers. But at last it became so overcrowded that the States decided to build a new one next door to the hospital. This cost £19,000, and its front remains one of the finest bits of granite work in the Island. In 1838 a house of correction was added, for persons whose irregular lives made them a public nuisance; this is now used for debtors, for imprisonment for debt is still legal in Jersey, though not largely enforced. Later, two additional blocks were built, one for men and one for women. It is rather horrible to think that as late as 1883 this was a show-place for trippers. A guide-book of that date says: "Visitors are allowed to inspect it on application to the obliging gaoler, and a pleasant hour may be spent within its walls." During the German Occupation a considerable number of prominent Jerseymen became residents in its cells, some for trivial breaches of enemy proclamations, others, innocent of any offence, because they had been seized as hostages. There are at present plans to build a new prison on the beautiful south coast, at La Moie.

Royal Square. The open space east of St Helier's parish church, once—before the houses encroached—much larger than it is now, was for at least 600 years the shopping centre for the Island. It was known as *le Marchi*, the Market. Before the Reformation its central feature was the Market Cross, where public proclamations were made and all new laws were published. The surrounding space was filled with stalls, piled with goods of every description, eggs, butter, poultry, vegetables, clothes, earthenware, hardware. The fish was laid out on flagstones, where the statue now stands. The corn-market was on the site of the National Provincial Bank, while the upper storey, now the premises of the United Club, was, in the 17th century, privately owned by Suzanne Dumaresq, Lady of La Haule, who kept it as a town house, building a fine granite hall in place of a previous wooden shed. A large room in this house was let for public meetings, and here John Wesley preached when he visited the Island in 1787. The butchers hung their joints where the other branch of the National Provincial Bank does its business. Chevalier gives a picture of the scene in 1643, when the Royalist cannon from Elizabeth Castle bombarded the town on market-day: "Twenty cannon fired a volley at two in the afternoon, when the Market was at its height, and all the Twelve Parishes were gathered together with their relations and friends, innocent ladies who had never taken any part in politics and children too young to discern their right hand from their left. Cannon balls fell like thunderbolts all about the Market. Everyone lay flat on the ground or rushed to take refuge in a house, overthrowing the stalls of the haberdashers and cobblers, and scattering their wares. Those who had money in their hands dropped it, and much clothing was lost, for everyone knew that cannon balls are no respecters of persons." A little later permanent shelters were put up for some of the trades. The butchers too had a long, low shed with two rows of stalls—"but," says one writer, "lucky was he who could get home without some grease on his clothes." The small building which now bears a large sun-dial was a guard-house for troops. The land on which it stands was ceded by the States to the British government in 1802, and was re-purchased from the latter in 1934.

The Market was also the place of public punishment. Some criminals were hanged on Gallows' Hill, but others met their end here. When a witch was strangled and burnt in 1648, Chevalier says: "Such crowds came to watch her execution that the Town was full. No one had seen so many people since the Prince came to Jersey. A multitude of men and women, young lads and girls, swarmed on the walls of the churchyard and the slope of the Town Hill." Unmarried mothers were flogged by the hangman from the door of the Court to the churchyard gate. The pillory was in frequent use. As late as 1835 three Jews were exposed in it for forgery. The stocks at the church gates seldom lacked an occupant. In 1619 Katherine Le Sauteur, "convicted of joining in night revels, dressed as a man and wearing breeches", was sentenced to sit all Saturday in the Market stocks with her breeches hung beside her.

Till 1697 prisoners who were marched in from Mont Orgueil were locked in a large iron cage at the east end of the marketplace to wait their turn to be taken into the Court. When a prison was built in the town, this was no longer necessary; so the States planned to erect in its place a monument 30 feet high, a Tuscan pillar on a granite pedestal with a globe-shaped sun-dial on the top. A man named Le Preuve contracted to build this; but he died with nothing done. So Abraham Gosset, proprietor of the Hôtel de l'Union, which stood on the west of the Court, offered to take over the contract in exchange for the narrow passage which separated his property from the Court-house. He suggested that, instead of a sun-dial, a gilded statue of George II should be placed on the top. After certain modifications of the original design, in 1751 the statue was un-veiled amid mighty thundering of cannon, and in its honour the

Market was renamed La Place Royale (Royal Square). But the fact that the King, according to an absurd convention of the time, was represented as a Roman gave rise to unkind stories. It was said that Gosset had bought cheap the statue of a Roman Emperor found on a Spanish ship captured by a privateer; but, if so, it is strange that an ancient Roman should be wearing the Order of the Garter below his knee! This is clearly part of the original moulding, and cannot have been added later. All the milestones in the Island are measured from this statue.

The most thrilling event in the history of the Market was the Battle of Jersey. In 1779 an abortive attack by the French, under the Prince of Nassau, had been made, attempting to land in St Ouen's Bay. They were repulsed by the local forces, but two years later it was a different story. In 1781 England and France were at war. Before dawn, on January 6, that dare-devil soldier of fortune, Philippe Charles Felix Macquart, Baron de Rullecourt, halted at the foot of the statue 600 French soldiers who had landed secretly at La Rocque. The surprise was complete. Corbet, the Lieutenant-Governor, was asleep in his bed, and de Rullecourt bluffed him into believing that the men in the marketplace were only the advance guard of an overwhelming French force that had occupied the Island. Then, by a threat that, if he refused, he would burn the town to the ground, he induced him to sign an order to his troops to lay down their arms. By the time Corbet had signed the capitulation order, the alarm had already been given. Captain Mulcaster, R.E., learning that the French were in the town, had ridden to the hospital buildings, where troops were billeted, and finding that they were already warned, rode to Elizabeth Castle to give the alarm. At the same time Captain Hemery, of the Jersey militia, was riding from town through the half-light of dawn to warn the Scottish companies stationed on Grouville Common. Soon the guns of Elizabeth Castle were sounding the alarm, and the bells of the parish churches were carrying it over the Island. All the senior officers of the Regulars were in England on Christmas leave. The decision rested with Francis Peirson, a Major of 24, who with half the companies of the 95th was quartered at a house called La Hougue in St Peter. Dare he disobey the written orders of his commander-in-chief? He marched into town, found 2,000 of the militia gathered on Gallows' Hill (now Westmount) wondering what to do, took command of the whole force, and gave orders to attack. He sent one party by a devious route to seize the Town Hill, where Fort Regent now stands. The old Court buildings were so low that from the hill it was possible to fire right into the Market. He launched his main attack up what is now Broad Street; while he himself led a smaller force by the back lane, La Rue de Derrière, which is now King Street, to burst into the Market by the opening now called Peirson Place, and take the enemy in the rear. The French were outnumbered and outmanoeuvred, and the fight did not last long. Copley's famous picture in the Tate Gallery has made the scene familiar. Peirson and de Rullecourt both lost their lives, but the victory was complete. "The enemy," wrote one who was present, "threw down their arms and fled for refuge, some into the Court, some into the Beef or Corn Markets, the rest into any houses that they found open." They were herded into the town church to await transports to take them to England. Peirson and de Rullecourt are both buried here. Major Corbet was court-martialled and removed from office, but granted a pension. Although he had found himself in an almost intolerable position, he must bear some blame for his conduct in this moment of supreme emergency.

As the population increased, so did the business of the Market, and by the end of the 18th century there were constant complaints about its congestion. Room could no longer be found for all who wanted stalls nor for the crowds of jostling customers trying to make their purchases. Moreover, business in the Royal Court was often seriously disturbed by the noise outside. So in 1800 the States decided to move the Market elsewhere. A new road, now Halkett Place, and named after Sir Colin Halkett, Lieutenant-Governor from 1821–30, was then being planned; so the land on which the present markets stand was bought, and one built there (a model of this is in the Museum), copied from one at Bath, and that in the Place Royale was closed. The chestnut trees were not planted till 1894.

Round the old marketplace the public buildings clustered. First came the Royal Court or *La Cohue*. Here the Jurats, 12 honorary judges, chosen once by the Optimates or Magnates of the Island, but since 1605 by popular election, have administered justice in all cases but treason, to use the phrase our forefathers loved, "from time immemorial". Their Cohue has, however, been rebuilt several

95

times. In the accounts of John de Roches, Warden of the Isles, in 1329 is the item: "For repairing the House in which the King's Pleas are held, 20 sols." Chevalier describes the Court, as he had known it in his youth, as "not much of a place to look at. From outside it resembled a barn. It had no chimneys, and only one storey, and was thatched with straw." He lived to see the new Cohue, which Sir George Carteret erected in 1647, a much finer building of Mont Mado granite, roofed with slates from France, with a gilt crown on its little belfry, "which," says Chevalier, "when the sun shone, dazzled the eyes of spectators." Sculptured arms on granite of the King, the Governor Lord Jermyn, and Sir George himself as Bailiff, were made by a mason from St Malo, and erected on the façade. The whereabouts of the former are unknown, those of Lord Jermyn are at the back of a small house in the town, and those of Sir George are now in the forecourt of the Museum.

After the Restoration dignity was added to this Court by the presence of the great silver-gilt mace presented by Charles II "as a proof of his affection towards the Island, where he twice found a safe retreat, when excluded from his other dominions." It is carried before the Bailiff on all ceremonial occasions, and laid before his chair when he presides in Court or States. It bears the inscription (in Latin), "Not all doth he deem worthy of such honour." It is almost the same size and weight as that borne before the Speaker of the House of Commons, and bears a strong resemblance to that also presented by Charles II to the Royal Society.

Carteret's Cohue lasted until 1764, when a new building was erected, and finished in 1769. There were complaints that it was cold and draughty, and it was again replaced a century later. The present building was completed in 1866, but again complaints continued about its lack of comfort, and only after final modifications had been carried out in 1896 does it seem to have been found satisfactory. Extensive redecoration was done in 1964, and at the same time the paintings were cleaned and restored. They include various portraits of past Bailiffs and other officials, and a copy of John Singleton Copley's *Death of Major Peirson* by Holyoake; the original hangs in the Tate Gallery. There is also a portrait of George III by the local artist Philippe Jean, and one of Field-Marshal Henry Seymour Conway, Governor 1772–95, by Gainsborough. Of the 1764 building we are told, "the entrance is a spacious vestibule, open to the public. At the end is the Court itself, where red-robed Jurats dispense justice with Rhadamanthine dignity. Upstairs are the office for registering contracts, rooms for keeping the records, and a large chamber where the Bailiff and Jurats meet for private consultation." One use to which the vestibule was put was the drawing of the lotteries. Two small boys in blue with red sashes stood by two great wheels. One put his hand into one and pulled out a number, which he held up for everyone to see. Then the other boy drew from the second wheel either a prize or a blank, while two Jurats sat at a table writing down the winning numbers.

The Bailiff's throne-like chair, with heraldic carvings, is said by experts to date from about 1500. The Lieutenant-Governor's which stands beside it, is dated a little later. These two chairs illustrate a point in constitutional history. After many disputes between the two officials the Privy Council in 1617 ruled: "We hold it convenient that the charge of the Military Forces be wholly in the Governor, and the care of Justice and Civil affairs in the Bailiff"; so in Court the Governor's seat is a few inches lower than the Bailiff's.

Adjoining the Court on the east is the States' Chamber, the home of the local Parliament, for Jersey has always had the privilege of Home Rule. In the Middle Ages the Royal Court not only administered justice, but ruled the Island also by issuing ordinances, which had the force of law. But in the 16th century the custom arose of sometimes consulting the Rector and Constable of each of the 12 parishes about the feeling in their parishes. What began as an act of courtesy came to be expected as a right, and gradually this meeting of Jurats, Rectors, and Constables became an established institution, known as *Les États*, the States. In 1771 the right to make ordinances was taken away from the Court, and the States remained the only legislative body. In 1856 they were made more democratic by the admission of Deputies elected by each parish. In the sweeping Reform Act of 1948 Jurats and Rectors were removed, and the Assembly consists today of Senators, Constables, and Deputies, all chosen by popular vote. For 400 years the States met in the same chamber as the Royal Court, but by 1809 they had secured a room of their own upstairs. In 1887 they moved into their present handsome quarters. Above the Bailiff's seat hangs a banner with the three leopards passant, the arms of the King of England which the

Bailiff has permission to use, as his official seal. This banner was made by the Royal School of Needlework in 1921. Like the Royal Court, the States Chamber has recently been redecorated, and both are now lighter and more colourful.

On the other side of the Court-house is the Public Library. Founded in 1736 by Philip Falle, the first historian of Jersey, who left over 2,000 volumes to the States, the library was originally housed in the street which is still called Library Place. But in 1886 the present stately home for them was opened in the Royal Square. The library now has 90,000 volumes, including a large collection of local books and newspapers. There is also a children's library housed in the New Street school building, a branch library situated at Les Quennevais School, and a mobile library service, serving the Island schools, and adult borrowers, in all the parishes. There is also a large reference section of dictionaries, encyclopaedias, etc., a number of works on diatoms in the science section, fiction, ancient and modern, French and English, and a well-stocked agricultural section.

Set into the wall, on the south of the Square, is a plaque commemorating Wace, the Jersey-born 12th century poet, who has been mentioned elsewhere. All passers-by should also notice the letters V and Vega, and the date 1945, let into the paving stones. This was done during the Occupation, and under the noses of the Germans, who never noticed. Vega was the name of the life-saving Red Cross ship which brought the supplies which were so desperately needed during those last months.

In 1934 the States extended this line of buildings still farther west by adding an imposing block of offices for their various departments; so now they occupy all the south side of the Square.

Rozel Bay. The name is taken from the manor (next article), not vice versa. In this quiet bay in the north-east corner of the Island nothing seems to have happened. When we have said that the barracks were built in 1810 as part of the precautions against Napoleon, and the pier in 1829 to provide accommodation for oyster boats which could not find anchorage in the overcrowded harbour at Gorey, nothing remains to tell. But on either side of the bay there is much to interest archaeologists. On the windswept promontory of Le Couperon, the eastern wing of the bay, there is a fine gallery-grave. A passage 27 feet long is roofed with seven great capstones, and the whole is surrounded by an outer wall of 18 uprights. Here, about 2000 B.C., some prehistoric chief, perhaps a contemporary of Abraham, was laid to rest by his tribe. The tomb was then made cavelike and mysterious by heaping a mound upon it, though for a time the passage was probably left open. The peephole in the end stone is found in similar graves on the Continent. Originally perhaps it may have been made to provide some means of communing with the dead, or for the escape of their spirits.

On the hill-top on the west of the bay are remains of a great earth rampart, the Castel de Rozel, which is still 20 feet high and 30 feet thick. Two hundred yards of it remain, but once it evidently extended right across the headland from Bouley Bay to Rozel; field names in the vicinity confirm this. The old theory was that this was a camp where Vikings dumped their spoil while they sailed on again in search of fresh plunder. But this has been disproved by the discovery of three hoards of Gaulish and early Roman coins buried within the defended area, showing that it was there many centuries before Vikings had been heard of. One of these consisted of 982 pieces, all of the type used in Gaul before the Roman conquest. Another, among its 700 coins contained a few Roman ones, of which the latest dates from 43 B.C. Since then, a jar has been unearthed in which there was one coin minted in 32 B.C. But none of the coins is later. So we may conclude that the Castel de Rozel is one of those prehistoric promontory forts, of which there are many in Brittany, Cornwall, and Ireland, erected to enable hard-pressed people to stand at bay against an invader. And we can add that, at some date not much later than 32 B.C., it was occupied by refugees, perhaps defending themselves against the Islanders, and who, in their terror, buried their treasure in its earthen walls.

Rozel Manor. *Rosel* is the old French form of *roseau*, a reed, but the reeds from which this manor took its name grew, not in Jersey, but in France. In Normandy, almost opposite Jersey, stands the Castle of Rosel, whose seigneurs had three reeds as their arms. One of them invaded England with the Conqueror and founded the famous family of Russell. In early Norman days these seigneurs held three fiefs in the islands, two in Guernsey, both called Rosel, and Rozel in Jersey. But the first seigneur of Rozel whose name has come down to us was Ingram de Fourneaux, who, like most of the Norman Barons, when John was expelled from Normandy, sided with the French King, and so lost his Jersey estates. Rozel was then given to Drogo de Barentin, Warden of the Isles, whose family held it for four generations. Two conditions of their tenure were: "If the King come to this Isle, you shall ride into the sea to meet him till the waves reach the girth of your saddle; and likewise you shall see him off at his departure. And, as long as he tarry in the Isle, you shall act as his Butler, and receive for your fee what the King's Butler hath."

A tragedy caused the last of the de Barentins to leave the Island. An old manuscript says: "One day the wife of Philippe de Barentin said to her sons, 'Jehannet de St. Martin has called me adulteress. Avenge this insult on your mother.' So the sons set an ambush, and put a boy to whistle when de St Martin drew near. When he came, they seized him, and tore out his tongue, where the Cross of Jehannet now stands on the road from St Martin to Trinity. The sons fled to Normandy. One, however, was arrested and hanged. The other made his home near Rouen." The site of this cross is not known for sure, but there is reason to believe that it may have stood at the cross-roads called La Croix au Maître. De Barentin then went to live in England, and sold his many estates to his two attorneys, of whom one, Guille Payn, took Samarès, while Rozel went to his partner, Raoul Lemprière.

The Lemprières held the manor for five generations. The old house did not stand where the present one does. Its position is fixed by an entry in Daniel Messervy's Diary: "1770 May 25. Went with my wife to dine at Rozel. The seigneur had masons and carpenters building a new house on Mont Ste Marguerite, near the Old Manor. They have demolished the Old Manor, which was behind the Chapel and almost adjoining the colombier. I gave the masons a crown." The fishponds, and the colombier remain where they have always been, as well as the chapel, which is in a most favoured setting, in the midst of beautiful gardens. It is the best surviving example we have of a seigneurial chapel. The seigneurial gallows in 1570 were on Mont Daubignie. The fief also owned Le Moulin de la Perrelle, in St Catherine's Bay.

Of these early Lemprière seigneurs the best known is Renaud,

Le Pinacle, St Ouen's

L'Ile au Guerdain, in Portelet Bay

Royal Square, St Helier:
The States Buildings
(*left*) and looking
west (*below*)

St Aubin's Fort

St Brelade's Church, from the south

Martello Tower at L'Archirondel

St Catherine's Bay and Breakwater

who in 1463, during the French Occupation, was accused of bribing a prisoner in the castle who was on parole to leave a gate unbarred, so that the French might be surprised and driven out. The evidence at his trial gives passing glimpses of life in the manor. Every day began with Mass in the chapel. Twice a week the seigneur rode to town to perform his duties as Jurat. When at home he worked with his men in the fields or went out fishing at St Catherine. In the evening he played chess. For his younger guests he had a fives court in the barn. He took great pride in his gardens, and every visitor was taken to admire them. He kept open house, and even the most unwelcome guest was expected to stay for dinner. At his trial he was acquitted, thanks largely to his gallant young wife, a girl of 22, who stood up for a day and a half to a gruelling cross-examination; some authorities say he was killed four years later in the final assault on the castle which expelled the French; others think he died, by fair means or foul, immediately after the trial. The account of the trial, a highly important document, is most unfortunately incomplete.

The fifth Lemprière seigneur died childless; so the manor passed to his sister, who had married a Guernsey Jurat named Perrin, and the Perrins were seigneurs of Rozel for five generations. In 1625 Abraham Perrin sold it to Philippe de Carteret, of St Ouen, and that family held it with their other estates till 1735, when it passed back by marriage to a junior branch of the Lemprières. By this time the old manor house had become uninhabitable, and Charles Lemprière, the new seigneur, continued to live for 35 years in his own home, Diélament Manor. But in 1770 he built a new house at Rozel. In 1820 his grandson doubled the size of this, adding the towers and turrets, and unfortunately smothering the fine granite work with Roman cement which had just come into fashion. Further alterations were made in about 1880 by the then seigneur, Reginald Raoul Lemprière, at whose death in 1931 the male line failed. But his grandson, the present seigneur, has taken the name of Lemprière-Robin, having inherited through his mother.

St Aubin. It is widely believed that St Aubin was once the capital of Jersey; but this cannot be true. From earliest times the Royal Court and the States have met in St Helier, and St Helier had a market centuries before St Aubin. St Aubin had no church till the

18th century. It would surely be odd if the capital were left church-less, while the Island was being covered with churches! Moreover, St Aubin has never had an independent civic existence. It has always been ruled by the Constable and Parish Assembly of St Brelade. It has never even formed a separate vingtaine. Half of it is in the vingtaine of Noirmont and half in the vingtaine of Le Coin, the mill stream of Le Moulin d'Égouttepluie dividing them.

The little town lies in a sheltered corner of the bay; so it is pos-sible that in quite early days fishermen may have built some huts there. But, though Charters, Extentes, and Assize Rolls exist, full of information about other places in the Island from the 13th century onwards, no document even mentions St Aubin till the 16th century.

When it does emerge into notice, it had gained its present name; how, nobody knows. Other places are called St This or St That from the dedication of their churches; but St Aubin had no church. The best guess is that some neighbouring chantry chapel (there were many such before the Reformation, that have now disappeared) was dedicated to St Aubin, the Breton bishop who was supposed to be a powerful protector against pirates, a very natural dedication for an undefended coastal village.

The hamlet grew through the fact that, when Jersey had no har-bour, this corner of the bay provided the safest anchorage in the Island. It was sheltered by Noirmont from south-west gales, from the south by the islet on which the fort now stands, and from the north and east by the sweep of the shore. Moreover, at low tide ships could rest on the sands and discharge their cargo into carts. The chronicler tells how in 1533 "a Spanish merchant had laden his barque with wheat in the harbour of St. Obin, when four vessels arrived flying the flag of Brittany, determined to take it to St. Malo. But the Spaniards repelled them so valiantly, and so many Jersey-men assembled when they heard the guns, that the Bretons had to retire." In 1546 a Privy Council minute runs: "A Flemish ship in the roadstead of St. Albyne, laden with cloth, was attacked by pirates, Englishmen from Brighton. They robbed her of the cloth, and, what more cruel was, cut her tackle, deprived her of sails, and demeaned the master and crew in very evil sort."

To guard against raiders like these a bulwark (i.e. an earth-work) with two guns was thrown up above Bulwark Bay, and a tower was built on the islet and four gunners placed in it. For a hundred years this remained a low, one-storied tower. In the Civil Wars the Roundheads made it a fort by building a bulwark round it, and then the Royalists replaced this with granite ramparts and added a storey to the tower. A century later the fort was remodelled to suit new conditions of warfare; but its present appearance dates from its reconstruction in 1840. During Victoria's peaceful reign it was let as a summer residence. The Germans, however, in 1940 made it once more an up-to-date fortress with Renault tank-turret guns and ferro-concrete casemates. They always utilised existing strong points.

Turning back to the harbour, a time came when the shelter provided by nature was felt to be insufficient. The Newfoundland fishing fleet began to winter at St Malo. So in 1649, when Charles II was in Jersey, he offered 500 *pistoles* towards the building of a pier at St Aubin. Twenty years later, when seated on his throne, he ordered part of the import duties to be used for this purpose. The States decided that the pier should run slightly to the south of the present south pier. A Nicolas Bailhache contracted to build it; but, as three years later he showed no sign of beginning, Sir Thomas Morgan, the Governor, took on the job. He, however, had his own ideas as to where the pier should be, and he built it in 1675 projecting from the fort. His work still remains. The present south pier was not begun till 1754. In 1790 the owners of land facing the harbour constructed the existing quay. The long gardens in front of the houses show how much land they reclaimed from the sea. The north pier was added in 1816. At first the little harbour was kept busy. In the last week of 1788, a quiet season, when many ships were laid up, there arrived at St Aubin the *Kingfisher* and the *Marie* from St Sebastian, the *Beaver* and the *Dauphin* from Santander, the *Betsy* from Gigón, the *Aigle* from Bilbao, and the *Mercure* from Cologne. In 1798 a visitor counted 30 ships tied side by side to the pier. But when St Helier's harbour was built it drew most of the shipping away.

The harbour created the town. Merchants began to build houses in St Aubin in order to be on the spot when their ships came home. The Old Court House Hotel is a typical wealthy merchant's mansion with enormous cellars to hold the goods his captains brought from abroad. The date, 1611, is carved over the fireplace. Another has initials and the date 1687 over the door; others have panelling of a later era, about 1740, which are apparently contemporary with the buildings. But less desirable imports were brought back by sailors. In 1626 there was a bad outbreak of plague. In five months 105 people died, and, as no one could be found to carry the bodies to St Brelade's churchyard, the funeral register frequently records: "Buried in his own garden."

The Civil Wars brought an English colony to St Aubin. The Gentleman-Porter at Elizabeth Castle had a house there, and, when the Castle was besieged, devised for his wife a code of signals through the washing hung on the line. For example, two sheets and two shirts meant "No news"; three sheets meant "Good news from England"; one sheet meant "Bad news." Sir George Carteret's privateering captains were mostly Englishmen, and they brought their families here, and some of their descendants remained for generations. Rich prizes were constantly brought in, and their cargoes sold by auction. The goods on one vessel, laden with provisions for Cromwell's army, realized £15,000, and, says Chevalier, "the cellars of St. Aubin's were filled to overflowing".

The great expansion of building, however, took place towards the end of this century. In 1685 Dumaresq wrote: "The conveniency of the pier has occasioned a small town to be built, consisting of about four-score houses." Two in the High Street and two on the Boulevard bear the date 1686.

During the 18th century St Aubin was a prosperous little mercantile community; and in 1715 a move was made to obtain a church. A group of merchants petitioned the Bishop of Winchester: "The town is distant from its Parish Church (St Brelade) about two miles. The road is difficult by reason of rugged ascents, and a great way on moving sands. [The present road was not yet made.] The inhabitants are exposed to great fatigue in summer by the scorching heat and in winter by tempestuous winds, from which there is no shelter. Such as come to Church cannot return home between Morning and Evening Service, but are compelled to stay at a Public House near the Church." They asked permission to build a Chapel-of-ease, and the Bishop granted his licence. But the foundation-stone was not laid till 1735, and the first service was not held till 1749. In 1887 this chapel was condemned as unsafe, and the present church was built in 1892, largely through the support of Miss Harriet Le Couteur of Belle Vue.

Towards the end of the 18th century the Methodists gained a footing amid fierce opposition. When they tried to preach on the quay, the local roughs mobbed them. When they obtained the use of a shed in Les Vaux, their benches were carried out and burnt. When another meeting-place was found, the police arrived with the militia drummers and drummed the preachers out of the town to the tune of the Rogues' March. Nevertheless, they persevered. They built their first chapel in 1817 on the site of their present hall. Their new chapel on the Boulevard was opened in 1868. Roman Catholics worshipped for many years in a hall in the Mont des Vaux, and have since opened a granite-built church facing the sea.

There was no road between St Helier and St Aubin till 1810. The only highway was the sands. When Richard Marsh in 1788 started a Saturday omnibus, it had to take this route, and could only run "tide permitting". Even when General Don made his military road in 1810, it stopped at La Haule. You had then to go up Mont au Roux and down the High Street. The extension from La Haule to the harbour was not made till 1844. A print of 1839 shows a shipyard, where the parish hall now stands, with three unfinished vessels on the slips. In 1854 the *Evening Star* (800 tons), which was launched here, made her maiden voyage to Australia with a large party of emigrants.

The coming of the railway was a great event. A company formed in 1846 accomplished nothing. A new company in 1861 met with many difficulties; but at last the track was laid. In 1870 the first train was greeted with a salvo of cannon, and the Dean read an eloquent prayer. Two hundred guests lunched in a marquee in the Noirmont grounds. And trains ran continuously to bring the whole Island to the fête and fireworks. In 1899 this line was extended to La Corbière. But the advent of the motor-bus eventually killed the trains, and in 1935 they ceased running. Later, the four-mile track from St Aubin to La Corbière was transformed into one of the pleasantest walks in the Island. The Germans relaid the lines when making their fortifications; but they have now been removed.

The chief legacy the Germans left to St Aubin is the immense tunnel which they blasted into the side of the hill to hold their reserve ammunition.

St Brelade's Bay. Some of the earliest inhabitants of Jersey lived here. At La Cotte Point, on the eastern side of the bay, is a cave which must have been hollowed out when the sea was 60 feet higher than its present level. This was for many thousands of years a camping site for prehistoric hunters during two periods; the first beginning about 110,000 B.C. and lasting to just after 100,000. Subsequently the Island was abandoned during the rise in sea-level which accompanied the meeting of the ice-sheet during the last inter-glacial period, approximately 95,000–65,000 B.C. With the advance of the last glaciation the sea-level fell and Jersey was once again joined to the Continent, and further groups of hunters resumed their visits to the cave. This second group practised what is known as the Mousterian culture, and fragmentary remains including human teeth, show that they belonged to the so-called Neanderthal race who inhabited the whole of western Europe about 65,000 to 36,000 B.C. The bones of creatures like the mammoth and woolly rhinoceros, that could not have swum the Channel, offer further proof that Jersey was then joined to France. Throughout the last glacial phase Jersey offers us no certain traces of occupation, but was probably visited by Upper Paleolithic man from time to time. When the last Ice Age drove out the last of the cave-men, Jersey probably remained for centuries uninhabited.

The appearance of the bay has changed immensely in recent years. From the days of the cave-men till well into the 19th century it was almost uninhabited. Legend said that when a church was being built in a convenient part of the parish, the Devil removed the stones by night to their present position, so that the church might be as far as possible from the people. As late as 1844 a guide-book rhapsodised: "You who love Nature in her wildest beauty, you pious souls who seek utter solitude to muse on godly things, come to St. Brelade's, and you will find the object of your search." And Durell wrote eight years later: "The bay is enclosed by barren hills covered with heath and furze. The sea-line is formed by a sandy down, yet even here the surface is overspread by a dwarfish, creeping rose." This rose still grows on sandy areas.

During the French wars the peace of the bay was for a time disturbed, for it was considered a danger-spot and had to be heavily fortified. Two martello towers were built, each with an 18-pounder carronade on the top. The sand-dunes were bristling with guns—

two 12-pounders on Le Grouin, three 24-pounders where the Hotel l'Horizon now stands, two 12-pounders near the St Brelade's Bay Hotel, three 24-pounders in the churchyard, two more on the point just behind the church, and at each extremity of the bay, at Beau Port and Le Fret, a battery. But when peace came, the gunners were withdrawn and the bay resumed it sleep.

Its loneliness made it an ideal spot for smuggling. In 1823 a British Custom House report said: "On March 17 a Cawsand boat took in at St. Brelade's Bay upwards of 300 ankers of brandy. On March 31 a Plymouth cutter took in at the same place upwards of 600 tubs of brandy and geneva. On June 10 a cutter from East Looe took in at the same place 690 casks of brandy, and during the same month a Cawsand boat took away a large cargo of spirits."

But the making of the road from St Aubin, down Mont Sohier, and round the bay to the church, led in time inevitably to the building of houses. The Fisherman's Inn, near the church, grew into a large hotel. Other hotels were built along the shore. Visitors from all parts of the world were attracted to St Brelade; among others, in 1889, General Boulanger, the man who might have been the first European dictator. As Minister of War he had become the idol of the French Army. Thousands of civilians, too, hailed him as the saviour of France who would sweep away parliamentary government and send the politicians packing. Paris returned him as its Deputy by a quarter of a million votes; and all was ripe for a *coup d'état* and a seizure of the Élysée. But the government issued a warrant for his arrest, and took care that the news should reach him three hours before the arrest was timed to be made. Then his nerve failed. He fled across the Belgian frontier and eventually came to Jersey. An eccentric Parisian curio-merchant, named Vanier, had built a villa at St Brelade, which was itself a curiosity. Its grounds were filled with Greek temples, Roman altars, and other fake antiques. He lent this to the General, who for the next two years could be seen pacing the sands surrounded by conspiratorial Frenchmen, weaving plans which always ended in smoke. At last, on a visit to Brussels, his mistress died, and he blew out his brains on her grave. The house has now been converted into flats.

Today tourism reigns supreme in the Bay. The sands in summer are sometimes reminiscent of Blackpool The anti-tank wall round the shore is a relic of the German Occupation.

A recent and delightful addition to the bay is the Winston Churchill Memorial Park, with its dedication stone of a large block of Jersey granite bearing a plaque of Churchill and the inscription: "The Right Honourable Winston Spencer Churchill, K.G., O.M., C.H. 'and our dear Channel Islands are also to be freed to-day.' 8th May 1945:" words graven on the heart of every Jerseyman, and an example of Churchill's supreme genius for choosing the right adjective.

St Brelade's Church. Every guide-book asserts that this was built in 1111 and that it is the oldest church in the Island. There is no authority for either statement. They first appeared in a local almanac for 1792, which printed *A List of the Churches in Jersey with the year and day in which the building was begun, drawn from the Livre Noir of Coutances*. But, as has been shown in the Foreword INTRODUCING JERSEY (page 9), this is now known to have been an impudent forgery.

We know, however, that St Brelade's was built before 1111, for William the Conqueror in a deed which is older than 1066, for he signed merely as "Duke of the Normans" not as "King of England", mentions eight of our Jersey churches, including St Brelade's. These were all standing before the Conquest, but which was built first no one can say. Whether St Brelade's is the oldest or not, it is certainly the most picturesquely placed, standing with its churchyard washed on two sides by the sea. There is some doubt about the dedication. St Brendan, the navigator saint, is highly probable, but St Bren Gwaladr, meaning a leader, was a companion of St Sampson, and so is quite likely to have visited these islands. His name would have become softened into Brelade, or Broladre, as occurs in Brittany. Perhaps the former story overlaid the latter.

It is useless to ask of our ancient churches, "When were they built?" for each took probably 500 years to reach its present shape and size. At some unknown date in early Norman days two little chapels were built side by side in the present St Brelade's churchyard. One, now called the Fishermen's Chapel, remained a private chantry, in which Masses were said for the founder's family. Its owners evidently took pride in it. During the 14th and 15th centuries they covered the walls with mural paintings—the Annunciation, the Massacre of the Innocents, the Palm Sunday

Triumph, the Scourging, the Crucifixion, the Resurrection, the Last Judgment. But no one outside the family used it. In time it became neglected. The very name of the saint to whom it was dedicated is forgotten. For 300 years the militia cannon were stored in it. Early in the present century the late Rector restored it. An old altar-slab with five consecration crosses was brought from Mont Orgueil, where it had been used as a gun-platform, and erected as an altar, and in 1933 the chapel was "reconciled" by the Bishop of Winchester.

The neighbouring little chapel, dedicated to St Brelade, now forms the chancel of the present church. It was probably built by one of the de Sotevasts, who at this time were large landowners in Jersey, for in about 1136 the son of a Roger de Sotevast confirmed his father's gift of the chapel to the Abbey of St Saveur le Vicomte in Normandy. The de Sotevasts had not kept their chapel to themselves. They had welcomed their neighbours; and by this time it had become the parish church. Then it was gradually enlarged. First, two transepts were added, one of which is the present vestry; later a nave, giving the church the form of a cross. Next, the saddle-back belfry was built, with five bells cast on the spot by a bell-founder from Normandy. And in 1754 a bell was cast for St Brelade by Maitre Jacque(s) Pitel, but this was replaced in 1883. Then the north wall of the chancel was pulled down and *la Chapelle de Ste Marie* erected. In 1537 the Parish Assembly announced: "Because our Church needs enlarging, we have begun a Chapel [i.e. the present north aisle] alongside of the Nave at the expense of divers of our number." At the same time the nave was lengthened by 10 feet.

The church still shows traces of those pre-Reformation days. A rood-loft must have stretched across the chancel arch bearing the great crucifix, for the corbels on which it rested remain, and the door through which the sacristan passed to trim the lamp upon it. Each altar has a piscina, at which the priest washed his hands before Mass; the main altar has a double one, severely rectangular in style and unornamented, and unlike others which have survived in some of the parish churches, dating from the time when he was ordered to wash the vessels also. The pre-Reformation font was thrown out by the Calvinists, and for 300 years lay hidden in the furze on a hillside near-by. In 1845 it was discovered by a picnic party and brought back to the church. The old sanctuary path from the churchyard to the beach has recently been reopened. It is the shortest and most direct of all the perquages.

At the Reformation the church was transformed into a Huguenot temple. The rood-loft was sawn down, the altars destroyed, the images, the stained glass, and all that recalled the old ways of worship demolished. The Calvinist régime lasted for 80 years, and even when Anglicanism was enforced, little change was made in the appearance of the building. In the 18th century, as the population increased, galleries were built against every available wall. There was even a *Galerie des Fumeurs* for men who wished to smoke during the sermon.

In 1843, however, a move was made to bring the church more into line with Anglican ways. Several of the unsightly galleries were removed. The Lady Chapel was turned into a chancel and a communion table placed there for the quarterly celebrations. But the big restoration took place while the Rev J. A. Balleine was rector. During his fifty years of office he removed the remaining galleries, stripped the inner walls of plaster, restored the chancel to its ancient use, placed an altar and choir-stalls there and a chancel screen, reseated the church with modern pews, replaced the big pulpit of painted deal with an unobtrusive oak one, and substituted granite tracery for the square, wooden sash-windows. In time this tracery was filled with fine painted glass by the Jersey artist, H. T. Bosdet.

The stone altar is a recent addition, its top being another of the altar-slabs with five consecration crosses, which had been built at the Reformation into the walls of Mont Orgueil.

The most prominent monument in the churchyard is the obelisk erected by the States to commemorate Mrs Marie Bartlet, the foundress of the General Hospital. The lych-gate was given by Lady Trent in memory of her husband, Jesse Boot, the chemist, later created Baron Trent. The fine arched entrance at the north-east corner of the churchyard was erected in 1851. Owing to the fact that in World War I six German prisoners had been buried in the churchyard, the Germans in 1942 commandeered all the unoccupied space to be their military cemetery; 213 German soldiers lay buried there for some years, later being moved and re-interred at Mont de Huisnes, Ille et Vilaine, in France. For parishioners, a new churchyard had to be made on the hillside across the road.

St Brelade's Parish. Other articles describe the CORBIÈRE, NOIRMONT, PORTELET, ST AUBIN, ST BRELADE'S BAY, and ST BRE-LADE'S CHURCH; but something more must be said about the parish as a whole. On the land side it is entirely bounded by St Peter. Its coast-line leaves St Peter where a brook runs into St Aubin's Bay just west of Beaumont. It passes St Aubin, Noirmont, Portelet, and St Brelade's Bay, which have already been described, till it reaches Beau Port, a beautiful bay which the owners, the family of the late Lord Trent, opened to the public, and Ficquet Bay, which takes its name from Mont Ficquet that overlooks it. Here is some of the most remarkable rock scenery in the Island. This is a good area on which to see the Spotted rock-rose (*Tuberaria guttata*) which only grows here, in Alderney and in Anglesey, in the British Isles, and which loses its petals at mid-day. Here, too, is the Fosse Vourin (Vourin is a now extinct Jersey family name). This is a huge funnel, 100 feet deep, from the top of the cliff down to a cave that communicates with the sea. When the British troops cleaned up the Island after the German Occupation and had hundreds of miles of barbed wire to get rid of, they discovered this great hole and dumped it all down there. No one will ever descend the Fosse Vourin again. The coast-line then passes La Moie Point, whose quarries were once one of the great industries of the Island (the granite for the Thames Embankment came from La Moie), and rounds La Corbière to Petit Port, whence a delightful walk round L'Oeillère, the Look-out, leads to La Pulente, one of the chief sea-weed-gathering centres, and continues for about a mile along St Ouen's Bay till it meets St Peter again just beyond Le Braye slip-way.

Being the south-west corner of the Island, this parish is exposed to the full fury of the south-west gales, with the result that two of its four vingtaines, La Moie and Les Quennevais, have become to a large extent barren. Tradition attributes this to a sudden divine judgment on the wrecking propensities of the inhabitants. A less sensational explanation is that strong west winds have blown sand up from St Ouen's Bay, and in time this has buried the fertile soil. The process is still continuing. As late as 1668 the Extente mentions: "Land in the Parish of St. Brelade's formerly belonging to Edmond Le Marquand and David Vaudin, which has been swallowed up by the sand and abandoned by its owners, has therefore passed into the hands of the King as unoccupied." Moie means a stack or hump, and probably refers to the promontory of that name, and Quennevais is derived from *chenevière* or *chanevière*, meaning an area where hemp was grown, a most important crop for rope-making during the period of ship-building in Jersey. The area is mainly sand-dunes now, and is partly occupied by a golf links, and also a rapidly expanding secondary town, with housing estate, shops, banks, and a very large modern secondary school. These sand-dunes are also the botanist's El Dorado, covered by dwarf trailing roses and tiny plants innumerable.

Though the parish contains no spectacular megaliths like some of those found elsewhere, it is specially rich in other prehistoric remains. The palaeolithic cave at La Cotte has been mentioned in the article on St Brelade's Bay. And, coming to Neolithic times, it is clear that about 1000 B.C. the district had many inhabitants. Two dolmens, now only heaps of fallen stones, looked down into Ficquet Bay, and a third on Mont Sohier was carted away about seventy years ago to make room for a tennis-court. On Les Quennevais stand three menhirs erected for long-forgotten religious rites. These great blocks of granite were clearly not placed there by nature, for each is held up by a circle of trig stones. Near the foot of the sand-hills, as they slope down to St Ouen's Bay, a burial-chamber was discovered containing bones of at least 20 persons. Near La Sergenté are the remains of a round hut which once had a domed roof; it is almost certainly a Neolithic tomb. To save it from destruction when a German anti-aircraft battery was sited nearby during the last war, it was buried in the sand, but was later opened up again. At Les Blanches Banques a settlement of these neolithic folk was found, from which many specimens of their pots and stone and flint implements were transferred to the Museum. One cooking pot was still upright and half filled with limpet shells, which suggests that some terrific sandstorm had driven the inhabitants from their homes while their meal was still cooking, and buried the pot without upsetting it.

The next arrivals were the Gauls, who came somewhere between 300–50 B.C. and a hoard of about 12,000 of their base silver coins was dug up on the Park estate. Throughout historical times St Brelade seems to have remained a quiet farming parish, producing no one of special distinction, till in comparatively recent years it gave birth to Martel, the brandy merchant, Dean Jeune, who became Bishop of Peterborough, Dean Samuel Falle, and Dr R. R. Marett, the famous anthropologist. It is surprising to notice how modern all the main roads in the parish are. There was no road to St Helier till 1809, the only way being across the sands; and then the road only started at La Haule. The final stage from St Aubin to La Haule was not made till 1844. The road from St Aubin to St Brelade's Church by Mont Sohier was made in 1810, the one up Mont de la Rocque in 1811, the one up La Marquanderie and across the Quennevais in 1812. The road to the Corbière was only made for the benefit of the lighthouse-builders in 1873. Before these dates the parish had nothing but narrow, winding lanes.

St Catherine's Bay. A bay facing east in St Martin's parish, lying between Verclut Point and La Crête. It took its name from a mediaeval chapel of Ste Catherine, which stood close to where L'Archirondel Tower now stands. One wall of this chapel with a long narrow window remained till 1852, when it was pulled down to make room for a tramway to carry stone for the new harbour. It had a fraternity attached to it whose members had the right to be buried round their chapel walls, and five skeletons were dug up when the tramway was made. Another chapel, dedicated to St Agatha, the ruins of which were still there in 1607, stood further along the shore.

It was a lonely spot, seldom mentioned in ancient records, though in 1500 a pirate was hanged there. As late as 1832 a guide-book said: "The road round the bay is not passable for any wheeled carriage, and was only cut to facilitate the movements of light infantry in the event of an attack on the island." Facing, as it does, the French coast, it was heavily fortified. In 1793 a martello tower was built on L'Archirondel Rock (in old records of the fief d'Anneville this is spelt La Roche Rondel), which was then an islet 200 yards below high-tide mark; another was half-way round the bay, while six batteries were snugly hidden at intervals among the sand-dunes.

In 1847 the British Government, alarmed at the growth of the heavily fortified French naval port at Cherbourg and at the fortifications that were springing up at Granville and St Malo, decided to make two naval stations in Alderney and Jersey. The site chosen in Jersey was St Catherine's Bay. Eight hundred workmen were brought here, who started quarrying the great rock called Gibraltar. The first step was to join L'Archirondel Rock to the shore, and to do this a steam tramway was made to bring the stone to the spot. The men then switched on to Verclut Breakwater, which was run out half a mile to sea; but in 1852, before they could resume work on L'Archirondel pier, which should have stretched out to meet the other, the work, on which half a million pounds had already been spent, was suddenly stopped. Some said that the French had protested strongly that a naval base within sight of their shore would be regarded as a threat to peace. Others said that the breakwater had so altered the set of the tide that in a few years' time the harbour would have been silted up. The reason was really that the advent of steam had made it unnecessary, since fleets were no longer dependent on wind and so did not need this harbour of refuge during contrary winds. In 1878 the breakwater was handed over to the States. The main use now made of it is as a resort for anglers.

St Clement's Church. In most of Jersey's ancient churches the oldest part is the chancel, and the rest has been added later. St Clement's is an exception, for the oldest part is the nave, though this is also the case in Grouville church. This was originally a small Norman chapel, with a low, thatched roof and narrow windows, two of which remain in the north wall. It was dedicated to St Clement, a Roman Christian of the 1st century, of whom nothing is known except that he wrote a short letter to the church in Corinth. But later ages added queer stories to our knowledge. First, a tradition asserted that he had been banished to the Crimea, where the Governor had him drowned with an anchor round his neck. Then 800 years later St Cyril, walking on the Crimean sands, noticed a bleached human rib sticking out of a sandbank. Scooping away the sand, he found other human bones, which seemed to his imagination to have a strange fragrance. He jumped to the conclusion that these must be relics of St Clement. When he brought them to Rome, the church whipped up enormous enthusiasm for their reception. There was a great epidemic of miracles. The lame walked, the deaf heard, the blind recovered their sight. The fame of St Clement spread throughout Christendom, even to remote Jersey, and the family who built this chapel dedicated it in his name.

114

Another little chapel, the one which now contains the organ, stood a few yards away, as the Fishermen's Chapel still stands close to St Brelade; but, for perhaps 500 years, they remained quite separate buildings.

Before 1066, however, St Clement's chapel had become a parish church, for William the Conqueror, while "Duke of the Normans" and not yet "King of England", granted to the Abbess of Mont-villiers in Normandy "half the tithes of the Church of St Clement in Jersey", and only parish churches received tithes. A charter of 1090 shows that by this time the church had passed to the Abbey of St Sauveur le Vicomte, and it remained the property of that abbey throughout the Middle Ages.

The 15th century was a great age of church building in Jersey. Then it was that St Clement's was enlarged by the addition of a chancel and transepts, giving it the shape of a cross. The date is fixed by the Payn arms, the three trefoils in the chancel showing that it was built while the Payns were seigneurs of the neighbouring manor of Samarès. The gargoyle at the east end is also of that period; and so are the wall-paintings. In the south transept are two dog's and two horse's legs, with a French verse underneath: "Alas, St Mary! Who are these three corpses who look so grim? It breaks my heart to see them thus piteous." This shows that the complete picture was a scene from the famous poem, *The Three Living and the Three Dead*, in which three hunters are accosted by three skeletons, who warn them of the vanity of all earthly pomp. At least 25 English churches and many in Normandy have scenes from this poem on their walls. In the north transept a large picture has been cut in two by an arch, showing that, when the picture was painted, there was a solid wall there and the chapel behind was still separate from the church. All that remains is part of St Margaret with a wing of her conquered dragon, and St Barbara standing by her tower. In the nave a rather scared-looking St Michael is trampling on his dragon. This has, in recent years, been most excellently restored.

When the church was enlarged, the roof was raised and made of stone, and the line of this roof can still be seen on the tower arch. Buttresses were built to support the weight. Other relics of this period are the finely sculptured font which, though thrown out at the Reformation, was discovered in the 19th century buried in the churchyard, and the two piscinae at which the priests washed their hands, one south of the present altar, the other in the north chapel, the latter being the less well constructed.

On the eve of the Reformation a further enlargement was made. The belfry and spire were built. That this was done later than the wall-paintings is shown by the fact that the belfry arch now fills the space where the three skeletons must have stood. The roofs of the nave and chancel were now raised to their present height, and the north chapel thrown into the church by cutting arches through the transept and chancel walls. In 1549, the Commissioners who sold all church property for the benefit of the Crown, sold an endowment which provided a lamp in the church.

In the Middle Ages there were no pews. Everyone stood or knelt on the rush-strewn floor. Only for the aged and infirm was a stone seat carved at the foot of each pillar, and one of these can be seen on the chancel arch. But in the 17th and 18th centuries the church was cluttered up with pews of all shapes and sizes, even the chancel being filled with seats facing the pulpit, and, when there was no more space on the floor, galleries were erected. The possession of a private or family pew became a matter of importance and many were the quarrels which took place on this score. But a big restoration in 1879 swept all these away and left the church as we see it today.

St Clement's Parish. The south-easternmost strip of the Island, extending from the slip at Le Dicq to within a quarter of a mile of La Rocque Pier; in area the smallest of the 12 parishes, covering only 1,044 acres, compared with St Ouen's 3,707.

Much of the parish lies below the equinoctial high-tide level, and so would frequently be flooded had not a dyke (*le Dicq*) like those in Holland been built at some early date to dam back the sea; but the forest bed, which lies only a foot beneath Grève d'Azette sands, shows that a considerable tract of land had already been lost. And the dyke has not always been able to hold back the enemy. In 1688 the sea broke through and flooded a large area. In 1796 it swept away the road at Le Hocq, and a new road had to be made farther inland. The worst inundation took place in 1812, when hundreds of vergées were submerged. This, however, forced the States to build the sea wall. But the ever greedy sea still makes its assaults beyond the sea wall, or finds gaps and weaknesses, and landowners constantly lose portions of their gardens during the equinoctial tides.

Looking back to prehistoric times, the first farming folk to settle in the Island, the pre-Celtic race commonly called the Iberians, who arrived probably about 3000 B.C., left traces of their presence here in the great passage-grave, which crowns Mont Ubé, overlooking the whole plain. Whether this was the tomb of a great chief or a communal burial-place is still a matter of debate. In the early 19th century it was used as a pigsty. Then in 1848 its cap-stones were broken up for building material. But its 28 uprights still remain, forming a passage leading to the burial-chamber, which, apparently like that in La Hougue Bie, had three side cells. The whole was originally covered with a mound of earth.

Another wave of immigrants who arrived later left a cemetery on La Motte, the islet 300 yards from the shore, popularly known as Green Island. A "motte" can mean a small island, but the word also has a megalithic inference. Here 18 cist-graves were discovered, some containing human remains. Several of these have been removed to the garden of the Museum to save them from being washed away by the tide.

Half-way between Mont Ubé and La Motte stands a menhir, 11 feet high, known as La Dame Blanche, this probably being a folk-memory from a time when such stones were worshipped. Here again we meet the limpets, which so mysteriously appear in almost all the remains of this period. Twelve feet from the menhir a pocket was found in the undisturbed clay, surrounded by a ring of stones, which was packed tight with limpet shells.

Coming down to historic times, in pre-Norman days the name of the district seems to have been Petravilla. As late as 1172 the Abbot of Mont St Michel wrote that his abbey possessed a chapel in Jersey "in the Parish of St Clement in Petraville", and six years later a Papal Bull confirmed the monks' right to the land they held "at Petraville in the island of Gerse". This suggests that, before the Normans came, the owner of the villa or estate had been some Gallic man named Peter; but when the church was built and dedicated to St Clement, the parish gradually assumed the name of its patron saint. The land mentioned above had been given to Mont St Michel about 1050 by one of the Knights of Duke Robert, the father of William the Conqueror, and a hundred years later the Bishop of Coutances had given the abbey permission to build an oratory on its "estate of Perreville, in the island of Jersey".

This was the origin of St Clement's Priory, which stood in the south-west corner of the present churchyard near the house now called the Priory. Its foundations were unearthed some years ago. It seldom housed more than two monks, whose duty it was to collect the rentes due to the abbey from the Island; yet it managed to fill more official documents than all the other Jersey priories and churches put together. For one thing, it was very rich. A list of the prior's income in 1381 calls up a curious picture of the two monks receiving their dues. Twenty-two people each had to bring "one goose, two hens, twenty eggs". Some brought less, "one hen, ten eggs"; others more, "three geese, three hens, forty eggs"; eight people owed one capon; five owed one pullet. Such payments were the usual dues to any overlord at the period. Moreover, a great abbey like Mont St Michel never willingly let any of its property slip. When the King claimed that the monks had encroached on one of his fiefs, there ensued a lawsuit which lasted for 23 years, till the Abbot at last won. And there were constant bickerings between the Abbey of St Sauveur le Vicomte, which owned the church, and the Abbey of St Michel, which owned the priory, till at last St Michel agreed that it was only by permission of St Sauveur that the priory had any rights in that parish. When monks lived far from the discipline of their abbey, scandals sometimes arose. There was an ugly one in 1268, when a murder was committed in the priory by the husband of a woman with whom the prior was said to be living in adultery. In 1414 this establishment was suppressed with the other alien priories.

St Clement had not as many mediaeval chapels as other parishes. Apart from the manorial chapel at Samarès, we only hear of one, dedicated to St John the Evangelist, and its probable site is known only by a field name. A priest was licensed to serve in this in 1495, but in 1540 Leland's map marks it as "in ruins".

In the 16th and 17th centuries St Clement became notorious as a centre of the witch movement. On the point called Le Nez stands a granite rock 40 feet high known as Rocqueberg. Here half-crazy men and women, who had solemnly consecrated their lives to the Devil, used to meet at midnight for their sabbath orgies. The fact that the top of the rock has been vitrified by lightning and that a ledge half-way down has dents like the hoof-marks of a goat may have suggested that this was a haunt of the Evil One; but more probably the utter loneliness of the place was the main attraction. Though today the rock stands in a private garden, 300 years ago Le Nez was one of the most desolate spots in the Island.

All witches were not women. In 1585 Jean Mourant of St Clement was sentenced to death, and the Act of the Court ran: "Having been so forgetful of his salvation as to make a covenant with Satan, he confessed with his own mouth his dealings with the Devil by mark and pact, confirmed by the gift of one of his members, by means of which he had committed infinite mischiefs, crimes, and homicides." The "mark" was the famous *merche du diable*, branded indelibly on the flesh of all who joined the sect; and he had apparently cut off a finger-joint as a sacrifice. In 1611 three St Clement's women were convicted of witchcraft and condemned to be strangled and to have their bodies burnt. When in 1625 the same sentence was passed on Marie Filleul, the seigneur of Samarès intervened, and insisted that his manorial gallows should be used for the execution, as she lived on his fief. But these were the unlucky ones. The secret was so well kept that the majority of the Devil-worshippers at Rocqueberg were never caught or suspected.

After the Revocation of the Edict of Nantes in 1685 swarms of French Protestants began to settle in this, and other parishes. The church register contains many entries such as this: "Sieur Isaac Queston of Angers, having been forced by persecution to take part in the idolatries of the Roman Church, after confessing his sin before the Ecclesiastical Court, made public confession of it in this Temple, and afterwards was received back into the peace of the Church."

One curious expense that fell on the church during the 18th century was the five annual bonfires, on St George's Day, Oak Apple Day, Midsummer Day, Guy Fawkes' Day, and the King's Birthday, for all of which the churchwardens had to hire men to go out and cut gorse.

The martello tower at Le Hocq was built about 1778, when France made an alliance with the revolted American colonies.

By the middle of the 19th century the town had begun to spill over into the western corner of St Clement, and the parish received its most distinguished resident, Victor Hugo, the famous French poet, novelist, and dramatist. Marina Terrace had been built facing the sea, and when he arrived in Jersey, a refugee flying from the wrath of Louis Napoleon, No. 3 in that terrace was to let, an unattractive house with whitewashed walls, which Hugo described as "a bit of built-up Methodism". Here he and his family lived for nearly four years, and here he wrote *Les Châtiments*, the bitterest poems of satire and invective ever penned. Other French exiles had fled to Jersey and looked to Hugo as their leader, and they printed a paper, *L'Homme*, to smuggle into France. But France and England were allied in the Crimean War, and Queen Victoria paid a visit to Napoleon in Paris. This roused the wrath of the exiles. *L'Homme* printed a letter to the Queen which declared: "You have sacrificed your dignity as a monarch, your pride as an aristocrat, your fastidiousness as a woman, even your honour." The Lieutenant-Governor promptly banished the editorial staff from the island, and, when Hugo protested, the Constable of St Clement's escorted him too to a steamer. For the next 15 years he made his home in Guernsey. To mark the centenary of his stay here La Société Jersiaise erected a commemorative stone to Victor Hugo, on a rock which came to be known Le Rocher des Proscrits, because he and his compatriots used to meet there to discuss matters. The rock is actually in St Saviour's parish, which has the smallest coastline of all the twelve parishes.

The little church of St Nicholas, at Grève d'Azette, was opened in 1927 through the energy of a retired clergyman, the Rev L. B. Lee, who bore the cost of the building, and made with his own hands all the interior fittings, pews, reading-desk, and chancel-screen, and ministered here till his death.

Separate articles will be found on ICHO TOWER, ST CLEMENT'S CHURCH, and SAMARÈS MANOR.

St Helier's Church. The oldest building in the town is the Town Church, and the oldest part of the church is the chancel. A glance at its outer walls will show that they are built of rough boulders from the beach, whereas the rest of the church is built of quarried stone. This was once a little chapel standing on the seashore, for, before the harbour and the houses were there, at high tide the waves used to wash what is now the churchyard wall.

A second little chapel, *la Chapelle de la Madelaine*, stood till the 18th century in the north-west corner of the present churchyard.

The first chapel was probably built about the 10th century, at a time when *The Passion of St Helier* was being read (see article on the HERMITAGE), for it was dedicated in the name of the hero of that story. By the 11th century it was receiving tithes as a parish church, for before 1066, when William the Conqueror was Duke of Normandy but not yet King of England, he gave away half these tithes to the Abbess of Montvilliers. Another charter shows that before 1090 the appointment of its rectors had been entrusted to the Abbey of St Sauveur le Vicomte in Normandy. After that, the church is frequently mentioned in ecclesiastical documents. In 1120 the Bishop of Coutances settled a dispute between the Abbot and the Rector. In 1140 he confirmed the Abbot in his rights. It is named again in 1160 in a charter of Henry II, and again in a Bull of Innocent IV in 1250.

When it became the parish church, the building was constantly enlarged and altered. First the west wall of the chapel was pulled down and a nave added. Later north and south transepts gave the church the form of a cross. In the 14th century the roof was raised; the narrow Norman windows were replaced by the present large ones with their flamboyant tracery; and the handsome, square tower was built to hold a peal of bells. In the next century, as the population of the town increased, a south aisle was added and a south chancel, swallowing up the south transept. Other additions to the church seem to have disappeared. Round-headed arches can be traced on the north wall of the chancel, which suggest that behind them may have been a lofty Lady Chapel, and it is possible that there may once have been a north aisle.

At the Reformation, statues of saints, stained-glass windows, and wall-paintings were swept away. Nothing was left to remind people of the old doctrines. Even the font and altar were cast out. The church became a Huguenot temple; and eight rectors in succession were French Huguenot ministers in Presbyterian orders. When Sir George Carteret in the Civil War held the Island for the King, the Anglican Prayer Book was introduced, and Charles II several times attended service in the church, first when he came as Prince of Wales, in 1646, and also when he came as King in 1649. On one occasion the solemnity of the service was seriously disturbed by a mad little Doctor of Divinity, who climbed grimacing into the pulpit pretending to be a monkey, and, when ejected, hurled stones through the window, one of which narrowly missed the King's head. When Cromwell triumphed, Presbyterianism again took possession; but at the Restoration Anglicanism was reintroduced, and a French translation of the Prayer Book remained in use till 1906, when a change was made to English.

The church has been used for many purposes besides worship. Before the Reformation criminals could take sanctuary within its walls, and, when you went to Church, you might find a burglar or a murderer camping in one corner. All the secular parish assemblies, for rating, street-widening, drainage, etc., were held in the church till 1830, and often were very stormy. Elections for Jurats and Constables took place in the church porch at the close of the morning service till 1831. The militia cannon were kept in the church till 1844. The church bell announced the opening of the market in the square.

The walls of the church are covered with memorials to famous Jerseymen. The oldest is one to Maximilian Norreys, who died in 1591 of wounds received while fighting in a force which Elizabeth sent to France. There is one to Michel Lemprière, the Republican leader, who was Bailiff under Cromwell; one to General Anquetil, the Jerseyman who perished with all his army when cut off by Afghans in the retreat from Kabul, in 1842, one to Le Capelain, Jersey's famous water-colour painter; another to Colonel Le Gallais of Boer War fame, who died in 1900, and whom De Wet in his book declared to be the bravest foeman he had met. But the memorial that attracts most attention is that erected by the States to the memory of Major Peirson, the hero of the Battle of Jersey (see article ROYAL SQUARE). His grave is at the foot of the pulpit. The only memorial to the French commander, who was also killed in the battle, is a block of granite in the churchyard inscribed with the word RULLECOURT.

The old church has had more than one narrow escape from disaster. When Philippe Falle left his books to the States to form a public library, they proposed to build a room to house them in the rectory garden, where the church house now stands. To save encroachments on his garden the Rector urged that the library should be built on the church roof. In 1842, when the growth of the town demanded more church accommodation, Dean Jeune got out plans for pulling down the church altogether, and building a new one on the site to seat three times as many people. He collected a considerable sum towards this; but fortunately the scheme came to nothing.

Between 1864 and 1868 his successor, Philippe Filleul, carried out a much-needed restoration. The seven galleries that had been built to provide extra seats vanished; and a new south transept and a lengthening of the nave, with a gallery in each, accommodated the evicted pewholders. The shabby, old, high box-pews, each with a locked door, were replaced by uniform modern seating. A communion table was placed at the east end, and choir-stalls in the chancel, and a font by the main door; and the windows were filled with stained glass. The church, as we see it today, is much as Filleul left it; though minor improvements have been made. Under Dean Falle the chancel floor was raised to its pre-Reformation level, as shown by earth-stains on the pillars, and new choir-stalls, a new altar, and a new organ were given. The chancel screen and the canopies over the clergy stalls commemorate Dean Falle's ministry, and the cross and candlesticks over the altar were given by the then Queen Consort, Her Majesty Queen Elizabeth the Queen Mother, as a thankoffering for the liberation of the Island from the German Occupation. Her Majesty attended a service here in 1963, when the Bailiff's mace was laid flat on the altar in recognition of the subjugation of temporal to divine power. The only other royal personage to worship in this church has been Charles II. The diocese of New Jersey has made generous gifts of a beautiful processional cross, and a Bailiff's chair.

A new church house, or hall, is in course of erection. It replaces the 19th century one, which was of no architectural merit.

St Helier's Parish. Elsewhere in this book articles will be found on FORT REGENT, the HARBOUR, HAVRE DES PAS, the HOSPITAL, the MUSEUM, the PRISON, the ROYAL SQUARE, ST HELIER'S CHURCH, VICTORIA COLLEGE, and WESTMOUNT. But there is more to be said about St Helier as a whole. The parish, which stretches from the Waterworks Valley to the Grands Vaux, is much larger than the town, which merely nestles in its extreme south-eastern corner. Of the four vingtaines into which it was for centuries divided, three were entirely rural; and even today there are four square miles of open country north of the streets before you pass into Trinity.

Perhaps the most ancient relic is a group of stones of a prehistoric cist found under the modern gas works, evidence of changes of level as the town gradually evolved through the centuries.

The town itself started as a tiny fishing hamlet. A few little boats found shelter in the mouth of the brook that ran into the sea close to the town church, and there the owners built their huts. No place could have seemed less likely to become the capital. Gorey, where the Governor lived, in the castle, or St Aubin, where merchants unloaded their ships, might well have secured this honour; but its market gave the victory to St Helier. At the Assize of 1299 the seigneur of Samarès stated that the land on which the town stood had been given by his ancestor to the abbey on the islet; and monks were good business men, quick to develop the financial value of any property they possessed. A very usual plan was to obtain a licence from the King to establish a market. The St Helier monks would have had no difficulty about this, for their abbey was founded under royal patronage. When the market was opened, farmers from all parts of the Island would come into St Helier every market-day. Where the market was taverns sprang up, and in time some permanent shops. Jurats, like other folk, rode in to market every Saturday, and found this a convenient place to transact their official business. A large shed was erected to be the Royal Court; and where the Court was, lawyers and other officials gathered. In this way the handful of fishermen's huts grew into a town. But for centuries it remained a very small one.

The hearth tax returns in 1331 show that five parishes at that time—St Saviour, St Martin, St Ouen, Grouville, and Trinity—all contained more houses than St Helier. When Poingdestre wrote in 1685, there were still only 210 houses in the town. As late as 1800 it was only a narrow strip extending from Snow Hill to Charing Cross, with a bulge at the end formed by Hue Street and old Street on one side and Seale Street and Sand Street on the other; and this bulge was comparatively new. Two houses in Hue Street bear the dates 1756 and 1767, and some appear to be older. In breadth the strip was no wider than from Hill Street to Hilgrove Street and from Broad Street to King Street. The back windows on the north of King Street looked out over green fields, those on the south of Broad

Street over sand-dunes to the sea. There are remains of the town wall, Le Muraille de la Ville, to be seen in roads off Bond Street, where a water mill used to stand, and foundations of houses in Broad Street show that the sea lapped their walls.

But the town was already growing. First had come swarms of French Huguenots flying from the Catholic Reaction, then a rush of French aristocrats flying from the Revolution, then a steady stream of English, largely half-pay officers and their families, flying from the increased taxation that the Napoleonic Wars made necessary, to a land where taxation was as yet unknown; for the States still paid all expenses out of the harbour dues, import duties, and the letting of the market stalls. New streets were springing up in all directions. Beresford Street was first mentioned in 1822, having been named after the Marquis of Beresford, Governor from 1821–54. In 1825 Halkett Place was opened. Bath Street, Belmont Road, and Great Union Road were spoken of as "recently opened" in 1827. When Falle wrote in 1734, the population was about 2,000. By 1800 it had quadrupled. By 1831 it had doubled again and become 16,000. In 1841 it was 24,000; in 1851, 30,000. In the last census, that of 1961, it was 26,000, and the total Island population is now in the region of 70,000.

The old street names were naturally French. Some of these were picturesque. Church Street was Rue Trousse Cotillon (Tuck-up-your-petticoat Street), because a little brook ran down the middle of it. Regent Road was Rue du Froid Vent (Cold Wind Street). Some of these names still survive. Colomberie took its name from the colombier or dovecot beside the road, which belonged to the manor of La Motte; and we have Havre des Pas, La Motte Street, and La Chasse. Others are found in the suburbs. The stream which flowed down Queen's Road formed a *bouillon*, French for a bubbling spring, at the bottom; and the oxide of iron that it washed down from the clay higher up gave the mud a reddish tint; so the district was called in Elizabethan days *la contrée du Rouge Bouillon*, Red spring district, and three hundred years later, when houses began to be built there, the road was called Rouge Bouillon. The hills that lead down to the town still retain their French names—Mont à l'Abbé, Mont au Prêtre, Mont Cochon, Mont Millais, the two former connected with ecclesiastical fiefs, and the two latter taking their names from local families.

Of the new streets many were named after some local celebrity, popular Governors like General Conway and Lord Beresford, Lieutenant-Governors like General Don and Sir Colin Halkett, or heroes of the Battle of Jersey, like Peirson and Captain Mulcaster, or national heroes giving us Nelson Street and Wellington Road and Waterloo Place. Some (e.g. Hilgrove Street, Lemprière Street, Dumaresq Street) took their names from the family on whose land they were built; others from some building that stood in them. The public library was once in Library Place, the public baths in Bath Street, a museum in Museum Street, the cattle market in Cattle Street. The militia cannon were kept in Cannon Street, and the Parade was levelled to be the parade-ground of the town regiment. But many streets owe their name merely to some personal whim; e.g. the wife of the builder of Almorah Crescent had been born at Almorah in India. This is a fine example of a crescent built in about 1815, with all the details of its façade being contemporary. Boyne Terrace, surprisingly however, derives its name from the maiden name of the wife of one, Thomas Sohier, a builder and speculator of the early 19th century.

Amid all this building there rose over 20 new churches and non-conformist chapels. Anglicans were handicapped at first by legal difficulties that made it impossible to form a new parish; but they cut the knot by opening proprietary chapels. No law could prevent a group of churchmen from erecting a private building, and engaging a chaplain of their own to hold services in it; nor could anyone stop them from inviting their neighbours to worship with them. St Paul's, St James's, and St Mark's all started life in this way. All Saints' began as a chapel-of-ease attached to the Town Church. The first new church to have a parish of its own was St Luke (though this is just outside St Helier's boundary and in St Saviour), as, by the time it was built, the Peel Act, which made it legal to form new parishes, had been registered by the States. Non-conformists had no such trammels. Roman Catholics built their church in Vauxhall and bought a chapel in New Street. Methodists had their great church in Grove Place, the largest place of worship in the Island, and for their English-speaking members another chapel in Peter Street, no longer used for religious purposes. Primitive Methodists, Bible Christians, Presbyterians, Baptists, Independents, Quakers, Plymouth Brethren, Unitarians, Swedenborgians, all had their meeting-houses. For a time a Mormon mission flourished, and a group who called themselves the Truly Pious. There used to be a Jewish synagogue in Halkett Place, but there is none at present.

Of secular buildings the markets attract most attention. When the stall-keepers were ousted from the Square in 1800, the States built for them a picturesque market, modelled on one at Bath, at the junction of Beresford Street and Halkett Place (a model of this is in the Museum). The flowers and vegetables, eggs and butter, were sheltered by a roofed colonnade round three sides of a square, while the butchers' stalls in the centre had a roof of their own. The whole covered about half the area of the present market. Other markets were added—the pork market in Hilgrove Street, the fish market in Cattle Street, and a second vegetable market on the farther side of Beresford Street. But by 1882 the old market had become so congested that the States pulled it down and built the present spacious one in its place.

The Town Hall, built in 1871, and recently modernised, is a purely practical building with the police-station and municipal offices on the ground floor, and above, a large public hall for electoral and other meetings; the latter rather surprisingly contains a fine collection of paintings, which includes some by Le Capelain, two by Walter Ouless, R.A., and *The Ironing Girl*, by David, the French painter of the Revolution, an outstandingly beautiful and valuable picture.

The theatre has never aroused much enthusiasm in Jersey. The first reference to it occurs in 1778 when the States passed an Act whereby no play was to be performed without the permission of the Bailiff. The first plays known to have been presented in the Island were put on by two French companies in 1788. The first building used as a theatre was the Long Room over the corn market, at the western side of the present Royal Square. The first regular theatre was probably the Theatre Royal, which was opened in 1802, and reconstructed in 1804. It occupied part of the site on which a block of flats now stands at Regent Road, which used to be known as La Rue de la Comédie. It was largely superseded after the building of the New Theatre Royal in the Royal Crescent in 1828; this one survived until 1863, when it was destroyed by fire. In 1865 the Royal Amphitheatre and Circus was opened in Gloucester Street, and three years later was sold to Wybert Rousby who changed its name to Theatre Royal, and ran it for some thirty years. He retired in 1898 and sold it, but it was destroyed by fire in the following year. It was rebuilt, and opened in 1900 under the name of The Opera House, the opening performance being "The Degenerates" starring Lillie Langtry. In later years the Opera House was used as a cinema, but reverted to its former use in 1958. Of the many well known performers who have appeared on its stage the most famous is undoubtedly Charlie Chaplin who appeared for four nights in 1912.

The statuary in the town is not outstanding. The one really impressive monument, the obelisk in Broad Street to the memory of Constable Le Sueur, has been ruined by a later Constable who built a public lavatory immediately behind it. The Cenotaph in the Parade is an uninspired copy of a hundred cenotaphs elsewhere. Of the remaining statues, there is the rather ponderous monument to General Don, Lieutenant-Governor from 1806–14, an immensely popular man; the four cannon at the base of the statue are not contemporary, and date between 1850–80. There is the spindle-shanked George II disguised as a Roman Senator, and the somewhat uninspired statue of Queen Victoria on the Weighbridge, erected in 1890, in honour of Her Majesty's jubilee. At Victoria College a statue of Sir Galahad forms the memorial to the World War I. A fine statue of George V forms the focal point in the Howard Davis Park.

The town is well off for open spaces. With the Parade, Westmount, the College Grounds, the La Collette Gardens, and now the beautiful Howard Davis Park, one of the many benefactions of Mr T. B. Davis to the Island, there are 50 acres of recreation grounds within easy reach of every house, to say nothing of those wonderful playgrounds for children and adults alike, the sands of St Aubin's Bay and of Grève d'Azette. Of the cemeteries only one need be mentioned, the well-kept war cemetery in Plaisance Road, which contains the graves of British and American airmen shot down over the Island by the German guns and of naval ratings washed ashore from ships sunk in the Channel. After the War the bodies of the American men were removed, and while the wishes of the relatives can be understood, it was a matter of regret to the Islanders to see them go. The graves are still marked, and the Stars and Stripes fly overhead with the Union Jack. Before each burial, the coffin used to lie in state in St Luke's Church which is adjacent.

A crematorium, within a pleasant park, has now been built on Westmount.

Of more modern buildings the most outstanding are the Roman Catholic Church of St Thomas with its lofty spire, and the great hotels that have sprung up everywhere to accommodate the swarms of tourists who flock to the Island every summer. St Helier today, with its crowded streets, its fine shops, its large bathing-pool, its daily paper, its cinemas and buses, its yacht club, its Green Room Club, established in 1909, its Rotary Club, its musical, literary, and debating societies, and branches of every imaginable organisation, religious, charitable, sporting, or social, is essentially a new town. In 1908 an Eisteddfod, a festival of arts and crafts, was established and is very flourishing today. The town contains more than half the population of the Island. The only ancient building left is its parish church. An interesting old house, Le Manoir de la Motte, was, regrettably, demolished in 1958. This was where Major Moses Corbet signed the capitulation to the French, early on the morning of the Battle of Jersey. A splendid stairway tower with pigeon nests in the top section, probably dating from the 16th century, and situated on the north of the Royal Square, fell before the advance of progress in recent years also. The town does, however, contain some fine Georgian and Regency terraces, as well as individual houses and architectural features which are most certainly worthy of preservation.

It is interesting to note that the first pillar boxes in the United Kingdom, called road-side letter boxes were introduced to Jersey in 1852, as an experiment, at the instance of Anthony Trollope. There were four of them, all in the town, and the letters were collected twice daily, at 6 a.m. and at noon, but on mail days the collection was to be made as soon as the mail steamer was sighted.

St John's Church. The oldest surviving document to mention this church is a charter belonging to the Abbey of St Sauveur le Vicomte in Normandy. This records that in 1150 Guillaume de Vauville gave to the Abbey the church of St John in Jersey. Another charter four years later shows that St John was already a parish church, for a Guillaume Suen transferred to the Abbey certain lands "in the parish of St John in Jersey". The church at this time evidently stood in an oak wood, for we find it called St Johannes de Quercubus and St Johannes de Caisnibus, which are both Dog-Latin for St John of the Oaks. No register makes clear after which St John the church was named. But, since in the Middle Ages the biggest fair in the Island took place in this parish on St John the Baptist's Day, and since these fairs were held as a rule on the patronal festival of the church, it is a safe assumption that this one was dedicated to the Baptist. This is indeed confirmed by a statement of 1447 that the Bishop of Coutances, when visiting the Island, ordained priests in the church of St John the Baptist.

Like all old Jersey churches, St John's grew bit by bit. If you stand in the churchyard to the north, you see at once that the chancel is a different building from the nave; its roof is higher, its stones are rougher, and the corner buttress still remains where the building once ended. This chancel is the original little church. Stand by the present pulpit and look east, and you see the size as it was about 1100. Neither nave had yet been built, nor the spire, nor the south chancel. The broken holy water stoup by the vestry door shows where the main door stood. There is also a blocked-up priest's door level with the north of the altar. Above it rather mysteriously is the date 1622, but the door itself is clearly older. On the south side, where the organ now is, there was a solid wall with narrow lancet windows. The large windows in the other walls are all later additions. The only windows in this little chapel were narrow unglazed slits. There were no seats. The people stood or kneeled on the floor.

Later, as the population increased, the west wall of the chapel was pulled down and the present nave added. Then at the end of the 15th century came a great enlargement, the building of the large south aisle and the tower and spire. The date is fixed by the fact that Thomas Lemprière had his name carved on the west gable with his arms and two Tudor roses, and fixed another slab with his arms on the steeple. He was seigneur of La Hougue Boëte in 1492 and Bailiff in 1495, and evidently played a leading part in the enlargement of his parish church.

At some unknown later date the south chancel was added; this must have been considerably before 1799, for in that year it was reported to be in danger of collapsing. The new aisle and new chancel now became the main part of the church, and the old chancel and nave were rather neglected. Then came a great pillar controversy. People in the south aisle could not see the pulpit because of a huge pillar. In 1828 the Assembly instructed the Rector to ask permission from the Ecclesiastical Court to remove this obstruction; but he hesitated, fearing lest its removal might bring down the roof. Three years later the parish appealed to the Court, but permission was refused. When a new Rector came, the Antipillarites returned to the attack, but he too thought their proposal too dangerous a piece of surgery to attempt on an old building. But Jerseymen never acknowledge defeat. One summer the Rector went to France for a holiday. On his return he found the pillar in the rectory garden, where it can still be seen, and the church was still standing. Architecturally the broad arch that was left, when two arches were thrown into one, may be a monstrosity; but from a practical point of view it was a vast improvement. The preacher can now see the congregation and they the preacher.

Meanwhile, the steeple was constantly giving trouble. In 1796, 700 livres tournois were spent on its repair, but in 1804 it had to be pulled down and rebuilt from its foundations. Alas, no one showed the builder that a steeple can be a thing of beauty! In 1881 it was given its hideous coat of cement, and the churchwardens were so proud of their work that they fixed their initials on it for all posterity to see! But the steeple was so badly built that a bush rooted itself in a crack half-way up, and it appears in many picture post-cards of the period. A parishioner performed the daring feat of climbing the steeple to remove it.

In 1754 a new bell was cast for St John's Church, by Maître Jacques Pitel. It weighed 1,200 lbs and was cast in the garden of a house in Colomberie, in St Helier. It failed because "the funnel which led the metal to the mould was too narrow and got blocked . . ." and a month later the work was done again, this time successfully. There is a good golden cock weather vane on the apex of the steeple. St John's Church also owns a very good example of the local type of collecting box, in copper with chasing, inscribed with the date 1677 and A.D.C., the initials of Abraham de Carteret, the donor.

In 1934 a thorough restoration of the old church was begun. The north chancel and nave again became the main portion of the church. The font was removed from its unusual position in front of the altar. A new vestry, a new organ, a new heating apparatus, new chancel furniture, new stained-glass windows, and electric light, were costly but useful improvements. After more than eight hundred years of service, the ancient building is still performing all the functions of a village church.

St John's Parish. No parish has a finer coast-line than St John, extending as it does from the Mourier Valley to the middle of the Havre Giffard. A strip of this was opened to the public for the first time during the German Occupation. When the enemy landed, many people were thrown out of work. Since no boats arrived, dock labour ceased; since no imports arrived, merchants needed no staffs; since no tourists arrived, hotels had to close, and their employees swelled the ranks of the unemployed. Soon the Labour Department had on its books 2,300 men asking how they could earn a living. Then someone suggested making a road from Les Mouriers to La Saline, a lovely stretch of cliffs which few had ever seen, because it was shut in by private property. The ground was bought, and the first strip made round La Saline (the salt-pan) and foundations laid for a second stage as far as Sorel; but work farther west was impossible, for the Germans placed the land between Sorel and Les Mouriers inside their military zone, which civilians were forbidden to enter. The whole is now completed and named La Route du Nord, and at its end is a stone inscribed, "This road is dedicated to the men and women of Jersey who suffered in the World War, 1939-45."

Glancing along the coast, the Mourier Valley is the loneliest spot in Jersey. Its three water-mills have disappeared; its knacker's yard is in ruins; the only sign of life is a pumping station of the Waterworks Company. Its utter solitude is impressive, and at its end, when it reaches the sea, an enchanting peep at St Mary's coast can be obtained. Sorel, the northernmost tip of the Island, is another glorious view-point. Here one looks right across the dangerous Paternoster Reef to Sark, and towards the east the coast of France is clearly visible. This is a good place for seeing shags, whose bronze-green plumage is a striking contrast to the snowy whiteness of the gulls. Between Sorel and Ronez at half-tide level is the Lavoir des Dames, the fairies' bath, or more correctly, Le Puits de la Chuette,

St Helier's Church, from the east

Royal Crescent

Morel Farm, St Lawrence

St Lawrence's Church, from the west

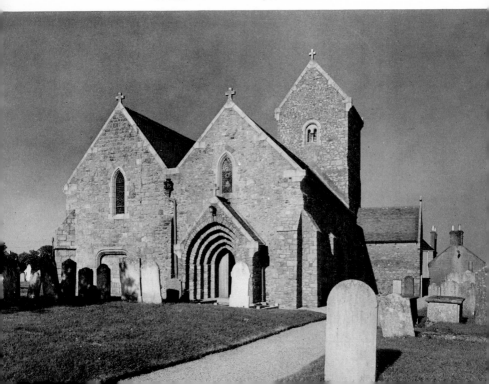

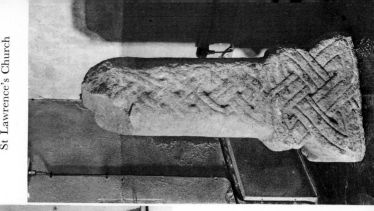

Carved pillar in
St Lawrence's Church

Wall painting in
St Clement's Church

Pre-Reformation font in
St Clement's Church

Priest's tombstone, built into
St Mary's Church

Faldouet Dolmen

The Reservoir at St Catherine's

a mysterious, rectangular hollow in the solid rock, 25 feet by 24, with a depth of 15 feet. Noury's *Géologie de Jersey* declares that it must be man-made; though why it should be made in such an out-of-the-way spot, and how it was made, when tons of sea water would have had to be emptied out of it during each brief low-tide spell before work could be resumed, are unsolved mysteries. Sinel, in his *Geology of Jersey*, argues that a block of soft shale may have been embedded in the granite, which became decomposed and washed away, leaving only the granite shell. But again it seems queer that the block of shale should have been so nearly rectangular. It is sometimes suggested that it was a "nourrice", that is a store room for lobsters. This again is unconvincing, as it is difficult of access at all tides. Very naturally, with an unsolved mystery, legends have appeared, one saying that if any man saw the fairies bathing here, he would immediately be struck blind, an effective way of frightening people away if the bath is in some way connected with smuggling.

Ronez itself is the one blot on the landscape. Once a delightful picnicking spot, a Concrete Company has acquired it, and its "Trespassers will be Prosecuted" boards now warn visitors off. We then reach the completed part of La Route du Nord; and at its far end a footpath round La Saline Point leads to the Wolf Cave, one of the finest in the island, 350 feet long, 60 feet high, and from 20 to 50 feet wide. The main entrance is scarcely ever left by the tide, and can only be reached by boat, but there used to be a side entrance down an iron ladder. The Germans, however, removed this, and, as it has not been replaced, at present it can only be visited by the help of ropes. Farther east comes BONNE NUIT, on which we have a separate article; and then at Havre Giffard we pass into Trinity.

Looking inland, the only prehistoric site of importance is La Hougue Boëte, a bowl-shaped mound, which was partially excavated in 1911 and the result published in a Paris periodical. Unfortunately, before the Société Jersiaise could examine it, the tunnel that had been made in its side had collapsed; so we have only the rather unsatisfactory report to guide us, and it is hoped that further excavation will be undertaken on this interesting site. The report says that a rectangular chamber was discovered, roofed with a great slab, and that in it were the bones of a man. As sherds of wheel-made Iron Age pottery were also found in the tomb, this burial probably dates

133

from just before the Christian era. It is a pity that the details could not be more firmly verified. La Hougue takes its name from the family of Boiste, who held the property before the separation from Normandy, and the mound was used as the meeting place for the seigneurial court; other instances are known or suspected where a prehistoric site was so used, as being an area sanctified by time in the minds of the people.

In the Middle Ages, in addition to the church and the priory chapel at Bonne Nuit and the seigneurial chapel attached to La Hougue Boëte Manor, there was the chapel of St Blaize, which still stands, though it has been so successfully transformed into a charming modern house that the only sign of its former use is one buttress, the name, and the legend. The Rue de la Croix, a house called La Croix, and another called Cross Cottage probably preserve memories of wayside crosses, and three of these are still remembered by name—la Croix de Hérupe, la Croix Jenette Benest, and la Croix ès Baudains.

For centuries one feature of the parish has been its great granite quarries. Mont Mado in early days was probably a tor-like hill; but even in prehistoric times the excellence of its stone seems to have been recognised. In La Hougue Bie one of the uprights was dragged all the way from this hill, and a quern (hand-mill) of the same material was buried in the tomb. In later years all the finest houses were at any rate faced with this stone; and the States always stipulated that their new buildings should be made of Mont Mado granite. Before long Mont Mado ceased to be a mount, and then, as the demand for its stone increased, it became a gigantic chasm. In 1650 Elie Brevint wrote: "These quarries are worth little now, for all the good granite is extracted"; but he was wrong. The quarry has gone on even deeper and deeper. Today the gash is 200 yards broad and about 200 feet deep, and this is only one of several granite quarries in the parish, but for economic reasons stone is no longer quarried there, and the great chasm is serving a useful purpose as an authorised rubbish tip.

Returning to town by St John's main road, we pass a neglected cemetery. In days when only Anglican rectors could take funerals in the churchyards, the Independents, who had already built themselves a chapel, procured a piece of land where they could be buried by their own minister, and called it Macpéla, after the burial-place that Abraham bought for his wife Sarah (the spelling is that of the French Bible). This little graveyard gained an international reputation. In 1848, the year of revolutions, most of which failed, exiles from many lands found a refuge in Jersey. Whenever one died, the whole colony marched to Macpéla behind the red flag, and Victor Hugo delivered one of his tremendous orations. The epitaphs in the cemetery testify to their love of rhetoric: "Here let him sleep in alien soil. If his home-town asks where he lies, answer, 'Died in Exile,' as our soldiers answer for La Tour d'Auvergne, 'Died on the Field of Honour.'" "One by one we outlaws die. The tyrant digs our graves. But the day comes when the grave will engulf the grave-digger."

A few yards south of the tall Methodist Chapel called Sion we cross the boundary into St Helier's parish.

St Lawrence's Church. No one can date our ancient churches. Like Topsy, they growed. Old parts were pulled down and rebuilt. New chapels and aisles were added. At St Lawrence's this process was so complete that no part of the original structure remains. The oldest document to mention it is a charter of 1198, by which John (then Lord of the Isles and later King of England) gave to the Abbey of Blanchelande in Normandy "the Church of St Lawrence in Jersey with all its appurtenances", and that abbey remained patron of the living till the Reformation. But the church may have been standing for centuries before John gave it away.

It probably began as a small chapel on the site of the present chancel. When the family that owned it threw it open to their neighbours, a short nave was built. As the population increased, this nave was lengthened. Then a tower and two transepts were added, giving the building the shape of a cross (the north transept was swallowed up later by the building of the north aisle; the south transept is now the south porch). In the 14th century the parish demolished the old nave and built the present one, longer and loftier than its predecessor (the stonework shows that it was added to the tower and not vice versa). The nave was now much finer than the chancel; so in the 15th century the latter was pulled down and the present chancel built. The two latest sections of the church can be dated exactly. In 1524 Louis Hamptonne, the Rector, built the Hamptonne chapel, which included a piscina, which must have

135

been the last one to be made in the Island, only twenty-three years before the Reformation fury hit Jersey. The date of the chapel is on the north-east buttress. It is the finest bit of ecclesiastical architecture in the Island. In 1546 the Royal Court authorised the sale of some rentes belonging to the church to pay for "the enlargement of the church by constructing a chapel [the present north aisle] alongside the nave." The building then attained its present shape and size.

Few relics remain of the church's earliest days. The oldest is a broken granite pillar 5 feet high, made of non-local granite, and designed like an architrave, to stand flush with the face of a wall, found 3 feet below the nave floor. It was originally a pillar in some secular building in which a local grandee was copying Roman fashions. Similar pillars are found in the ruins of 4th century Roman villas. This building was destroyed, and probably towards the end of the 6th century the pillar was picked up and placed in a Christian church. A Celtic inscription was then carved on it in lettering, known as insular majuscule, that belongs to the end of the 6th century. Only the last half of each line survives which reads:

> . . . US DI
>
> . . . LIAUSI R
>
> . . . RITON ⟋

If the missing letters of the first line are SERV, we get Servus Di, the Servant of God, the regular title of a monk. The second line would then be the man's name. The missing letters here are merely a matter of guesswork. Inscriptions of this kind generally end with the place the man came from. Many place-names in those days ended in —riton, e.g. Darioriton and Vagoriton. Unless the other half of the stone, with the left hand portion of the inscription, is found, we can only say that in the 6th century this Roman pillar was used as a tombstone for some Celtic monk. But it shows that Celtic monks were in Jersey as early as 600, spreading Christianity from this central position in the Island, long before parishes, or parish churches existed. In those troublous times if there was a church of any sort, it was probably destroyed, for the pillar was used for a third purpose. In the 9th century an elaborate pattern was carved on it of three-cord plait with interlaced loops, a pattern common at that period. It then became an architectural ornament in what must have been a church of some dignity, which was probably swept away during the Viking invasions. But the fact that the stone was found under St Lawrence's nave suggests that a centre of worship has been on that site since the 6th century. It is, perhaps, the most interesting and important single historical object in the Island.

Apart from the walls, not much in the present building reminds us of pre-Reformation days. Some crudely carved stones, taken probably from parts of the old church now demolished, are built into the buttresses of the chancel; those showing a cross with a circle round the intersection are Celtic, of the 9th century. Those with a Calvary cross, that is to say with steps rising up to the Cross, are later, Norman, work. The recess in the porch probably contained the reredos of an altar, when this was the south transept. The few fragments that remain of the rich mediaeval glass have been placed in the west window. A comic face in the north transept, within the church, reminds us of days when humour was the ally of religion.

The long Calvinist communion table, which was placed before the pulpit on the four Communion Sundays, now stands in the north porch; and the bell, the oldest in the Island, belongs to this period. It bears the inscription: *"Cete cloche est pour la paroisse de St. Lorans a Jarze. 1592. I.W."* The door at the end of the north aisle was made curiously broad to run in and out the parish cannon, which were kept, from Elizabethan to Victorian times, in all the parish churches.

In the 17th century Jersey gentry prided themselves on their skill as Latinists. A good example is the Hamptonne tombstone outside the chancel wall. Translated, it runs: "All is dust!" (this is in Greek: the rest is Latin). "Hail, passer by! I would have a word with thee for a moment. Within this Temple lies buried that illustrious man, Laurens Hamptonne, who deserved more than well of his country, once Vicomte of this island, and Lieutenant-Bailiff, and Captain of this Parish, now, alas, snatched from us. Born, 1600. Unborn 2 Feb., and buried 5 Feb. 1664. Also Edouard Hamptonne, Junior. If anyone in this island was polished, it was he. He too was Vicomte, and now, alas, has been torn from us by an untimely death. Ripe for Heaven, he was taken away, 27 Jan. and buried on the 29th, 1660. Born, 1628. Farewell, passer by. Live in the light. Remember Death and Heaven."

St Lawrence's was the last church in the Island to be restored. Till 1892 it retained all the old Puritan arrangements—its three-decker pulpit, its high-backed pews, its great square boxes for the gentry filling the chancel and the space in front of the pulpit, each with its stove and chimney, and two of them with a private door into the churchyard. In that year all this lumber was swept away, and the church was thoroughly modernised. The colours of the St Lawrence Battalion of the militia were then deposited in it, including two actually carried at the Battle of Jersey. Many additional improvements have been made in recent years, the most noticeable being the refurnishing of the Hamptonne Chapel to be a Lady Chapel.

St Lawrence's Parish. The central parish of the Island. Bounded on the south by a mile of St Aubin's Bay from the Mill Brook to the brook by the perquage, its eastern boundary runs for three-quarters of a mile up the Waterworks Valley, then swerves till it meets the Bellozanne Brook, which it follows to its source; its western boundary starts at the brook, which flows beside the perquage, but after passing Quetivel Mill it deserts the main stream for a rivulet coming in from the north, and then straggles by a devious route till it reaches St John a mile and a half from the north coast.

The parish is divided into five vingtaines, four with the prefix Coin (district), Coin ès Tourgis Nord, Coin ès Tourgis Sud, Coin du Motier, probably a form of "moustier", a monastery, and Coin ès Hâtains. The Tourgis and the Hasteyns were once leading families in the parish. The fifth name, La Vallée, explains itself.

The outstanding feature of the parish is its brooks. Down the winding St Lawrence Valley, now called the Waterworks Valley, ran one of the swiftest streams in the Island, which with its fall of 380 feet in less than three miles was powerful enough to turn six watermills and so was known as the Mill Brook. Four of these ground corn: Quetivel, the King's mill, to which Crown tenants in the parish had to take their grain; the Moulin des Écoliers, at the foot of the Côtil de Dannemarche, which by its name must once have belonged to a Dane—this helped to support the scholars whom the Baudains Trust sent to Oxford; Vicart (a personal name), and the Petit Moulin du Prieur, which belonged to the priory on the Islet. There were also a paper-mill and a mill for crushing sugar-cane. In addition there was a windmill at Bel Royal.

Milling was an important trade when the Island produced its own flour, and down to the middle of the 19th century it was still prosperous. There was no corn-tax; so wheat could be brought in Jersey vessels straight from Russia, ground into flour, and exported to the colonies, where as British produce it landed free of duty. But steam flour-mills drove the leisurely water-mills out of action. A new use was then found for St Lawrence's water.

By 1847 it had become obvious that the old system of street pumps was inadequate for the rapidly increasing population of St Helier. A meeting, attended by the Bailiff and the Lieutenant-Governor, stressed the need of a public water supply; but not till 1863 was the first Waterworks Company formed. This decided to draw its water from the St Lawrence Valley, and in 1869 the Lieutenant-Governor cut the first sod. But the work was badly planned; the town's new taps ran dry, and in a short time the company went bankrupt. The present company began work in 1882. One by one it built the big reservoirs that line the valley today, making it look like a glen in the Westmorland Lake District—Millbrook in 1892, Dannemarche in 1908, and Handois, on the site of the old China Clay Quarries, in 1929; and the pipe that is seen pouring a torrent into the last tells of neighbouring valleys tapped and water being pumped up from St Peter and Le Mourier Valley.

The parish is not as rich as some in prehistoric remains. At Blanche Pierre Farm as late as 1870 stood the menhir, La Blanche Pierre; but it has disappeared. On Mont Félard are two great blocks of granite, brought either from the Elizabeth Castle Islet or from the Town Hill, which are all that is left of some destroyed dolmen. In an orchard on the Mainlands estate a hoard of the Bronze Age was discovered—axes, broken swords, spears, knives, and lumps of molten metal—the stock-in-trade of some travelling smith, who, perhaps about 500 B.C., had buried his wares and never lived to unearth them. But the most interesting relic of this period is the Pierre des Baissières, a large block of red granite, which marks the spot where the three parishes of St Peter, St Mary, and St Lawrence meet. As it stands in a shale area, it must have been brought there for a purpose, and it has five cup-marks on it. If the theory is correct that these mysterious marks were an early form of heraldry, or some form of writing, a tribal mark put there in this case probably to warn intruders from encroaching, it suggests the intriguing possibility that our present parish boundaries may be roughly the same as those of the prehistoric tribes, but this peradventure rests on a very slender foundation. It cannot, however, be a coincidence that it stands at the junction of three parishes.

A well-known legend (told in the article on LA HOUGUE BIE) speaks of the dragon of St Lawrence, which lurked in the marsh later called Goose Green, where Bel Royal is now. It is said to have held the whole island in thrall, till the brave Knight of Hambie crossed from Normandy and slew it.

The parish today is famous for its farms and manors. A good example is Morel Farm, now the property of the local National Trust, which Marguerite Langlois brought to the Morels on her marriage in 1560. Another old house, Cap Verd, in La Ville Emphrie, has two bénitiers, and a fine spiral stone staircase; though much renovated in recent years, it is among the oldest houses in the Island. Turning to the larger mansions, St Lawrence was never dominated by one great manor as St Martin was by Rozel or St Clement by Samarès, but it contained at least four manors of some importance. Two possess colombiers. One can be seen not far from the church on the fief Jourdain Payn, and a stone records that the colombier was rebuilt in 1669. The Payns were a Jurat-breeding family in St Lawrence, and the old manor, which still stands on the left of the present dwelling-house, though now much altered, was built by Jourdain's son Raulin, who was Jurat in 1350. The newer house, which is called Le Colombier, was built in 1776.

Of greater importance was the house which for three hundred years has been called Hamptonne. In 1445 the Duke of Gloucester, who was then Lord of the Isles, gave Richard Langlois leave to build a square colombier on his land, an unusual privilege to grant to a house that did not possess a fief, and unusual too, in that all other colombiers but one are circular. In 1637 this house was bought by Laurens Hamptonne the Vicomte, and he largely rebuilt it, and called it by his own name. A stone on the entrance arch has the date 1637, and the pillars at the main door bear his arms. His son Edouard, in 1649, obtained leave from Charles II to rebuild the colombier which had fallen into ruins, but the date on it shows that this permission was not used till 1674. A family tradition said that King Charles II stayed in this house, and the bed in which he slept used to be shown; but this is hard to reconcile with the explicit statement of Chevalier, who kept a day-by-day diary of the King's visit: "If any of the island gentry invited the Duke [i.e. the King's brother] to their house, neither he nor the King ever accepted the invitation, but the Lords of the Court used to accept, and the King counted this a compliment paid to himself." Nevertheless it is reasonable to think that in his rides round the Island, the King would have visited, and accepted meals in the houses of his friends. Indeed Falle, writing not many years later, suggests just this. In 1649, however, the King granted Hamptonne Letters Patent (from which the house was sometimes called La Patente), by which the property was held by Knight's Service, could never be divided, and the owner was always summoned to appear at the Assize d'Héritage. This was virtually the creation of a new fief, though the owner does not in fact, now, appear at the Assize d'Héritage.

Les Saints Germains, a house that must once have been linked with some forgotten chapel dedicated to St Germain of Auxerre and St Germain of Paris, gave its name to a third fief. In the 14th century an English soldier named Wallis married the widow of the seigneur of Handois, who also owned the fief Pinel at St John, the fief Grainville at St Saviour, and the fief Morville at St Ouen. These four fiefs then began to be considered as one, and were called the fief de St Germain, because the Wallises chose this house as their home. But a later Wallis fell fighting on the Yorkist side at the Battle of Barnet, and so his estates were confiscated by the victorious Lancastrian King. Henceforth these fiefs belonged to the Crown, but were later granted to other persons.

A fourth manor is Avranches. In the 13th century the Le Franchoys, whose name survives in the district called La Ville ès Franchoys, held in this parish the fief of Amorers (for which every Michaelmas they had to give a dinner to the Bailiff, the Vicomte, and the King's Receiver), and the fief des Arbres. This latter fief passed in time to the Tourgis, and the Dumaresqs, and then to the Maretts. The fief d'Avranches, which had once belonged to the Bishop of that See, but had been confiscated by the Crown in 1415, was sold to Hélier de Carteret in 1649, to assist in paying Charles II's debts. In 1749 it was bought by François Marett, who lived in the house referred to above, and he gave the name of his newly acquired fief to it. Its 50 acres of grounds include two large ponds. During the Occupation it was used as a German petrol dump, and

750,000 gallons were secreted there. It was rebuilt in 1818, and it is that Regency house which we see today.

A much less-distinguished house, but one notorious throughout the Island, was the Hangman's Cottage, which stood between Mainland and Bel Royal. This was provided for every hangman as part of his pay.

The two churches, the parish church and St Matthew, have separate articles in this book, but there were also before the Reformation a number of smaller chapels: Ste Claire, which gave its name to the fief de Ste Claire, St Eutrope, St George, perhaps the seigneurial chapel of Handois, and possibly St Christopher. The Fontaine de St Martin, one of the old sacred springs, whose waters were supposed to have healing properties, still bubbles up beside one of the roads. But the most interesting ecclesiastical survival is the perquage. In olden days every parish church had a perquage or sanctuary path to the sea, by which criminals who had taken sanctuary in a church could make their way to the shore unarrested, and escape by boat, a convenient way of inducing undesirables to deport themselves. But the right of sanctuary disappeared at the Reformation, and one of the few surviving pieces of a sanctuary path is half a mile of the St Lawrence perquage, which comes down to the sea just east of Beaumont, which was ceded to the States by the Société Jersiaise, and must be maintained as a public path for all time.

A relic of the Occupation is the German Underground Hospital, quarried out of the side of a hill with 130 feet of solid rock above its roof as a safeguard against bombing. This was the work of Russian and other prisoners-of-war, who had been marched across Europe from the Ukraine, guarded by S.S. men and large, savage dogs. Most of them arrived barefooted. About 14,000 tons of rock were excavated by them, and many of them were killed by falls of stone. Their bodies are said to be buried behind the concrete walls. The hospital was planned to consist of four parallel tunnels, each about 100 yards long, with seven connecting tunnels crossing them at right angles. Two of the long tunnels and six of the short ones had been completed before the Liberation. These contained 600 beds, an operating theatre, a dispensary, doctors' and nurses' quarters, store-rooms and kitchens, and were supplied with central heating, air-conditioning plant, electric light and power, and all the amenities of a modern up-to-date hospital. This hospital forms a great tourist attraction.

Three additional place-names may be mentioned. Modern tradition has linked Bel Royal with the visit of Charles II, but its origin is much less romantic. *Bel* in Norman French meant "a yard". There is a Bel au Vent in the north of the parish, and the yard in the town where the market-women left their donkeys was known as the Bel ès Anes. And the Bel Royal was merely the King's Yard, where some of the cannon were stored. La Maison Charles, next to it, may refer to a certain Charles Le Roux, who lived somewhere near there in the mid eighteenth century; there are so few houses of that date in the immediate vicinity, which was sand dunes before the building of the sea wall, that it is reasonable to guess he lived there.

Mont Cambrai has only a remote connection with the French town of that name. In the Extente of 1331 we find two families of Cambraes holding land in St Lawrence. They may originally have come from Cambrai, but the hill takes its name from them and not from the town.

The Carrefour Selous (Carrefour means "a place where four roads meet") bears the name of an English soldier, Philip Slow, who in 1652 married a Jersey girl and settled in the Island. The family name became Jersified later into Selous, and from them descended Selous the dramatist, Selous the painter, and Selous the mighty hunter.

St Lawrence claims to possess the best ghost story in the Island. It is said that, if you are in a certain lane that leads down to the Waterworks Valley on a certain night at midnight, you will hear a peal of wedding bells, which is strange, as St Lawrence lost most of its bells at the Reformation. Then you will see a coach with six grey horses come spanking down the hill. The coachman has white ribbons on his whip, and inside sits a bride all in white; but, as she passes, you see with horror that she has no face, nothing but a grinning skull. The story goes that years ago she drove to the church to be married; but the bridegroom failed to arrive, and the poor girl returned home and committed suicide. And still on every anniversary of her wedding-day she drives through the parish seeking for her faithless swain. Everyone knows the story, but no one can produce a witness who has actually seen the coach.

St Martin's Church. Jersey had been Christian for generations before the Normans came. Each estate had its wooden chapel for the family and its serfs. When pagan Northmen overran the Island, these chapels went up in flames; but the people remained Christian. In 911 the Normans accepted Christianity, and knights, who had seized the north-east of Jersey, built stone chapels on their estates. There were many of these in the present St Martin's parish, and one of them, dedicated to St Martin, grew to be the parish church. In 1042 William the Conqueror, Duke of Normandy but not yet King of England, granted to the Abbey of Cérisy "the Church of St Martin the Old in the isle of Jersey with its land and a third part of its tithe of grain." This shows, not only that the church was standing as early as 1042, but that it was regarded as old in comparison with St Martin's, Grouville. The mention of tithes indicates that it was already a parish church.

The chancel of the present church was the original chapel, and bit by bit it grew into the building that we know today; but it has been restored so drastically that it is impossible to date dogmatically the various additions. First a nave was added; then two transepts were thrown out, giving the building the form of a cross. Next, a south chancel was built; then, perhaps a century later, a south aisle. Look at the south wall of the church from the churchyard, and you will see that the east part is built of boulders from the beach, while the western half is of quarried stones, and the roof of the two halves is not quite the same height.

St Martin used to be considered the leading church in the Island. Its endowment was larger than any of the others, and many of its rectors were deans. Of these the most vigorous was Dean Mabon (1514–43), and for a time he was Bailiff as well as Dean. He made a pilgrimage to the Holy Land, and on his return built a chapel of the Holy Sepulchre on La Hougue Bie; and towards the end of his life he began to add a new chapel to the north-east corner of his church. He planned it on noble lines, as the walled-in arch on the north of the chancel shows, but he died before it was finished. In 1740 the churchwardens applied to the Ecclesiastical Court for permission to pull it down, stating that it had never been roofed or used and that its ruins disfigured the church. The eastern part was then demolished, but the western end was preserved to house the militia cannon. In recent years this has been transformed into an organ-chamber and vestry.

The pre-Reformation perquage, the path by which criminals who had taken sanctuary in the church could escape to the sea, crossed the north wall of the churchyard by a stile, plunged down the valley to the brook, and followed the stream till it reached the shore near St Catherine's Tower. It was last used in 1546, when Thomas Le Seeleur escaped the gallows by walking down it to a boat that took him to Normandy.

The Reformation did its work thoroughly. No church in the Island shows fewer traces of the old worship. Altars, images, stained-glass windows were swept away. All seats were turned to face the pulpit, and the chancel was boarded off to be the parish school. The account book for 1582 begins with the entry: "Paid to Edward Baudains for sundry missions for the building of the spire, 4 nobles 19 groats." Does this give the date of its first building, or only a rebuilding after destruction by lightning?

No church has more buttresses than St Martin's. Soon after the Reformation the weight of the stone roof made the walls bulge ominously. The first set of buttresses were built then, and priests' tombstones can be seen, used ruthlessly for this purpose. Another stone has an elaborate coat-of-arms, much weathered, and probably 15th century, but as yet unidentified.

In 1616, on a Sunday morning, as the people were going into church, the spire was struck by lightning, and broke off in the middle, which caused widespread panic. It was taken as a warning that God's wrath was about to smite the Island, for it was written, "Judgement must begin at the House of God." The spire, however, was rebuilt in 1618.

During the 18th century, as the population increased, two large galleries had to be made to hold the congregation. In 1745 the north wall began to bulge again, and fresh buttresses had to be added, which are easily distinguished from the others because they are of blue granite. In 1749 we find an amusing instance of Jersey thrift. The churchwardens petitioned the Ecclesiastical Court for permission to substitute windows for two of their doors. They explained that they had four doors but only two almoners; and at whichever door they stationed these officers to take the collection, many of the congregation slipped out through the others.

In 1837 the spire was again destroyed by lightning, but this time, when it was rebuilt, a lightning conductor was added. The chancel was still boarded off as a schoolroom, and in 1842, when Dean Jeune suggested moving the school elsewhere, the parishioners would not hear of it. Three years later, however, the parish assembly sanctioned a restoration, "provided that it cost the parish nothing". The school was removed, the partition pulled down, and the chancel restored to its former use, with a communion table under the east window. A new pulpit and several painted glass windows were added, and the present vestry made in the remnant of the Mabon Chapel.

The next restoration took place in 1877, the cost being covered by printing bank-notes, a form of finance much favoured in the Island at this time. This work was done thoroughly, and the Rev. William Lemprière, seigneur of Rozel, refurnished the chancel at his own expense, with choir-stalls, altar-rails, and east window, and also presented a new font and lectern. The chief glory of St Martin's is its coloured glass. No church in the island has finer. One of the latest gifts is an ancient wooden statue of St Martin dividing his cloak with a beggar, which Lady Trent bought in the south of France and presented. The head of a girl saint, with a Mona Lisa smile, evidently knocked off at the Reformation, was found under the floor at the last restoration, and is now in the Museum.

St Martin's Parish. Les Ecréhous, which form part of this parish, are only seven miles from France, and Mont Orgueil itself is only 14 miles from Carteret, a fact which gave rise to the tradition that, when early bishops of Coutances came to hold their confirmations, they merely laid down a plank, referred to as La Chaussée des Bœufs, and walked across the narrow channel. This, however, is more than doubtful. The strait had almost certainly broadened centuries before there were Christians in Coutances, but the story may have been meant to symbolise the close link between Jersey and Normandy. Granite from Les Ecréhous was extensively used in building houses in this parish.

St Martin extends from the middle of Gorey village to the brook that runs into the northern end of Rozel Bay, and is almost wholly agricultural, 85 per cent of its land being under cultivation. Most of the interesting spots have been dealt with in separate articles, LES ECRÉHOUS, GOREY, MONT ORGUEIL, ROZEL BAY, ROZEL MANOR, ST CATHERINE'S BAY, and ST MARTIN'S CHURCH. This article merely gathers up the fragments that remain.

The Le Couperon gallery-grave has been mentioned in the article on Rozel Bay, but there is a fine tomb of more elaborate design on the hill-top overlooking Mont Orgueil, the Faldouet dolmen, which takes its name from the vingtaine in which it stands. This is a passage-grave, in which a corridor 16 feet long leads into a central chamber, where a group of cists was discovered containing human bones, and beyond this is an inner sanctum capped by an enormous stone, which weighs at least 23 tons. Finds in it suggest that it may have been made a thousand years later than Le Couperon. When Poingdestre wrote in 1682, most of it was still covered with a mound, which was not removed till 1839, when the owner of the ground began a treasure hunt.

Anne Port gets its name from the fief of Anneville behind it, which, before the separation from Normandy, belonged to the seigneurs of Anneville-en-Saire near Cherbourg. Many tales are told to explain why one rock in this bay should be called Geoffrey's Leap, or in French *le Saut Geoffroi*, but all are merely guess-work. Who Geoffrey was is a matter of legend.

A most attractive walk is that round Saie Harbour, which the National Trust saved from the bungalow-builders by buying the côtil leading down to it. Both halves of the name are a trifle puzzling. There is a Saie Bay in Alderney, but the old Jersey spelling was apparently Scez; and "harbour" seems an inappropriate name for such a rock-bound coast. But a hooked reef of rocks, which at low tides rises 27 feet out of the water, gives shelter to little boats that anchor under its lee.

To judge by the number of chapels it possessed, St Martin should have been the most religious parish in the Island. In addition to the parish church and the chapels of St Mary and St George in the Castle (and the second of these was so popular a resort that the Government grew nervous lest the fortress should be rushed by enemies disguised as worshippers), the chapels of St Agatha and St Catherine in St Catherine's Bay, the manor chapel at Rozel, and the lonely chapel on Les Ecréhous, there were the chapel of St Barbe at Faldouet, of St Etienne at La Quéruée, of St Julian where the Fontaine St Julien still bubbles by the roadside, of La Croix immediately north of the parish church, and that of Sire Augustin Baudains just to the south-east, built only shortly before the Reformation, and therefore enjoying only a brief life. At 13 altars in this parish Mass was said every morning, and, since the hill overlooking the Castle was called Mont St Nicolas, there was probably also a chapel of St Nicolas there. But of all these the one in the manor alone remains in use, and the crypts of the two in the Castle can still be visited.

The Germans left their usual scars on the parish, but they did one good deed. By damming the brook down the Rozel Valley they created a great reservoir from which neighbouring farms in time of drought can draw inexhaustible water. As well as this they created an automatic nature reserve, and perhaps the loveliest inland walk in the Island.

Explorers of St Martin must be warned, however, about Constable Messervy, an insatiable curio-collector, who, not content with bringing home from abroad many unusual souvenirs (he presented to the Methodist chapel a stone from the Temple at Jerusalem), spent large sums on creating entirely bogus antiquities. At La Chasse cross-roads stands a mysterious little granite building with 1626 carved over the door. It was built about 1900 by this eccentric old man, and has never had any conceivable use.

In the garden wall of the house called Wrentham Hall, a big 19th century structure, is the upper section of a pre-Reformation cross, the survivor of La Chapelle de la Croix on this site. Half-way down the hill opposite, called Les Vaux, is a roadside fountain dated 1846, bearing the initials of those who lived near and had the right to use it.

St Mary's Church. The origin of this church is clear from its ancient name. In the oldest documents it is called St Mary of the Burnt Monastery (*arsi monasterii*). So, in early days, there must have been a monastery here, perhaps an offshoot from St Magloire's in Sark, which had been destroyed by fire, possibly during Viking raids. Many houses in the parish claim to be, or to incorporate the remains of, the burnt monastery, but in no case is there any supporting proof. It is more likely that a small chapel survived, built of rough stone from the beach, or at least the memory of such a one, and that this evolved into the north-east chancel of the present church. By 1042 it had become a tithe-receiving parish church, for in that year William the Conqueror granted a third of its tithes to the Abbey of Cérisy near Coutances.

The parishioners added a tower and spire, and later a nave. If you stand in the road, you can see that the nave is a separate building, higher than the chancel. In 1342, and not 1352 as has often appeared in print, as the date can still be deciphered on the gable, a fine new chapel was built on the south side of the chancel. After that, building ceased for nearly 500 years. The south aisle was not added till 1840. Few relics of pre-Reformation days remain, only a piscina in the south chapel decorated with the somewhat rare rope moulding, and with a stone shelf within its niche, and the tombstone of a priest in the west wall, on which is cut a chalice and a fish.

Like all Jersey churches at the Reformation St Mary's was transformed into a Huguenot temple. Altars, images, stained glass were swept away. Every pew faced the pulpit. Even the east window was blocked with masonry, that tiers of seats might rest against it. The Calvinist communion table now stands facing the north door. When the parish bought cannon as a protection against Spain in Elizabethan days, these were housed at the end of the church, and a gallery built over them to provide seats for those who had lost their pews.

St Mary has the smallest population of the twelve parishes, but for 70 years the church bell was a cause of bitter contention. During the Calvinist régime there were no Christmas services, but the custom arose of ringing the bell for 24 hours without stopping. This custom, observed in St Peter and St Ouen as well, almost certainly has its origin in the French Occupation of 1461–68, when it appears that these parishes were the last to be subjugated and the first to be freed. For the lads of the parish this was a spree, and often a drunken one, for a barrel of cider was rolled into the church, from which they could quench their thirst. As the bell-rope came down beside the pulpit, it was impossible to hold a service while this was going on. Rector after rector tried to stop this, but in vain. In 1788 one appeared before the Court with his head in bandages, complaining that the ringers had assaulted him; but the Jurats decided that they were justified in resisting any interference with so old-established a custom. When the next two rectors locked

149

the doors, the ringers took them off their hinges. When they appealed to the police, the police refused to help. Then came a young rector who determined that a service should be held. On Christmas Eve, 1858, he put new locks on the doors, and removed the bell-rope and the bell-clapper and the ladder that led to the belfry. But the ringers were just as determined. A handbill was distributed through the parish:

Enfants de Ste Marie
Vos droits sont envahis!

(Children of St Mary, your rights are assailed!) They broke the locks, and deposited the doors in the rectory garden. They fetched a ladder, and climbed to the bell. One galloped into town to get a new rope. Others woke the blacksmith, and worked his bellows, while he forged a new clapper. And the parish assembly asserted: "If there was any disturbance, it was due to the pig-headed behaviour of the Rector." This established the custom so firmly that it has continued, though now it is purged of its more unseemly features, and it no longer prevents the holding of the Christmas services.

Many alterations were made in the church during the 19th century, some wise, some otherwise, the most curious being the removal of the pillar between the two chancels and the throwing of two arches into one. The discarded pillar can be seen today as a gatepost of the farm called Le Marais in La Rue de L'Église, with a cross on the top, the base of which is in the garden of the same house. In 1930 a big change was made. The altar was moved into the south chapel, which was transformed with choir-stalls into a chancel, and the south aisle then became the main body of the church.

St Mary's Parish. A small parish with only two vingtaines, Nord and Sud. It extends along the north coast from GRÈVE DE LECQ (on which there is a separate article) to the Mourier Valley. This mile and a half of steep precipices split by narrow gorges provides some of the most glorious cliff-scenery in Jersey. The promontory known as Le Col de la Rocque, which has been presented to the local National Trust, is perhaps the finest viewpoint anywhere in the Island. Many of Jersey's three hundred caves are found in this strip of coast; of these the most imposing are one under L'Ane, and the tunnel through the Ile Agois, and the one which char-à-banc drivers have christened the Devil's Hole, though its right name is Le Creux de Vis (Screw Hole, or Vice.)

The Ile Agois is a small islet, 500 yards square, separated from the main Island by a narrow gorge with cliffs 250 feet high; but seawards there is a slope carpeted in spring with primroses and bluebells. It is in Crabbé Bay, and on its slopes can also be found the royal fern (*Osmunda regalis*). On the top 14 ancient hut-circles can be traced. This most inaccessible spot was perhaps only used as a refuge, and may not always have been an island, but it was undoubtedly inhabited about the 9th century B.C., and again in the 9th century A.D., for Neolithic pottery and flint arrow-heads are plentiful, and seven coins of Charles the Bald, who died in A.D. 877, have been dug up here. The next headland to the east, Le Col de la Rocque, is National Trust property, and offers a superb viewpoint of the north coast, as well as slopes carpeted with Lent lilies in the spring.

The parish ends at the deep Mourier Valley. Here a stream, before it plunged over the cliff in a waterfall into the sea, used to turn three water-mills, one of which belonged to the King; but today it is dammed by the Waterworks Company, and its water pumped over the hills into the Handois Reservoir.

Inland a circular mound, known as the Hougue Mauger, was explored by the Société Jersiaise in 1914. This had undoubtedly once covered a dolmen, but the stones had been dug out and broken to wall the surrounding field. In the centre of the mound, however, 22 querns were discovered, 19 of which had been deliberately broken. These granite bowls in which Neolithic women ground their corn were far too solid to get broken accidentally, and the breaking must represent some prehistoric burial rite. Lugged urns were also unearthed. In 1936 this hougue was entirely destroyed and a modern house built on the site.

Gigoulande Mill, another of the King's mills, is mentioned as early as the Assize Roll of 1274. In 1309 it was burnt down "through the negligent custody of the miller", and the King's tenants were ordered to provide material for its rebuilding. Till recent years it was the most picturesque mill in the Island, as well as being an extremely rare type, having two wheels one above the other, so that the water, having turned the top wheel, fell on to the lower one and turned that also. Alas, it is now a ruin.

In the days when knitting was a major industry of the Island, St Mary was one of the chief sheep-breeding parishes, and field names testify this, and it is still full of farms. Les Colombiers, looking down into Grève de Lecq Valley, once for some unknown reason possessed three colombiers; two of these have disappeared but the third has been well restored, with a cantilevered stone roof, re-using the original stones. The most typical farm, however, is the one known today as The Elms; though comparatively modern— the back arch bears the date 1734—it was built according to the old traditions, and the builders evidently used stones from some ruined mediaeval chapel, dedicated, there is reason to think, to St Simon, for many fragments of ecclesiastical architecture can be seen in the house and outhouses. The large arch on the south is a very early example and has most interesting carved chamfer stops, and, on the keystone, an emblem of a cross rising out of a rose. This may be a symbolic reference to the birth of Christ (the Rose of Sharon, the mystic Rose), or it may be indicative of a Tudor date.

St Matthew's Church. Architecturally St Matthew's, Millbrook, is the ugliest church in the Island, an oblong box cased in cement, with the kind of tower that a child would build out of its nursery bricks; yet every char-à-banc stops at its door and pours out its passengers to inspect it. For 90 years it had carried on an inconspicuous work in the housing district that had sprung up half-way round St Aubin's Bay. Then in 1931 Lord Trent died. He was the Jesse Boot who had established chemists' shops in every town in England. His widow offered to decorate this church as a memorial to him. She had admired in Paris the work of René Lalique, a French artist who, after making a fortune as a designer of expensive jewellery, had abandoned this for a new and daring method of glass-modelling, producing anything from minute perfume flasks to the enormous glass fountain in the Esplanade des Invalides. Lady Trent conceived the idea of creating something never seen before, a church entirely decorated with Lalique glass. Behind a glass altar stands an immense luminous cross, 15 feet high, composed of glass lilies. This is flanked on either side by 12-foot-high glass candlesticks of the same design. In the side chapel four glass angels watch over a glass altar. A lofty screen of glass lilies shuts off the vestry from the chancel, and opposite a similar open-work screen surrounds the Lady Chapel. A screen of translucent glass divides the chancel from the nave. The font is of glass. Glass angels guard the door. The windows are filled with wavy glass. The bowls of the lamps are of Lalique's choicest design. The result is a church quite unlike any other, but strangely restful.

St Ouen's Church. This church began life as a little thatched chapel on the site of the present chancel; and, as the de Carterets later regarded it as their private property, it was probably built by some early seigneur of that family. No one knows its date; but, since William the Conqueror mentions it in a charter which he signed before he conquered England, it must be older than 1066. No altar could be consecrated in those days unless it contained a relic; so the founder secured, probably at a high price from some church in Normandy, a tiny splinter of a bone of St Ouen, a famous 7th century Archbishop of Rouen, and henceforth the chapel was known as St Ouen's.

In 1156 Robert of Torigny, Abbot of Mont St Michel, visited his kinsman, Philippe de Carteret, at St Ouen's Manor, and Philippe presented the church to the abbey. His son, "moved by the counsel of evil men", tried to recall this gift, but eventually "humbly repented of this wicked thought", and confirmed it. When the church became the property of this wealthy abbey, it was gradually enlarged and beautified. The south wall of the chapel was pulled down and a second chapel added, divided from the present chancel by round Norman arches. Then a third chapel was built, where the organ is now. The pointed arches show that this was later work. Next the parish coveted a peal of bells, so a tower was erected to contain them. Then a nave was constructed towards the west, and, as the population increased, the broad north and south aisles, each as large as the nave itself, were added. Two shields over one of the windows, showing the three leopards and the Tudor portcullis, mean that the north aisle dates from the reign of Henry VII.

A sensational incident took place in the church during the Civil War. When the Roundheads occupied Jersey, Stephen La Cloche, the Rector, like other Royalists, fled to St Malo. Some months later orders came from the King to Captain George Carteret to take a force of a thousand men and recapture the Island by force. But news had reached La Cloche that Jersey's enthusiasm for the Parliament's cause was cooling, and he asked permission to try to accomplish the task without bloodshed. He landed near Plémont on a Saturday night after dark, and next morning appeared in his church, where a Puritan minister was preaching, read from the pulpit the King's proclamation offering a free pardon to all who would lay down their arms, and in a passionate harangue called on his parish in the name of God to march on the town and overthrow the Parliamentary committee, and take them by surprise. But he had over-estimated his influence and the Island's discontent. St Ouen's refused to rise, and he was lucky in being able to escape to Mont Orgueil, which was still holding out for the King, before the Parliamentary governor arrived with troops to arrest him.

Until the Reformation there were no pews. In church you either stood or knelt on the floor. But when hour-long sermons became a central feature of the service, seats had to be provided. This gave rise to a plague of pew quarrels. Your status in the parish largely depended on the position of your pew. Round the pulpit were four square horse-box-like erections, furnished apartments where seigneurs could snooze through the sermon unobserved by the common herd. Two belonged to St Ouen's Manor and one to each of the Vinchelez. Behind these, according to rank, were pews for the lesser folk. On one occasion Jean Le Marchant's wife "created a great commotion and uproar to the disturbance of the hearing of God's Word" by seating herself in a coveted pew and refusing to leave. For the next two Sundays she had to sit in the churchyard with her feet in the stocks. A few years later, when the owner of a certain pew arrived, it was not there. Two rivals had entered the church in the night and chopped it into firewood. A never-ceasing stream of lawsuits about pews flows through the Court records.

A great restoration was carried out between 1865 and 1870. The unsightly galleries that filled the church, including one for smokers (*galerie des fumeurs*) near the south door, were swept away. The militia cannon were ejected from the south aisle where they had been stored for centuries. After long negotiations the owners of the clutter of pews that were at this time scattered higgledy-piggledy through the church consented to an orderly and uniform system of seating. The chancel was vaulted and lengthened 8 feet. A new organ was provided. A new pulpit, font, and lectern, the last a striking piece of work by a local craftsman, were presented. And the windows were filled with stained glass; but here the committee was swindled. The glass was much admired at the time, but it was of such inferior quality that in many cases the figures have faded away.

St Ouen's Manor. For at least eight hundred years this has been the home of the de Carterets. Though the present owner is a Malet de Carteret, whose grandfather only assumed the name de Carteret by Sign Manual, he did so because he was a direct descendant of a daughter of the famous Sir Philippe de Carteret of Civil War fame. The house has never passed out of the family. Simply, when the male line failed, it passed to the female line.

The Normans added Jersey to their Duchy in A.D. 933, and it is possible that the de Carterets obtained St Ouen in that first division. But it does not follow that they at once came to live there. Their family seat was at Carteret in Normandy, and at first St Ouen was only an outlying corner of their estate. Two de Carterests fought at Hastings; but if either of them had come from Jersey, Wace, the Jersey poet, who describes the battle, would almost certainly have mentioned the fact.

But there came a time when the family decided to build a house on their Jersey estate. We know for a fact that that house was standing in 1135, for in that year a Philippe de Carteret granted to the monks of Mont St Michel two plots of land in Jersey "adjoining his own house". Of that original manor very little remains except the site, and perhaps the old portions of the two square towers with the intervening hall, drastically altered as it has been.

When John lost Normandy in 1204, and Norman barons who held land in Jersey had to decide which King they would serve. Renaud, Philippe's son, chose the English allegiance, and henceforth the interests of the family centred wholly in Jersey. For centuries the seigneur of St Ouen was accepted as the senior seigneur. When he became a Jurat, he sat next to the Bailiff. If a Governor died, he automatically took command of the troops.

Inside the house is the picture of a large black horse, which is believed to have been buried in the grounds. This recalls a famous de Carteret story. In 1461 the French surprised Jersey, and held it for seven years. During that time they suspected that the Philippe de

Carteret of that day was preparing a resistance movement, and determined to arrest him. The old chronicler says: "It befell one day that he went to fish in his pond near St Ouen's Bay, and the French came stealthily along the beach between the shingle and the sea, thinking to catch him unawares, and bring him captive to the Castle. But the seigneur ever kept a good horse, and he sprang to the saddle, hoping to reach his manor. But, ere he could get to the crest of the hill, another troop appeared, striving to cut him off, and he was constrained to swerve towards the Val de la Charrière. Therefore, since he could not gain the end of the track, he made his horse leap the sunken road at its deepest place, where it is 22 feet wide, and, spurring towards Les Landes, so made his escape. But ere he could reach the manor, his horse fell dead beneath him; whereat the seigneur was sorely grieved, and he would not suffer it to be devoured by dogs or birds, but caused it to be buried in his garden for the good service it had done him." A horse's shoulder-blade, which experts declared to be several centuries old, was dug up in the grounds in 1904; but whether this was really Sir Philippe's horse, no one can say.

The oldest part of the existing manor, of which we can be sure, dates from 1496. The Philippe de Carteret of that period had been a minor when his father died, and when he came of age, "alders did grow in the hall of his Manor through the covetousness of those who had custody thereof during his nonage". He married Margaret, the 16-year-old daughter of Sir Richard Harliston, the famous Yorkist governor, and set to work to restore his house. His father-in-law gave him leave to crenellate it: "Whereas our dear friend Philippe de Carteret, has made clear to us, that through the propinquity of his house to the sea his goods and servants are in grave peril from malefactors and the King's enemies, we grant him leave to fortify his Manor within and without with towers, battlements, bulwarks, moat, drawbridge, and artillery for the defence of himself and his household." To this restoration is probably due the central part of the manor. One relic of this period is the fountain, a large tazza on a leg which stands beside the chapel. It has the de Carteret and Harliston arms on one side, and other heraldry which has defied identification, but the most likely date seems to be about 1550.

Margaret was the heroine of a story that Jersey will never let die. When the Red Rose finally conquered the White at the Battle of

Bosworth, Harliston, the loyal old Yorkist, was replaced as governor by a Lancastrian named Baker. He naturally looked with no friendly eyes at Harliston's son-in-law, the seigneur of St Ouen. A nine years' feud between the two ended in Baker presenting to the Court a letter, which he said had been picked up in the road by one of his men, in which de Carteret offered to betray Mont Orgueil to the French. Philippe at once swore that this was a forgery, but the Lancastrian Bailiff ordered the matter to be settled by Ordeal of Battle, a form of trial that by this time had become almost obsolete. De Carteret was imprisoned in a dark cell on bread and water, while the hefty ruffian who was to fight him was fed like a fighting-cock. But Margaret came of fighting stock. She would not lose without a struggle her husband and her home, for, if Philippe were convicted of treason, all the St Ouen property would be escheated to the Crown, and she and her children would be penniless. Though, three days before, she had given birth to her twenty-first baby, she rose from her bed, slipped across to Guernsey in an open boat by night, and persuaded Jurat de Beauvoir, whose mother came from St Ouen, to take her in his cutter to England to appeal to the King. Baker also had crossed the Channel, for de Carteret had friends at Court, and it would not be safe to execute him without the King's consent. It was now a race betwen Margaret and the governor, which could get the King's ear first, and Baker had several hours' start. When Margaret's boat reached Poole, to her dismay she saw Baker walking on the pier. But, says the old chronicler, "since God always takes care of His own", a heavy hail-storm drove him indoors, and she landed unobserved. She took horse to Henry VII's palace at Sheen, and by the help of Bishop Foxe of Durham was admitted to the audience chamber. The King was impressed by the story of her breathless rush to save her husband's life, and signed an order that the case should be tried before the Privy Council. Foxe took the precaution of having the order sealed with the Great Seal, and as she left the palace she passed Baker on the stairs. It was still a race against time, whether she could get home before the day fixed for the ordeal. But again her luck held. She found a boat at Southampton, and arrived on the night before the battle. The Bailiff dared not disobey the King's Seal. De Carteret was sent to Westminster for trial, and there he was honourably acquitted.

Two of his sons later gained posts at Henry VIII's Court through their prowess as athletes. The field where they trained is still called the *Clos de Quintaine,* the quintain field, where they tilted on horseback to spear a ring suspended from a pole. Old documents call it also *le Jardin de la Ville de Troye,* which strongly suggests the presence of a maze.

Heraldry helps us to date the next alterations to the manor. On the eve of the Civil Wars the Sir Philippe, who later held Elizabeth Castle for the King, married an English girl, Anne Dowse, and his mother, who outlived him, was a Poulet. On the entrance arch to the manor are de Carteret, Dowse, and Poulet arms, showing that it was built by him, in about 1600, the approximate date of the latter marriage.

Big additions were made by the Sir Philippe of the Restoration, an immensely wealthy man, who always drove through the narrow lanes in a coach with six horses. It was he who built, about 1676, the two wings and the vast kitchen, now converted into living-rooms. However, as already stated, there is reason to suppose that the central portion, with its beautiful door, dates from the 15th century. To the right is a tiny aperture called *le ouie-chi* (for hearing and seeing) which made it possible for the inmates to check a visitor before admitting him.

Then the de Carterets grew too big for their manor. They spent most of their time in Westminster at the King's Court, and the old house grew more and more neglected. For years it remained empty. During the French wars it was turned into barracks for French Royalist refugees enlisted to fight the Republicans. A few years later its privacy was ruthlessly invaded, when General Don made his military road from St Ouen's Church to Beaumont. He ran it along the line of the present avenue, where the old avenue had been, and for 50 years all the main-road traffic rumbled under the windows of the house.

When Colonel Malet de Carteret inherited the property in 1856, it was almost a ruin. He carried out a drastic, perhaps over-drastic, restoration. The house, as it is today, is largely his creation. He got rid of the main road by presenting to the parish the road which now skirts the grounds. He built the lodge and remade the avenue. Externally he added tops to the two towers and a porch to the main entrance. But internally he transmogrified the whole building. The magnificent manorial hall, with its splendid staircase and gallery above, which looks as though it had dropped out of one of Sir Walter Scott's novels, even the oaken heads supporting the rafters representing past members of the de Carteret family, were all the work of the romantic colonel and his extremely skilful local carpenter. The only really old thing in the hall is the oak panelling. These panels, which are definitely mediaeval, were discovered stacked in a cellar when the restoration was in progress. Some earlier seigneur must have bought them, perhaps in Brittany, brought them home, and never used them; and there they had lain forgotten. One pane shows the legendary Trusty Servant with two heads, who was thus able to look both ways in defending his master's interests.

The manorial chapel, dedicated to St Anne, has passed through many changes. Here, in the Middle Ages, the seigneur and his household began each day with Mass. In the 18th century it was a barn, and a floor was put in above the windows to make a hayloft. Colonel Malet de Carteret restored it to its former use as a chapel, and the Bishop of Winchester "reconciled" it. Then came the Germans, who turned it into a butcher's shop for their troops, and used the altar as a chopping board for their joints. The present seigneur has again restored it as a chapel. The stone altar-slab with its five consecration crosses came from St George's, the seigneurial chapel of the fief of Vinchelez. When that chapel was destroyed, at the Reformation, it was left lying in the grounds, till rescued and brought to St Anne's.

The colombier or pigeon-cote is a modern one, built by Colonel Malet de Carteret. In old days St Ouen must have had one, for this was the hall-mark of every manor of importance; but in the period of neglect its very site had been forgotten.

In March 1941 the Germans made the manor a barrack for their troops, and burnt out the south wing by overheating one of the huge stoves they inserted in all their billets. This wing has not been rebuilt, and remains, in one sense, a war memorial. A tragic story belongs to this period. During the German Occupation of Brittany 16 young Bretons escaped by boat to join the Free French forces in England. Unfortunately, when they sighted Guernsey, they thought it was the Isle of Wight. They landed, singing the "Marseillaise", and were promptly arrested and sent to Jersey for trial. Four were condemned to death, the others to long terms of imprisonment.

159

Only one was executed, François Marie Scornet, a lad of 20, who accepted responsibility as leader of the expedition. He faced a firing squad in the manor grounds, shouting: "Vive Dieu! Vive la France!" A granite slab marks the spot where he fell. After the Liberation his body was removed to his native Plougean, where the square has been named Place François Scornet.

St Ouen's Parish. This covers the whole of the north-west corner of the Island. It is the largest parish of the twelve, having an area of 3,707 acres; but about half of it is uncultivated, consisting of heathland and barren sand-dunes. It is divided into cueillettes, not vingtaines. The word is derived from cueillir, to gather, and refers to certain dues that were gathered from each district. It was not always peculiar to this parish. St Peter once had a Cueillette de St Anastase and a Cueillette des Augrès; but like many old words and customs it survives only in St Ouen.

The parish begins at St Ouen's Pond or, to give it its old name, La Mare au Seigneur, the largest sheet of natural fresh water in the Channel Islands. The Société Jersiaise maintains the pond and surrounding reed beds as a nature reserve, by kind permission of the seigneur of St Ouen. The animals and plants, some of which grow nowhere else in the Island, are protected. The Société also operates a bird-ringing station, and as the southernmost observatory in the British Isles it has great importance in studying bird migrations, and it was here that the first Channel Island records were made of aquatic warblers, Cetti's warblers, and bluethroats. In olden days, when all houses were thatched, the reeds around it were a valuable crop. Carp may be seen leaping from the water and fresh-water eels abound. The small islet in the middle is certainly man-made, but whether or no it was the foundation of a primitive lake dwelling is an open question.

The Waterworks Company built an impressive dam here in 1962, just above the site of an old water-mill, Le Moulin de la Mare. Above the dam a large reservoir has been formed, partly in St Ouen and partly in St Peter's parish.

The Germans believed that, if the British tried to land, they would choose St Ouen's Bay; so this was heavily fortified. Every building that obstructed their line of fire was levelled to the ground. The beach was studded with iron posts, each with an explosive charge guaranteed to blow to smithereens any boat that touched it. The shore was lined with an anti-tank wall with guns in small turrets. Then came the mine-field and miles of barbed wire; and at either end of the pond they dug long canals, so that if tanks came thundering over the dunes, they would plunge into this hidden moat and find a watery grave. Some of the heaviest guns they possessed were placed on the hills beyond.

Not far from these gun emplacements stands the fine Neolithic passage-grave of Monts Grantez, so called from the Granteys family who owned land here in the 14th century. Till 1912 there was nothing visible but a mound, like one of the long barrows found in many parts of England. When this was excavated, a roofed passage 14 feet long was unearthed, which led to an oval chamber out of which opened a smaller side cell. In the passage a skeleton was found seated with its back to the wall. In the main chamber there were seven burials, in all of which the bodies were crouched on their sides, and offerings laid on their tombs included two bushels of limpet shells and a number of coloured beach pebbles evidently chosen for their beauty. In the side chamber there was also at least one grave.

Surrounded at half-tide is La Rocco Tower. This curious name is likely to mean Rocque-hou, or rocky island. On it a martello tower was built between 1796 and 1800. Severe breaches were made in the masonry by the Germans, who used the tower for target practice, but the intervening years without repair, and the erosion of the sea, have reduced it to a perilous condition, which cannot stand many more winter storms. A focal point in the bay, there is, at the moment of going to press, a scheme for its immediate restoration, which is now in progress.

Walking round the coast, and one of the most exhilarating walks in the Island is that over the heather-clad moorland from L'Etac to Grosnez, we come first to L'ETAC, then to LE PINACLE, then to GROSNEZ, on each of which we have had a separate article. On a headland a quarter of a mile east of Grosnez is a cave, perched 60 feet above the present sea level, called La Cotte à la Chèvre (Goat's Cave). Here men lived at a period contemporary with the oldest levels excavated at St Brelade, that is over 100,000 B.C. In addition, the cave may well have been briefly visited during the last glacial and early post glacial phases. The flints they left round their hearths here are of a very archaic type, as old as anything found in the Island.

At Grève au Lançon, Sand-eel Beach, we reach a group of the best-known caves in the district. But, apart from these, St Ouen is the cave-hunters' paradise. There is a double tunnel under the Pinnacle, and a fine one beneath Rouge Nez. Between Rouge Nez and Grosnez is one of the largest caves in the island, but this can only be entered by swimming. East of Le Chêne is another 375 feet long and a third big one at Le Petit Becquet close to a natural bridge. The high-level Cave ès Fraudeurs, Smugglers' Cave, at Le Grand Becquet is worth a visit, and so is the pretty cavern at Douet de la Mer with a waterfall at its mouth. But the caves along this coast are too many to enumerate. At GRÈVE DE LECQ, on which we have a separate article, we pass into St Mary's parish.

Turning inland, we have had articles on ST OUEN'S CHURCH and ST OUEN'S MANOR. But there was another fief almost as important as ST OUEN. This was the fief of Vinchelez, in early documents spelt Winceles, which suggests that it may have been given by the King to one of his English followers called de Winchelsea, a name which Jersey would soon soften into de Vinchelez. Other seigneurs had to present gilt or silvered spurs to the King, but the seigneur of Vinchelez was the only one who received a gift of this kind. One of his sub-tenants had to present him annually with a pair of spurs and a pair of gloves. The manor had a chapel of St George, mentioned in 1156, and the usual colombier. One of this family served as Bailiff of Guernsey; several became Jurats, and two were the King's Receivers; and for several centuries they held the island of Bréchou, near Sark. But more than once when a seigneur died, the fief was divided between sons, and in 1607 this division became permanent. On opposite sides of the road today stand the two manors of Vinchelez de Haut and Vinchelez de Bas, Upper and Lower Vinchelez. They shared St George's Chapel, and were jointly responsible for its upkeep and for that of the cemetery round it, and the steps over the wall remain, which were built to enable the de Bas household to visit the chapel easily. St George's has now disappeared, but its altar-slab, after lying for years in the grounds, has been restored to its former use in the chapel of St Ouen's manor.

A new St George's Chapel was built in 1880 in the north-west corner of the parish to be a chapel-of-ease to the parish church.

St Peter's Church. No one knows when the first stone of this church was laid, but a charter signed by William the Conqueror, before he became King of England, shows that before 1066 it had been promoted from the rank of a chapel to that of a parish church, for it was then receiving tithes, which were paid to parish churches only, and William transferred half of them to the Convent of the Holy Trinity at Caen. The original chapel must therefore be considerably older than 1066. Its walls still stand, nearly 4 feet thick, built of rough stones from the beach, and form the chancel of the present church. It extended to the point where the pulpit now stands, and the ancient door can still be traced on the south wall. The windows were then narrow slits like those at the west of the nave. Because it stood near the edge of the sandhills that stretch down to the sea, it was described in official documents as St Pierre du Désert. By 1090 the appointment of its rector had been entrusted to the Abbot of St Sauveur le Vicomte in Normandy, in whose hands it remained till the Reformation.

There is no documentary evidence as to its early years; but the walls tell their own story. The first enlargement of the church took place, probably in the 12th century, when the west wall of the chapel was pulled down and a nave and transepts added, giving the building the shape of a cross. The west wall of the nave is still almost in its original condition, except that its round window was added in 1856. There were as yet no side aisles. The north wall, before it was demolished to make the new aisle, had narrow lancet windows; so the same is probably true of the south wall also. At this time the tower was built; but it had as yet no spire, only a saddle-back roof like that at St Brelade's and on many churches in Normandy. Like hundreds of churches in France and England, the chancel leans slightly to the right. Modern books say that this was meant to suggest the drooping of our Lord's Head on the Cross. But this explanation has not been found in any ancient author, and seems merely a 19th century guess. An exhaustive article on the "Orientation of Churches" in *The Antiquaries' Journal* (vol. xxx, p. 51) decides: "The deviations were accidental, due to faulty laying out when a new part of a church was added to the old. There is nothing to show that any symbolic meaning was in question."

Then, possibly in the 14th century, two chapels were added, one (in later years used as a vestry and organ-chamber) on the north of the chancel, the other, now pulled down, stretching from the north transept half-way down the north wall of the nave. The east window of the surviving chapel is the original one, though not, of course, the glass.

Towards the end of the 15th century the great south aisle was built, broader and higher than the nave, and swallowing the south transept. A curious feature of this is the ruthless way in which tombstones were used to support the outer buttresses. The most interesting of these has on it a cross, two horse-shoes, a hammer, and pincers, evidently the memorial of a blacksmith. Similar tombstones depicting trades are found in the north of France; one, for example, has the sole of a shoe and a set of cobbler's tools; on another a hatchet, square, and hammer mark the tomb of a carpenter. At the same time as the aisle the spire was added to the tower. It is 120 feet high, the highest in the Island.

Only two later alterations were made to the building. In 1856, part of the south transept was rebuilt. The north aisle, an entirely new feature, was added in 1886. The sole relic of pre-Reformation days is the piscina beside the altar, and the other one at the east of the south aisle, where once an altar must have stood.

The spire was more than once in trouble. In 1612 it was destroyed by lightning as the people were going into church. In 1843 it was struck again, and the cost of repair was met by printing 275 one-pound notes issued on the security of the parish; but five years later it was brought down again. It carries on its tip today something unique among church decorations, a red light as a warning to night-flying aeroplanes.

In 1649, during the Civil War, the bigger of the two bells was recast by workmen from the famous foundry of Villedieu in Normandy. It was a French custom to name bells after some lady in the parish, and this one bears the inscription: *Mon nom est Elizabeth la Belle*. One wonders whether this was a compliment to Lady Elizabeth Carteret, the very beautiful wife of Sir George Carteret, the Lieutenant-Governor, he having property in the parish.

The tombstone of Clement Le Montais, described as *mercator dives*, a rich merchant, always attracts attention. He was Sir George's brother-in-law, and looked after the business side of Sir George's privateering, selling the captured prizes and paying the crews.

In 1698 there was a tussle over a communion service. The rector

St Ouen's Pond

St Ouen's Manor, from the south

The sweep of St Ouen's Bay, showing Le Pinacle and La Rocco Tower

St Saviour's Church, from the east

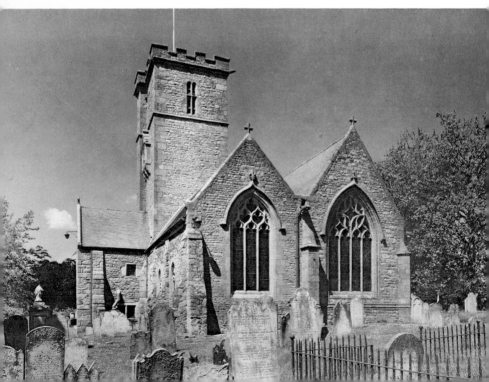

Samarès Manor: The
south façade (*above*)
and the Colombier
(*below*)

Victoria College

Le Ponterrin, a 16th century farmhouse

wished to hold one on Christmas Day. But it was customary at this time for the Communion to be celebrated only on the four Sacrament Sundays, and the Constable and churchwardens forbade him to hold this additional service, not on any doctrinal grounds, but merely because the parish would have to pay for the extra wine. For this, Dean Le Couteur excommunicated them in such outspoken terms that they prosecuted him for defamation of character before the Royal Court, and the old Dean was sent to prison.

The 19th century brought gradual improvements. In 1829 a permanent altar was placed in the north transept. In 1835 the small stone font that is still in use was bought, but no one knew quite what to do with it. At first it was placed beside the altar, then at the foot of the pulpit. In 1841 the militia cannon were removed from under the west gallery. In 1855 the altar was transferred to the chancel, and the main door moved from the south transept to the north.

The big restoration, however, took place in 1886. The troops were marched from St Peter's barracks to church every Sunday morning, and the church, though it seated nearly 900, was too small for its congregation. So the old north-west chapel was pulled down, and the present north aisle added. As there was now plenty of room, the galleries were pulled down. The church was reseated with oak pews. A new altar, reredos, and altar rails were put into the chancel.

The latest improvement has been the removal of the organ from the old north chapel, which has now been restored to its former use as a Lady Chapel. In 1951 a piscina was found in a nearby house, which was being demolished for airport extensions, and it was installed in the church, in the Lady Chapel.

St Peter's Parish. This parish is bounded on the north by St Ouen and St Mary, on the east by St Lawrence, and on the south by St Brelade. It touches the sea at two points. At Beaumont, for a quarter of a mile, it skirts St Aubin's Bay, and at the opposite end of the parish its boundary borders St Ouen's Bay for a mile as far as the middle of St Ouen's Pond.

The only prehistoric remains in the parish are Les Trois Roches, three upright blocks of granite, brought from Les Landes more than two miles away and set up in the sandy soil south of St Ouen's Pond, and a fourth two hundred yards away. They are likely to be the sole remains of some long-forgotten dolmen, the more manageable stones having been taken long ago for building material.

But in the Middle Ages there were several places of interest in St Peter. There was a priory. In England a priory was a household of monks, not big enough to be called an abbey, but with sufficient members, usually about 20, to maintain the monastic routine. But in Jersey, with the one exception, the Abbey (later Priory) of St Helier de l'Islet, a priory was a small house where two monks lived together, who acted as business managers for some great Normandy abbey and collected the rents and tithes due to it. The Abbey of St Sauveur le Vicomte near Carteret owned much property in St Peter. The parish church had been handed over to it, and it paid the rector his stipend. Other gifts to the abbey were lands presented by the seigneur of La Hague, by Ranulf a priest, by Richard of Orville, and the bequest of another priest, Tostain, who was lame included a water-mill in the valley which for centuries bore his name, and was later called Le Moulin de la Hague, but which has now been demolished. In some way this priory was a Royal Foundation, for in 1274 complaint was made that, though it was bound to keep two monks there to say Masses daily for the souls of the Kings of England, their founders, the house had been let as a farm and no monks were in residence. All the temporalities of the abbey were seized until this was put right. In 1331 we learn that the prior owed a dinner once a year to the Bailiff, the Vicomte, and the King's Receiver. The house seems to have escaped the dissolution of the alien priories in 1413, for in 1461, during the French occupation, the monks complained to the French King that his soldiers had turned them out of their house, and he ordered it to be restored to them. They were still in possession in 1485; but after that we hear no more of them, but in the Exténte of 1607 the priory site is called Flocktree, evidently a corruption of La Flocquetterie, from Robert de Floques, who came with Jean de Carbonnel in charge of the invasion force.

Another institution was the Leper House of St Nicolas, which stood near the house called Oak Walk. In the Middle Ages Europe was full of unfortunate lepers, outcasts forbidden to mix with the rest of the population; and it was an act of Christian charity to provide homes for them. There were over a hundred of these in England, and the one in Jersey had enjoyed royal patronage, for

King John had granted it 40 sols a year from the receipts of the mill Ruaval, situated in Grouville, and an additional 20 sols for the lamp in its chapel; and in 1234 this gift was renewed by Henry III. The present vingtaine of St Nicolas takes its name from this house.

But the institution with the longest life was the Chapel of St Anastase, named after an Italian scholar "learned in Latin and Greek", who was Classics Master, first to the monks of Mont St Michel and then in the Abbey of Cluny. He was admired for his wild attempt to convert the Moors in Spain, whom he challenged to accept mass baptism, if he proved the truth of his religion by passing unsinged through the biggest bonfire they could build. They ignored his offer; but his fame reached Jersey, and someone built a chapel in his honour in a lane on the east of St Peter's Valley.

In 1494 Jean Néel and Vincent Téhy (see article VICTORIA COLLEGE) built their grammar school for the boys of the western parishes alongside the chapel of this ancient classical schoolmaster. The education was free, but the boys had to work hard. Lessons began at six in the morning and lasted till six at night. Not only was Latin taught, but the teaching was given in Latin, and the States kept a sharp eye on its quality. In 1705 they threatened to dismiss the Regent if he used any grammar but Lely's.

But St Anastase did not entirely fulfil the expectation of its founders. There were constant complaints about it. One trouble was that the regents were appointed for life, and many an old man hung on to his job long after he was past work. Pierre Pipon, who became regent in 1602, remained for 62 years, and his son, who succeeded him, held the post for 52. In 1800 the States tried to set the school on its feet again. They entirely rebuilt it, and they put in the regent's house 22 rooms, showing that they hoped to attract a good number of boarders. But the opening of Victoria College killed it. Today its endowments are used for bursaries at the college, and the building is now a private house, still called St Anastase.

There were other chapels in the parish. The ruins of one known as La Gloriette stood at the edge of the churchyard till 1841, when they were pulled down to make room for the parish hall. The word means a rough hut made of branches, and may indicate that the building was of inferior workmanship. The perquage, instead of following its own parish brook down St Peter's Valley, cut across to the brook that flows by Pont du Val and Pont Marquet through St

Brelade to St Aubin's harbour. At the crossroads at the top of Jubilee Hill, called La Croix ès Bruns, is the base of the mediaeval wayside cross from which it took its name. One of the very few in its original position, the cross which fitted into the socket has long vanished, having been smashed and scattered by the reformers of 1547.

The most important manor in the parish was La Hague, which takes its name from its first owners, the de la Hagues, who probably came from the district of La Hague in the Cotentin. One duty of this fief was to provide a prison, 12 feet by 12 with irons, and to be responsible for the prisoners' safe-keeping. At some early date the de la Hagues had absorbed the neighbouring fiefs of Nièmes and Nobretez, and by 1309 they had become possessed of the fief des Blancs Esperons too, so called because its seigneur had to present to the King yearly a pair of white (i.e. silver) spurs. By 1489 the four fiefs had passed by marriage to the Malets, and a century later they were sold by them to a junior branch of the de Carterets of St Ouen. The estate passed into the hands of the Le Bretons, Pipons, and Le Cornus. François de Carteret built the colombier in 1629 and rebuilt the house in 1634; Thomas Le Breton rebuilt it again in 1753; and Colonel Le Cornu made extensive alterations in 1871. During the German Occupation it became infantry barracks, and the lawn was covered with wooden huts containing ammunition.

Of the mills the most important were the Moulin de Tostain already mentioned, and Gargate and Quetivel Mills, which once belonged to the Crown, but were sold by Sir Hugh Poulet, when Governor, and passed into private hands. The windmill in the north of the parish was built in 1837 by the issue of one-pound notes guaranteed by its three proprietors. It has a weighbridge in front which was in use until recent years.

The parish possesses one interesting relic of Tudor times. The most famous gunmakers of the 16th century were the Owens of Houndsditch. Six of their guns have survived, two in the Artillery Museum at Woolwich, one in the Tower of London, one in Carisbrook Castle, one in America, and the sixth stands at the Beaumont crossroads. It is a bronze falcon, 7 feet 3 inches long, capable of throwing a ball of 2¼ lb., and it is inscribed JHON OWEN MADE THIS PESE ANNO DNI 1551 FOR THE PARYSHE OF SAYNT PETER IN JERSSE. A merchant named Madolani Robin was ordered by the Governor to charter a boat and bring this cannon from London, but it cost him a two years' lawsuit to recover his expenses from the parish. It was rediscovered in London by Colonel Le Couteur in 1839, and by the help of the Lieutenant-Governor he secured its return to the parish for which it was made.

In the Civil War the decisive battle was fought in St Peter's parish. In 1651 Cromwell, having won the Battle of Worcester, had time to attend to little outlying pockets of Royalists like Jersey. A fleet of 80 sail under the famous Admiral Blake appeared in St Ouen's Bay. Sir George Carteret with the Castle garrisons and the Island militia marched to meet them. Numerically the forces were about equal. Carteret had 300 cavalry and 2,000 foot. The Roundheads numbered 2,200. But in morale there was no comparison. The invaders were seasoned veterans of Cromwell's victorious New Model Army, coming straight from their triumph at Worcester. Some of Carteret's men were Parliamentarians at heart, and even those who were Royalists felt no desire to die for a cause that seemed lost. Blake used brains to save bloodshed. For two days he moved his ships up and down the coast, now round to St Brelade then up to L'Etac, and Carteret had to keep his weary men marching and countermarching through a continuous drizzle, no one knowing where the enemy meant to land. Then at eleven on a pitch-dark night Blake threw his men ashore just south of St Ouen's Pond. Carteret's cavalry charged the boats and there was a fierce fight in the shallow water; but the Roundheads got ashore. When the sun rose and they climbed the hill, Carteret's army had fled. He himself had withdrawn to Elizabeth Castle, where 50 days later he surrendered, having no alternative after his stock of ammunition had been blown up by a bomb fired by the invaders from the Town Hill. For the next nine years Cromwell ruled Jersey.

Now a new use has been found for one corner of St Peter's parish. When aircraft first began to come to Jersey, they landed on the West Park sands, which meant a daily change of timetable in order to suit the tide. But in 1937 the States opened the Airport at St Peter at a cost of £128,000. At first it covered 83 acres. The Germans increased it to 119 acres, and used it for fighters that escorted bombers from France, when they passed to attack England. The States have now increased the area to 231 acres, and at week-ends it sometimes transports over 12,000 passengers daily. Nearby there used to stand St Peter's barracks, gaunt brick buildings of the late 19th century, where infantry battalions of the British Army were stationed until about 1927.

The Germans dug themselves in very deeply at St Peter. They established their battle headquarters near Panigot in an innocent-looking house, which they connected by telephone with every fire-control post, every strong-point, and every barrack in the Island. It even had a direct line to Guernsey. Here was a wireless room, a teleprinting room, a coding room, and, when the expected attempt by the British to recover Jersey began, the German commandant would have sat here and issued his orders. The district was heavily fortified. One dummy house, for example, which looked quite harmless with its lace curtains and a geranium in the window, had walls of reinforced concrete 6 feet thick, and was a formidable fortress with heavy machine-gun armament. Near the parish church there is a privately owned German Occupation Museum, within a German bunker.

St Peter's Valley was once considered the beauty-spot of the Island. When Queen Victoria, on her second visit in 1859, asked to see the loveliest view in Jersey, she was taken for a drive up this valley. But the German Occupation has left ugly scars upon it. As one goes up the valley today one meets first one of their power stations, then a pumping station, now used in connection with the Island water supply; then we pass three gigantic ammunition tunnels driven deep into the hillside, with many cross tunnels and a light railway running from end to end, and thousands of tons of stone and rubble that were quarried out of these have been dumped, but are gradually getting grown over and becoming less conspicuous

Many spots preserve the names of early parishioners. The Augereys, after whom the Vingtaine des Augerez is called, were once important people. William des Auguereys was a Jurat in 1274 and Raoul des Auguereyes in 1299. The Vingtaine du Coin Varin gets its name from the Varins. In 1331 a Richard Varin was one of the jurors of St Peter. Raoul Naymes was a juror in 1324, and the fief of Nièmes once belonged to his family. The Fondans, another St Peter family that produced a long string of Jurats and Constables, gave their name to Mont Fondan. And the Carrefour à Cendres has nothing to do with cinders. In old documents it appears as Carrefour Alexandre.

St Saviour's Church. No church in Jersey made a more unexpected start than this. It began life as four separate chapels. When the present churchyard became the burial-ground for the neighbourhood, someone built a little thatched chapel 30 feet long, in which Masses could be said, and he dedicated it in the name of "the Holy Saviour"; and, since in those days no altar could be consecrated unless it contained a relic, he possibly secured what purported to be a thorn from Christ's crown of thorns. There was an immense trade in this particular relic in the Middle Ages. Credulous pilgrims brought back so many of these from Jersulem that, even after the enormous destruction of relics at the Reformation, there are still, according to *The Catholic Encyclopaedia*, more than seven hundred of these thorns in European churches today. This tiny chapel then became known as St Sauveur de l'Epine, St Saviour of the Thorn. An alternative explanation of the title is that he obtained a thorn from the sacred thorn-bush at Glastonbury, which was supposed to have sprung from the staff which Joseph of Arimathea was said to have cut in the Garden of the Resurrection and stuck into the ground when he arrived in Somerset.

Then someone built another small chapel alongside this on the north, and dedicated it to St John. Later, two more chapels were erected a little to the west, with a gap between them and the other pair, the northern one dedicated to St Martin, the southern one to the Virgin. These four private chapels were at first quite unconnected; they were owned by different families and served by different priests.

But a time came when connecting walls were built to join the Chapel of the Virgin to the Chapel of the Thorn, and they were thrown into one to form a parish church; the walls were raised and a stone roof substituted for thatch. This happened before 1145, when a Papal Bull spoke of "the tithes of the Church of St Saviour in Jersey", for only parish churches received tithes. In the 13th century this little church was lengthened at both ends east and west. In the 14th century the great central tower was added. Later the other two little chapels were thrown into the church and it became its present size, and the narrow lancet windows were replaced by large flamboyant ones. The Archdeacon of Val de Vire had the right of appointing the incumbent, whose official designation seems to have been uncertain. Though all the other parishes had rectors, the priest of St Saviour's is called "Rector and Vicar, or rather Perpetual Curate".

Jehan Hue, who became rector in 1461, was evidently a good man of business. He compiled a register of the church's property. He gave full particulars of the priest's income; which fields paid tithe and which two cabots of wheat. Five houses were responsible for finding wax for the church candles, eight for supplying corn to make the *pain béni*, or holy bread for communion, eleven for supplying wine for the Mass. From another source we learn that one farm had to lay "two hundred reeds on Christmas Eve from the presbytery to the church for the priest to walk on as he went to the Midnight Mass."

Hue recorded the Rules of the Fraternities, which played in those days so large a part in the life of every parish. In St Saviour there were four—the Clerks of St Saviour, the Clerks of St Katherine, the Clerks of St Nicolas' Winter Feast, and the Clerks of his Feast in Summer. Every member absent from the Fraternity Mass was fined two *pots* of wine. Every sister had to provide a capon for the community supper. He listed too all the recent benefactions to the church. Richard Le Viellard had presented an image of St Sebastian. Madame Philippe de Carteret had left rentes to maintain a candle before the Crucifix. Madame Poingdestre had left rentes for a candle before our Lady of Pity, etc.

An alcove in the south-west buttress reminds us of another devotion very popular at this time. It bears the initials, very much weathered, of George Lemprière, who was Constable in 1464, and the cockle-shell shows that he had made the pilgrimage to the shrine of St James of Compostela in Spain, for which a ship crowded with pilgrims left Jersey every year, and had erected here an image of St James on his return.

Then came the Reformation; and the Calvinist purge was even more thorough in St Saviour than elsewhere. No trace of the old worship was left, not even a piscina. In 1563 the Royal Court held its meetings in the church while the plague was raging in the town.

In 1901 it underwent a thorough restoration. The communion table was moved from the Chapel of St John to its ancient place in the Chapel of the Thorn. Ugly galleries were swept away. Ancient windows and doors were unblocked, and every effort made to restore the building to its original form. A public-house, which stood in the corner of the churchyard, was bought and a lych-gate put in its place. This was erected in memory of Dean G. O. Balleine, father of the original writer of this book. St Saviour's today is one of the most impressive churches in the Island.

St Saviour's Parish. This looks as though it should have been a compact inland parish, but it runs a wedge down south, till its tip just touches the slip at Le Dicq, giving it the shortest coastal boundary of any parish, so that surprisingly St Luke's Church is in the civil parish of St Saviour, and it sends a mile-long corridor eastward at right angles to its normal boundary, till it includes the mental hospital at the top of Queen's Valley. More surprising still, it has three enclaves inside other parishes, one in Grouville and two in Trinity. Early in the 18th century some readjustment of boundaries must have been made, for the Extentes of 1607 and 1668 show that La Hougue Bie was then in St Saviour, but from 1713 onward it has been part of Grouville, though one of the vingtaines of St Saviour is still called Sous la Hougue. Once the parish was a purely agricultural community, but its western half is rapidly becoming a dormitory for town workers.

In addition to the church, which has been described in the previous article, there were in the Middle Ages the seigneurial chapels of the manor of Longueville, dedicated to St Thomas à Becket; of Maufant probably dedicated to Our Lady, and that of Bagot Manor dedicated to St André, permission to build the latter being given in 1496. There were also the chapels of St Symphorian, of which the site is unknown, and St Mannelier (see below), and La Mare de St Etienne, St Stephen's Pond. The parish was also full of wayside crosses, the Croix de Bois at Five Oaks, the Croix Besnard where Bagatelle Road meets Les Varines, the Croix ès Mottes near Maufant, the Croix de la Rue in Les Pigneaux, and the Croix Machon near Longueville. All these were swept away at the Reformation, but St Saviour possesses a modern one, erected by Mr Athelstan Riley in the Grands Vaux at the spot where his daughter-in-law in 1928 fell from her horse and was killed.

Of the ancient chapels the best known was the one dedicated to St Magloire, the Breton Apostle of Sark whom Jerseymen changed to St Mannelier. In 1477 Jehan Hue, the rector of St Saviour's, added to this a grammar school, and endowed it with a field that he had inherited from his mother. Nineteen years later the endowment was increased by two other Jerseymen, Jean Néel, who was senior chaplain to the young Prince of Wales, and Vincent Téhy, who had been Mayor of Southampton. This was for nearly four hundred years the leading school in the Island. John Wesley visited it in 1787, and wrote in his *Journal*: "It is a free school, designed to train up children for the University, exceedingly finely situated in a quiet recess surrounded by tall woods." One of the last pupils, Jurat W. L. de Gruchy, wrote of it as he had known it in 1848: "I have only most pleasant recollections of my schooltime there and intense gratitude for the careful and thorough way in which we were taught." It had in succession three very able men as "regents", the title given to the head master. His own regent was an Italian scholar, who inspired him with a love for Dante; "and," he adds, "there was included in the curriculum what must have been rare in those days, a course in Natural Science." But the foundation of Victoria College killed St Mannelier. The last pupil left in 1863. Its endowments today provide bursaries to send boys to its victorious rival. Since the States rebuilt the school in 1833, very few traces of the old buildings remain. The house is now converted into flats.

The western edge of the parish is the valley called the Grands Vaux, once a rural paradise, but in recent years being rapidly filled up with housing estates. Here are three water-mills, the King's two mills of Grand Val and Malassis and the one still known by the name of Louis Paul, who was miller in 1548. Between these mills there is a recently constructed dam and reservoir. The stream here was a constant source of litigation. Every miller complained that his rivals were wasting the precious source of power, and the farmers resented the millers' monopoly of the water which they needed for their meadows. One of the lanes leading down to this valley is known as the Rue à la Dame, because one of the Island's ghosts was supposed to haunt it at night; La Dame has legendary significance as a place name; if the Virgin is meant the form used is Notre Dame.

Much of the parish lay within the King's fief; but there were four considerable manors. Longueville has already had an article. Maufant, in the north, was the home of Michel Lemprière, Cromwell's Bailiff; there is, however, no fief of Maufant, and this appellation, which goes back to the 17th century, is curious. Grainville, in the west, had to present the King every year with a pair of gilt spurs. The manor-house has now been demolished. It dated from approximately 1830, but was built upon the remnants of a house a century older; it was, until its sale in 1873, the home of the Poingdestre family. And in the south was a manor with two names. It was sometimes called Gorges, and so gave its name to Georgetown, but more often Bagot, from the family who owned it in the 15th century. The old house was pulled down in 1935. It had the various manorial appurtenances, a colombier, and a chapel dedicated to St André; this chapel is presumably the origin of the unusual double piscina, now at the Museum, which was found in the old part of the house.

Among more modern houses is Government House. In early years the Governors used to live, first in Mont Orgueil, then in Elizabeth Castle; but in the 18th century they found it convenient to rent a house in the town. In 1781 Corbet lived in what was called Old Government House, which formed a corner of Grosvenor and St James's Streets, now demolished, but it was here that, on the morning of the battle of Jersey, he was captured by the French. But the first official Government House was bought in 1802. This stood in King Street, opposite the gap where Peirson Place enters the Square, and its gardens extended back as far as Burrard Street. In 1822 Sir Colin Halkett exchanged this for the present house on St Saviour's Hill, and the new proprietor of the King Street site made a small fortune by selling the gardens as building sites. The St Saviour's house, which was called Belmont, had been built in 1817. The drive had been a public lane to the church, known as the Ruette du Sacrement, but it had been closed when the new main road took the place of the old St Saviour's Hill.

On the other side of the church is the rectory. Here in 1853 was born the world-famous beauty Lillie Langtry, the lovely "Jersey Lily", actress and racehorse owner. She was the daughter of Dean Le Breton, the rector. After her marriage in St Saviour's Church to a wealthy young Irish yachtsman, she visited London, and was acclaimed as the world's loveliest woman. She was painted by Millais, Watts, Whistler, Poynter, Burne-Jones, and Leighton. Oscar Wilde composed a poem about her, comparing her to Helen of Troy. Le Gallienne wrote of her: "To have been the representative

175

of Beauty in one's own time, its very symbol, is a peculiarly aristocratic form of immortality." She was always devoted to Jersey; when she married a second time, to Hugo, (later Sir Hugo) de Bathe in 1899, she chose St Saviour's Church for her wedding; and when she died at Monte Carlo in 1929, she left instructions that she was to be buried in St Saviour's churchyard, where a marble bust by a French sculptor keeps watch over her grave. The portrait of her at the Museum, by Poynter, shows her to have been indeed of exceptional beauty.

Bagatelle, which gave its name to Bagatelle Road, was first the home of Philippe d'Auvergne, Prince de Bouillon, and was later rebuilt by Sir Thomas Le Breton, the Bailiff. Its grounds were one of the show-places of the Island, and Sir Thomas had to appeal in the Press to his lady visitors not to wear pattens, as they cut up his gravel paths. In 1931 it was sold and turned into the Palace Hotel. But when the Germans came, they occupied it; and in 1945 it was blown up in a mysterious explosion that shook the whole town. A number of officers lost their lives, and rumour said that it was caused by sabotage on the part of their own troops.

Of the old farms, the most picturesque and interesting is the one at Ponterrin. The venerable house at the back of the yard, which dates from about 1500, contains three magnificent hearths and a good deal of curious carving. The front wall is pierced by a double round arch, and the keystone of the pedestrian arch, now, alas, converted into a window, bears the date 1643 and the initials of Richard Falle.

Samarès Manor. Salt is a necessity of health; and the old way of securing salt was to let the sea flood low-lying land, then block the channel, and leave the water for the sun to evaporate, when a deposit of salt was left. Samarès takes its name from one of these salt-marshes. *Salse* was Old French for "salt water"; so *salse marais* means "a salt-water marsh". In the Assize Roll of 1309 it is spelt Sausmarys. The low ground between the manor and the sea, still known as Samarès Marsh, was in those days a valuable source of income to the seigneur.

There have been seigneurs of Samarès from early Norman times; but the manor has often changed hands. The first owners of whom we know anything were the de St Hilaires, who held it from about

1160 to about 1337. All that remains of their manor-house is the crypt of their manorial chapel, dedicated to St Martha, the bustling housewife of Bethany, a very rare dedication. The only place where she was venerated seems to have been Tarascon, where she is supposed to have tamed a dragon, which suggests that the de St Hilaires may have had some link, perhaps by marriage, with the south of France. This crypt is most unusually sited, lying north–south instead of the regulation east–west. It bears a strong resemblance to the only other surviving crypts, the two at Mont Orgueil Castle, both 12th century. An interesting item to survive here is a deeply carved window in the west wall.

The de St Hilaires certainly held estates in Normandy; and, when the Hundred Years' War broke out, they, like other seigneurs who held land both in France and Jersey, had to decide for which of their Kings they would fight. They chose the French allegiance, and so lost Samarès, but were rewarded with part of the de Carteret property in the Cotentin. Before this happened, however, a younger branch of the family had settled in Guernsey, still calling itself by the name of its Jersey manor, and these de Saumarez became one of the leading families in that island.

In 1367 the manor was bought by the Payns, who held it for nearly 200 years. Two small pieces of evidence suggest that towards the end of their tenure the house was rebuilt. In 1498 the Bishop of Coutances issued a licence to "the noble lady Thomasse, widow of Philippe Payn, late Seigneur of Samarès", for Mass to be celebrated in her manor chapel; which implies that a new chapel had been erected. And in the garden there is a stone, evidently removed from this second manor at some later rebuilding, which displays the Dumaresq scallop-shells and the Payn trefoils, and so must have been carved soon after 1500, when Mabel, the last of the Payns, married Jean Dumaresq.

For the next 200 years the Dumaresqs held the fief. During the Civil War Henri Dumaresq was one of the Parliamentary leaders, and when George Carteret captured the Island for the King, Henri was hanged in effigy, but saved his life by escaping by night to London. Carteret cut down all the timber on the Samarès estate, and made the house an internment camp for the wives of the Parliamentarian exiles, till two years later he expelled them to France. Henri's son, Philippe, was a man of quiet tastes, and he was the first to make the Samarès gardens famous. To drain his grounds he dug a canal a quarter of a mile long. He wrote to his friend, John Evelyn: "I have planted a score of cypresses from France and some borders of phillyrea (the jasmine box), whereof most were from slips. I have this year begun a little plantation of vineyard." The vines evidently flourished, for they are mentioned 70 years later in a deed of sale. In 1678 he patriotically transferred the Town Hill, which was part of his fief, to the Vingtaine de la Ville, in order that a fort might be built on it; but it was more than 100 years before the first stone was laid.

His daughter, Deborah, was a strong-minded lady, who fought the King for the possession of the Minquiers, which she claimed as part of her domain, but the Privy Council decided against her. Bit by bit Samarès had been swallowing the neighbouring fiefs—La Fosse, Crapedoit, and Le Homet. The latter carried with it the curious custom that, whenever the Dame had a baby, the Rector of St Clement's had to bring a white horse and escort her to church to be churched. In 1695 William III added to Deborah's inheritance the Fief ès Faisants.

Like the lords of Rozel and Augrès, it was the seigneur's duty, whenever the King came to Jersey, to ride into the sea to meet him, till the water covered his spurs. But we hear more about his rights than his duties. He had his own private gallows on which to hang his tenants. At the Assize of 1309 this prerogative was challenged, but he replied that his ancestors had always possessed it; later it was confirmed under the Great Seal, and ratified again as late as 1695. The position of this gibbet is uncertain, but, since in 1517 the Governor borrowed it to hang a particularly obnoxious criminal, because the market-place was not large enough to hold all who would profit by witnessing his fate, it looks as though it may have stood somewhere near the present signal-post on Fort Regent. And it was no empty symbol of authority. Tenants not infrequently swung from it. But the culprit would have had to be sentenced by the Royal Court, and not by the seigneurial court, as is so often supposed. A vast crowd assembled in 1625 to see a witch hanged and burnt.

The windmill, to which all his tenants had to take their corn to be ground, is mentioned as early as 1218, an exceptionally early mention for a windmill. In 1299, its sails were confiscated, because they had slain a man, and so under the law of deodand they were forfeit to God, and they were sold to buy a breviary for the Castle chapel. The colombier or pigeon-cote which enabled the seigneur always to have pigeon pie at the expense of his tenants' crops, is the oldest in the Island. In 1647 it was the scene of a tragedy. Sir George Carteret ordered a man named Wright to climb it to catch some young pigeons, but, while using the nesting-holes as footholds, he slipped and was killed.

The seigneur had the right to license a taverner and a baker for his fief; and as late as 1763 his tenants were compelled to make his hay, to cart it, and to thatch it, to fetch his wood and wine and all that the manor needed for repairs, to clean out the colombier when necessary, to place their carts two days every year at his disposal, and to carry him to four ports of Normandy once in each tenant's lifetime. These duties were not peculiar to Samarès, as most of them referred to all other important fiefs.

Deborah Dumaresq, being childless, sold her fief to the Seales, who 15 years later sold it to the Hammonds, who after three generations sold it to the Mourants. They, too, only held it for three generations, when it was bought by a merchant from Japan, who in 1924 sold it to the late Sir James Knott. Each owner in turn altered it, modernised it, added to it, till it has lost all appearance of an ancient house. Only the immense thickness of some of the walls remains to show that part of the old building is still there behind its modern façade.

It was the wealth and enthusiasm of Sir James Knott that created the gardens which are now the glory of the manor. When he bought the estate, the lower part of the grounds was a swamp and Dumaresq's canal was still useful. When Jurat Mourant went to the States in the 1870s, he used to make the first part of the journey by boat and mount his horse on the road. Sir James drained the marsh, and filled in the canal, bringing thousands of cartloads of earth from every parish in the Island. South Europe was ransacked for subtropical plants, and for 40 years 40 gardeners were employed. He is said to have spent £100,000 on his hobby. The result is a garden of outstanding beauty, now run on modern lines, aimed at being self supporting by the sale of produce. The present owner, Mrs E. Obbard, previously Lady Knott, is most generous in lending the grounds for charitable purposes.

Seymour Tower. An islet, called L'Avarizon, lies out at sea about a mile and a quarter from La Rocque Point. Somehow this rock became associated by tradition with the famous Breton, St Samson. We know, from an almost contemporary Latin life of him, that about A.D. 530 he visited Jersey, if only as a recruiting sergeant. In the tribal wars so frequent among the Bretons, Judual, Samson's candidate for the chieftainship, was driven out. "So Samson set out for Lesia [i.e. Guernsey] and Angia [i.e. Jersey], islands of the sea, and, as he was well known to the men who dwell there, they crossed to Brittany with him at his request, and God gave the victory to Judual, and he overthrew the usurper." What St Samson's link with this particular islet may have been no one can now say, but the tradition was long-lived; in 1747, in a case tried before the Royal Court, when the seigneur of La Malletière made good his exclusive right to cut vraic on "the rock called Avallison", one boundary of his property was fixed at "a certain rock called *les Settes Samson*"; and when, in the same century, a redoubt was built on this islet, it was always known as "*le Boulevard St Samson*". And in 1786 the States, considering defence, speak of "the guard house and magazine of St Samson at La Rocque point". The guard house, abutting on to a martello tower, is still there, and part of its walls may be the remains of a chapel dedicated to St Samson. There is a germ of truth at the back of every legend, and behind every place name.

This redoubt may not have been occupied by a permanent garrison, for when in 1781 de Rullecourt was preparing his raid on Jersey, his plan was to land his men on this islet on a moonless night, where any noise that was made would not be heard from the land, and where he would be beyond the range of the shore cannon; he then meant to march at low tide up the narrow channel that led to the harbour, where his approach would be hidden by rocks on either side. But his expedition was delayed by contrary winds, and, when at last he sailed, the state of the tide made it impossible to carry out this plan, and he had to take his boats right up to the shore.

In the year after the raid the States built the present square tower to guard the entrance to the channel, and named it either after General Seymour Conway, the Governor, or after Sir Edward Seymour, Lord Protector, and Governor in 1540, when an earlier tower was built there. The tower is now only used by fishing parties and occasional troops of Boy Scouts.

Trinity Church. This is a church about which history tells us little. In the 11th century a wave of super-orthodoxy swept over Normandy, laying great stress on the teaching of the so-called Athanasian Creed. The result was that churches were no longer dedicated in the name of some saint, but to the Holy Trinity, for example, the great Abbey aux Dames at Caen (1062), the Abbey of Lessay (1080), and the oldest church in Cherbourg. Holy Trinity, Jersey, probably belongs to this period. But the first document to mention it is a charter issued before 1172 by Henry II, in which he gives it to the Abbey of St Helier, which had been founded a few years before where Elizabeth Castle now stands. But this gives no indication as to when the church was built. It may have been 100 years old when it was presented to the monks.

The original little Chapelle de la Sainte Trinité stood on the site of the present chancel. Later a nave was added, then transepts, which gave the building the shape of a cross. A spire was then built, and a Lady Chapel side by side with the chancel. The fine arch in the west wall of the north transept shows that once there must have been a north aisle, but this has entirely disappeared, together with the south transept.

Twice the States met in the church. Once in 1541 to hear a letter from the Earl of Hertford, the Governor: "I am informed that divers inhabitants of the isle do show themselves rather like brute beasts than men in refusing to contribute to such charges as have been thought requisite for the defence of the country." A hundred years later in 1643 they met again in the church, when Captain George Carteret recovered the Island for the King. As the town had strong Parliamentarian sympathies, he chose Trinity as a safer place to be sworn in as Bailiff and Governor.

The Church stands on high ground, and three times in nineteen years the spire was struck by lightning. In 1629 a large part of it was destroyed, which Chevalier the diarist regarded as a manifest sign of God's wrath at "the pontifical grandeur of the Dean". In 1646 it was struck again and more than 12 feet demolished. The repairs had only just been completed when in 1648 a thunderbolt destroyed it as far as the bell, made great holes in the roof, and shattered all the glass in the windows. Yet no one thought of fixing a lightning conductor till 1937.

The finest mural monument in the Island is that to Sir Edouard de

181

Carteret, who was Usher of the Black Rod to Charles II. The quality of the work has suggested the possibility that it was sculptured by Sir Henry or Sir John Cheere, but there is no proof of this whatsoever. He died while on a visit to St Ouen's Manor in 1683. Arrangements had been made to bury him in St Ouen's Church; but, as the procession was about to start, a clap of thunder startled the six horses that drew the hearse, and they could not be checked till they stopped of their own accord at Trinity Church, where the road rises steeply. The mourners, who had followed this mad stampede right across the island, took this as a sign that he wished to be buried in his native parish, and adjourned to the manor while a grave was dug beside his family pew. The funeral was finished by torchlight.

The present church bell bears the inscription, in French, "I was refounded in the year of grace 1690 in the reign of our sovereign William Henry of Nassau and Marie Stuart, King and Queen of Scotland, France, and Ireland." If you wonder which reign this can be, it is what we generally call the reign of William and Mary. But it is rather strange that whoever drew up the inscription completely forgot England. The bell bears the arms of the de Carteret, Lemprière, and Dumaresq families, who happen to have been the most influential names in the Island at that time.

The chancel was once divided from the Lady Chapel by two arches. In 1830 the central pillar was removed and the two arches thrown into one. A ridiculous story has become firmly implanted in parish tradition that this was done surreptitiously in a single night by a family whose view of the pulpit was blocked by this pillar. If they had attempted such a thing, they would probably have brought the roof crashing down on their heads. But the Acts of the Ecclesiastical Assembly show that the alteration was discussed there and duly authorised, and the cost met by the sale of the pew that was placed where the pillar stood. Three parishes in all, St John and St Mary as well as Holy Trinity, have successfully accomplished this rather risky architectural feat.

Trinity has the distinction of owning the earliest piece of silverware in the Island. It is a pre-Reformation chalice, sadly mutilated, but retaining its pristine beauty.

Trinity Manor. The *Franc Fief de la Trinité* is one of the five chief fiefs in the Island. The first place among them has always been conceded to St Ouen, but long and ruinous lawsuits have been fought by the other four—Mélèches, Rozel, Samarès, and Trinity—over their order of precedence. Except, however, for one brief triumph, Trinity has always had to be content with the fifth place.

Its first two manor-houses probably stood opposite the present avenue gates on the other side of the road, for the field there has been known for centuries as Les Grands Manoirs. Of the present building the oldest part, the great hall with the cellars beneath and the bedroom above, is Elizabethan. The arms of de Carteret and Lemprière, the latter using the bearings of the de St Martin family from whom they had inherited the fief and the manor-house, are on the south façade, recording the marriage in 1578 of Amice de Carteret and Catherine Lemprière. Two bays to the west were added in 1642. Benjamin La Cloche's diary says: "In 1641 Amice de Carteret, Seigneur of Trinity, began to build his manor anew. He pulled part of it down in order to reconstruct it; but in October 1642, when the new walls were finished, they fell to the ground." Early in the 19th century the house was doubled in size by the addition of rooms on the north. Between 1910 and 1913 came the great restoration by Mr Athelstan Riley, who, taking over a building that was then practically a ruin, remodelled the whole into the likeness of a French château.

The earliest seigneurs of whom we have record were the de St Martins, who held the fief in the 14th, 15th, and part of the 16th centuries. They provided the Island with four Bailiffs and at least nine Jurats, but they were often under a cloud because of their pro-French sumpathies. The last de St Martin to hold Trinity died childless in 1515, and the fief passed through a nephew to the Lemprières. It was during their régime that the oldest part of the present house was built. The fief possessed two water-mills, the Moulin de Haut and the Moulin de Bas, the latter of which still stands. And, since the fields on the left as you enter the avenue, are known as the Grand Parcq St Maurice, the Petit Parcq St Maurice, and the Pré St Maurice, it is practically certain that a Chapel of St Maurice must once have stood there. One curious condition is attached to this fief. Whenever the sovereign visits the Island, the seigneur must present him with two mallards, a species of duck.

After 85 years the male line of the Lemprières died out, and the fief passed through a married daughter to a branch of the de Carterets of St Ouen, who held it for the next 240 years. It was Amice de Carteret, the third of this line, who rebuilt the manor-house. He took great pride in his grounds. Even the rector of Sark wrote in his diary of the tulips in Trinity Manor, and the peacocks, and the wild duck, and the rabbits of many colours. Amice's younger sister, Marguerite, may have lived with him. In 1646 the Prince of Wales, the future Charles II, then a boy of 15, took refuge in Elizabeth Castle from the victorious Roundheads, and remained there ten weeks. Marguerite, who was then 20, no doubt like other Island ladies made her curtsy to the prince, but for 200 years no one ever breathed a word against her chastity, till in the 19th century a Dr Hoskins of Guernsey started the idea that she had given birth to an illegitimate baby of which the Prince was the father. The story was quickly elaborated. The bed was shown in which they had slept, and the stone table in the garden at which they had revelled; and Marguerite figures as the Prince's mistress in several "historical" novels. Certainly 22 years after the Prince's stay in Jersey a young Jerseyman, Jacques La Cloche, showed to the Jesuits in Rome letters (which on examination prove to be forgeries) in which Charles acknowledged him as "born to us, more through the frailty of early youth than of deliberate wickedness, of a young lady of one of the leading families in our Kingdom". The only arguments brought forward to suggest that this young lady was Marguerite are: (1) that ten years after the Prince's departure she married a man named La Cloche; so if she had an illegitimate son, he might have been called by this name; but this is no proof that such a boy existed; (2) that part of a page has been removed from a Trinity Church register. This may have been cut out by the rector, because he had made some mistake in it, or some lazy solicitor's clerk may have found it easier to rip out an entry than to make a copy of it. But, in any case, it is unlikely that it was done to conceal the birth of a royal baby, for the Prince left the Island in 1646, and the damaged page deals with events in 1648. In any case, Jacques was a mere impostor and no son of the king; and he can never have claimed Marguerite as his mother, for he pretended that his mother's rank entitled him to the throne, which must have meant that she was of royal blood. No girl has ever had her reputation blackened on flimsier evidence.

The next seigneur, also an Amice, died at St Lô in Normandy, and left orders that his heart should be sent home to his native parish. The stump of a broken cross in the garden was supposed to mark the spot where this heart was buried; so the cross was restored, and a suitable inscription placed on it. But this was apparently a mistake; for in the 18th century St Lawrence had a chatty rector, who jotted down in his church register notes on all sorts of subjects. In 1737 he recorded that, when a grave was being dug in Trinity Church for Charles de Carteret, the seigneur, a leaden casket shaped like a heart was discovered, inscribed: "Amice de Carteret, seigneur of Trinity, died at St Lô, 1664, aged 25."

The most famous of the seigneurs was Admiral Philippe de Carteret, who on his voyage round the world in the little *Swallow* between 1766 and 1769 discovered and annexed for the Crown dozens of Pacific islands. His sister Anne kept house for him at Trinity while he was at sea, and on his return the manor was his home for 11 years, and the flag of the *Swallow* floated above the roof. Then the revolt of the American colonies recalled him to active service, and the manor was let to the Government for 100 guineas a year as a barrack. The result was disastrous. Three years later his solicitor wrote that the soldiers had broken the windows, burnt the banisters, smashed the furniture, destroyed the table-linen, and allowed the garden to become a wilderness of weeds. Nevertheless his son came to live in it, and, when he died, it passed first to a sister, who had married Sir William Symonds, then to another, who had married a Swiss nobleman, the Comte de St Georges. He and his son and grandson became seigneurs of Trinity, but they lived in Switzerland and left the care of their Jersey estate to an agent, and the fine old house began to fall badly into disrepair. In 1872 a Colonel Swan bought it, but, when his son inherited it, he soon ceased to live in it, and through neglect it rapidly became uninhabitable. When Mr Athelstan Riley bought it in 1909, the greater part had to be gutted, leaving nothing but the walls. The restoration was carried out by Sir Reginald Blomfield. Entirely new are the chapel, which was consecrated by the Bishop of Winchester in 1914, the colombier, the entrance court with its fountain which is a copy of a 17th century fountain at Lucerne, the porch, the east wing with its offices and kitchen, the library, the winter garden, the high roof and chimneys. The result is an extremely handsome mansion, though critics have been heard to lament that a typical old Jersey manor has been transformed into a French château. In order to have weathered stone available he bought a ruined house, L'Ancienneté in St Brelade, and incorporated its splendid fireplace in the dining room, the tourelle staircase in the garden, and the window surrounds in the various additions.

Trinity Parish. A large parish, of which the coast-line runs from the northernmost brook in Rozel Bay, round Bouley Bay and Belle Hougue Point, till it meets St John in the middle of Havre Giffard. Its southern boundary divides it from St Helier near the second milestone from the Royal Square. Previous articles have described BOULEY BAY, TRINITY CHURCH, and TRINITY MANOR; and Le Câtel or Cæsar's Camp, one of many examples of rendering to Cæsar things that were never his, has been discussed in the article on ROZEL BAY.

Prehistoric remains are not very plentiful here. At Les Platons, the highest point in the Island, 534 feet above sea-level, a large mound was found to cover a small cist containing two urns, in one of which were the half-cremated bones of a woman and a child. On a ridge of rock overlooking Vicard is a stone 15 feet by 13, called La Pierre de la Fételle. This looks uncommonly like a fallen menhir, and the field is known as Le Clos de la Pouquelaye, but it rests on solid rock, in which it would be impossible to dig a tomb. A farm in the south of the parish is called La Blanche Pierre Farm, and here a large stone, which is now built into the garden wall, is almost certainly a fallen menhir, for it is of a kind of diorite that is found nowhere nearer than the Hermitage.

An interesting find was, however, made at Belle Hougue. This wild windswept promontory is one of the finest viewpoints in the Island, and some students, scrambling down its eastern cliffs in 1914, found a narrow cave 33 yards long, containing the best local examples of stalactites and stalagmites. The entrance had been concealed by an ancient fall in the roof, but this same fall opened a shaft down which it is possible to climb. Here were discovered antlers, teeth, and bones of some small prehistoric deer, of a sub-species unknown elsewhere, which has been named *Cervus elaphus jerseyensis*. There were also quantities of sea gravel containing shells, including one species only found in warmer waters than ours. There are no human remains at all, and these animal relics probably date from a period between the two inhabited eras at La Cotte, say approximately an interglacial period of about 75,000 B.C. A surprising find was a polished stone axe of Neolithic period, but this must have been dropped there by man, thousands of years later. In 1965 a second cave with stalactites and deer remains, was found. Although not yet excavated, it seems highly probable that there was also a pre-historic or iron age promontory fort here, and this belief is supported by field name evidence.

On the promontory itself is a mineral spring known as La Fon-taine ès Mittes. One early writer declared that it had "the miracu-lous power of loosening the tongue, nay even of giving speech to the dumb, provided that the draught be taken before sunrise". It is, not surprisingly, the subject of a legend, and the water was, until modern times, believed to be good for eye complaints. On analysis it is found to contain chlorides, sulphates, and carbonates of sodium, calcium, and magnesium.

On a farm called Les Câteaux is all that remains of a great earth-work, which a contract of 1382 calls Le Chastel Sedement, "though," wrote Poingdestre in 1682, "who this Sedement was or when he lived appears not". It was a high embankment surrounded by a moat, which enclosed about 20 acres, and provided a camp of refuge, where thousands of people could seek safety when raiders overran the Island. In the centre was a keep as a place of retreat should the outer rampart be stormed. Since there would be huts for the women and children, it could reasonably be called a *ville*. When Hector de Pontbriant and Pero Niño landed in 1406 and won the Battle of the Dunes, Niño learnt from his prisoners (so his armour-bearer tells us) that "the other folk were in a *ville*, the largest in the Island, enclosed with palisades and moats filled with water, wherein they had their goods, wives, and children, and that those who had escaped from the battle had also retreated thither, and moreover that they held inflexibly to a rule that, if anyone tried to seize it, they must die to the last man, before this was permitted". Next day he marched north to reconnoitre, and envoys from the camp met him: "We are sent to tell you that this *ville* is our peculiar possession. Never has Frenchman or Englishman ever entered therein; and we are sworn in no wise to yield it either to friend or foe, while a single one of us is alive. If you ask gold or silver, we will give what we can. But draw not near our *ville*. Even if you chance to take it, it will cost you many a life; and you will have to kill every man, woman, and child therein, and that will be a weight on your conscience that God will never forgive." In the end the raiders accepted a ransom of 10,000 golden crowns, and sailed away down the Channel.

There were other manors in the parish besides the one described in the last article. The largest of these was Diélament. The origin of the name is obscure. One guess is that it was originally Le Manoir de Gilles Hamon. In the 14th century it belonged to the de Barentins, three of whom became Wardens of the Isles. In 1413 it was bought by the Lemprières of Rozel for 1,000 crowns and 2 pipes of Gascony wine, and they held it for more than five centuries. When they lost Rozel in 1534, they made Diélament their home; but when they regained Rozel by marriage in the 18th century, they rebuilt that manor and went to live there. Later they sold the house at Diélament, but retained the fief. The colombier, which is the largest in the Island, was rebuilt in 1573 on the foundations of one that is mentioned in 1409. The fine 17th century gateway, which was once linked to the house by a noble avenue of trees, now stands forlorn in an open field. The house itself has been so modernised that little that is ancient remains.

Another interesting house is that known as Augrès Manor. The fief of Augrès is in a different part of the parish, and this house actually stands on the fief of Diélament. In 1634, however, Elie Dumaresq, whose family had dwelt here for more than a century, bought the fief of Augrès; but, as he and his descendants continued to live in their old home, this became called Augrès Manor. The walled courtyard with its arched entries, bearing the Dumaresq arms, dates from the 16th century, but the old house was pulled down in 1771, when the present house was built. The cross over the main entrance may have come from La Croix Jehannet, and the stone on one of the outbuildings with a cross and the letters "S.T." stand, perhaps for Sainte Trinité. The grounds now contain a zoo, connected with the Jersey Wildlife Preservation Trust, which, under the inspired leadership of Gerald Durrell, zoologist and writer, seeks to preserve all forms of wild life which are in danger of extinction.

Like other parishes in the Middle Ages, Trinity had its chantry chapels—St Maur, on the site of Rose Cottage, St Symphorian, and St Cosme, as well as the manorial chapels at Trinity Manor, dedicated to St Maurice, and at Diélament Manor, dedicated to La Vierge. And there were as usual a number of wayside crosses—Les Hautes Croix in the Vingtaine de Ville à l'Evêque, La Croix in the Vingtaine des Augrès, La Croix du Pot du Rocher in the Vingtaine de Rozel, the Cross near Trinity Manor, and La Croix du Sacrement. The Vingtaine de Ville à l'Evêque took its name from the Bishop of Avranches, who held *"Le fief qui fut à l'Evêque d'Avranches"*, an area now often referred to as Bishopstown, from this origin.

In 1769 Trinity became famous for a successful revolt. Charles Lemprière of Rozel and a junta of Jurats were ruling the Island as dictators; but the men of Trinity held secret meetings and drew up 13 demands, which included a reduction in the price of corn (an unexpected proposal to come from a farming parish), a reduction in the Crown tithes, and the abolition of seigneurial rights. The leader was Thomas Jacques Gruchy, a well-to-do farmer, churchwarden, and militia captain. Three hundred men armed with bludgeons marched into the town, and men from other parishes joined them. They forced their way into the Court, where the Assize d'Héritage was sitting, threw the usher over the railings, and banged on the benches with their cudgels, uttering such bloodcurdling threats that the terrified Jurats granted all their demands. Three days later, however, the States fled to Elizabeth Castle, and sent a deputation to Westminster, complaining that the mob had caused the King's laws to be erased from the Statute Book. Colonel Bentinck was sent as Royal Commissioner to investigate, and he saw at once that drastic reforms were needed. He proclaimed an amnesty and released Gruchy and all who were in prison for their share in the revolt. The Trinity Three Hundred had cleared the ground for the building of a democratic constitution, which resulted in the Code of 1771, clarifying and stabilising the Island's laws.

The States run a modern agricultural advisory and research station, situated near the parish church, which was among the many benefactions of the late T. B. Davis, and given in memory of his son, who was killed in World War I.

Victoria College. From an educational point of view Jersey has always been fortunate. As far back as 1477 Jehan Hue, rector of St Saviour's, founded and endowed a grammar school, which he attached to the chantry chapel of St Mannelier in his parish. And a "grammar school" in those days always meant one in which Latin grammar was taught. Nineteen years later two Jerseymen, who had prospered in England, Jean Néel, who had become senior chaplain in the household of the young Prince of Wales, and Vincent Téhy, who was twice mayor of Southampton, increased the endowment of St Mannelier, and founded a second grammar school for the western parishes next door to the chapel of St Anastase. Both schools survived till the middle of the 19th century, but were always crippled by lack of adequate funds, their staffs seldom being larger than a regent and an usher. Yet they did good work. The long Latin inscriptions in our parish churches (e.g. on the tombs of John Poindexter at St Saviour's, Laurens Hamptonne at St Lawrence, and Sir Edouard de Carteret in Trinity) show that long before Victoria College was founded the Island had no lack of competent Latinists.

In 1636 the Charles I scholarships, covering both Jersey and Guernsey, were founded, originally being termed fellowships. They were to send local boys to university, being allocated one each to Exeter, Jesus, and Pembroke Colleges, Oxford, the intention being that such scholars should take holy orders, and return to serve the Island as rectors. The Don Baudains Trust, founded in 1611, had the same objective. Many local boys have profited from these benefactions, but they are no longer exclusively for careers in the Church.

But in the 17th century Sir George Carteret felt that something larger was needed. In 1669 he persuaded Charles II to issue an Order in Council: "There are wanting three things especially necessary. First, a College where the Islanders may have fitting Education without much expense"; and he authorised the Court to impose import duties on wines and spirits and to set aside 2,000 livres tournois of the amount annually "towards the erecting of the said School, College, or Academy". The money was raised, but it was used for various public works, like the building of the pier at St Aubin which seemed more urgent, and in time the college was forgotten.

But in 1846, when the young Queen Victoria thrilled the Island by

her visit, the States decided that some lasting memorial must commemorate this event. Various plans found eager advocates, but
General Helier Touzel urged persistently the revival of Carteret's
scheme for a college. He converted the Lieutenant-Governor, and
he won over the assembly of Governor, Bailiff, and Jurats, which at
this time adminstered the Impôt. The States, though unanimous in
the desire to build the college, disagreed over the amount of land
to be purchased: the Bailiff gave the casting vote for the larger
amount.

A joint committee of the assembly and the States then got to
work. They engaged Mr J. Hayward as architect. They bought a
fine estate on the edge of the town known as Mount Pleasant. They
built their college of grey granite on the brow of the hill, but they
made a mistake in using Caen sandstone for the quoins, for this has
not stood up well to the Jersey climate. They left standing the
Greek Temple, an eighteenth century "folly" that had been built as
a smoking-room in the grounds, an interesting relic of the days when
no gentleman would contaminate with tobacco a house in which
ladies were living. Then came the appointment of a headmaster.
One of the rejected candidates was Dr Westcott, who later became
the famous Bishop of Durham. But their choice was a happy one,
Dr Henderson, a Fellow of Magdalen College, Oxford, who later
became Dean of Carlisle.

The college opened on September 29, 1852, with a salute of 21
guns; 109 boys were enrolled, and this number rapidly increased
to 223, and it has now increased to 560, including the preparatory
department. All wore a black or dark green jacket, waistcoat, and
trousers, and a mortarboard. The Queen took a personal interest
in the school that was called by her name. She presented copies of
portraits by Winterhalter of herself and Prince Albert, which hang
in the Assembly Hall. She endowed an exhibition to be held at one
of the universities. She gave three gold medals annually for classics,
mathematics, and modern languages, and later added £10 worth of
books for the best historian.

Dr Henderson found that the new school presented many problems. What, for example, should be done about the difference
between English and Jersey weights and measures? Indignant parents protested against false information being stuffed into their boys'
heads by English arithmetic books, when everyone knew that in

Jersey 13 pence made a shilling and 11 inches a foot. But he gradually overcame his difficulties, and he and his successor, Dr Cleave, managed to establish an amazingly high standard of scholarship. A glance at the honours' boards on the school walls shows that in those early days Victorians gained six fellowships at Oxford, 17 of the big university prizes, 23 first classes, and 24 open scholarships, a record which probably no other school of the same size could surpass. The grounds became the townsfolk's fashionable promenade, and the regimental band used to play in them once a week.

Many additions have been made to the buildings in recent years. Among others, a boarding-house was built in 1899. In 1911 five new classrooms and two laboratories were added. In 1922 the preparatory school, which had begun as a private venture, was taken over by the States as an integral part of the school. In 1924 the Sir Galahad statue was unveiled as a memorial to the 128 Old Victorians who fell in World War I. In 1935 the Howard Hall was presented by Mr T. B. Davis in memory of his son Howard who was killed in the war. Then in 1952 the Old Victorians Assocation erected an art school in the grounds to commemorate those who lost their lives in World War II, and a school pavilion was presented by the Laurens family in memory of their son. In 1963 a swimming pool, built mainly through contributions from Old Boys, was completed in memory of A. H. Worrall, a former headmaster. Enlargements are continuing all the time to this, and indeed to all the local schools, in an effort to keep up with the increased population, and the intensified desire for education.

In 1919 the old endowments of St Mannelier and St Anastase were turned into bursaries to enable promising boys from the elementary schools to receive free education at the college. On the eve of the German Occupation, about 40 of the boys left the Island with their parents, and were hospitably received as members of Bedford School; but the majority remained in Jersey. The Germans took over the college buildings for their Hitler Youth Cadets, and the local boys and masters had to migrate to the Halkett Place Elementary School; but work went on as usual. When the Liberation came, the school rapidly recovered, and soon had 520 pupils. The Jersey College for Girls, which was founded in 1880, was taken over by the Education Committee in 1936, and is now run as a sister institution to Victoria College.

Westmount. A steep hill on the west of the town 250 feet high. It is now laid out as a public recreation ground, and from its summit a magnificient view of the bay can be obtained; but till recently it was always known as Gallows Hill, or, in French, Le Mont ès Pendus or Le Mont Patibulaire, the Mount of Hanging. Four gaunt pillars crowned the hill, where a little summer-house now stands, four to show that these were the King's gallows. Seigneurs who had hanging rights were only allowed two. At first these pillars were of wood, but in 1632 they were replaced by columns of solid granite at the request of the eloquent attorney-general, who amused the Court by pleading: "Then they will last for ever and serve for us and our children." Across two of these a beam was fixed when there was an execution, and executions were frequent in those days, when one could be hanged for a theft of anything worth more than a shilling. The Island kept a permanent executioner or, as he preferred to be called, *Maître des Hautes Œuvres*, who was given a cottage near Bel Royal and 25 crowns a year, and collected threepence from every stall-keeper in the market after each execution, and retained the clothes of the criminal. The last was a valuable perquisite, for the dead man's relations would often buy them back at an exorbitant price to prevent the body being left dangling on the gibbet naked.

Executions always took place on market day, and were proclaimed in all the churches on the previous Sunday. They were made as public as possible, in order that everyone might be reminded that the wages of sin is death. Schoolmasters were ordered to close their schools and bring all their pupils to see what lawbreaking leads to. The prisoner was marched by halberdiers from the prison to the hill, except in the case of exceptionally atrocious crimes, when he was dragged on a hurdle to show that he was deemed unworthy to tread this earth. On at least two occasions the solemn ritual of the ceremony was rudely interrupted. In 1640 a desperate ruffian threw the hangman off the scaffold, and swarmed up a pillar of the gallows and dared anyone to fetch him down. The Vicomte prodded him off his perch with the scaffold ladder, and he fell with the halter round his neck, and so he was duly hanged; but the question was seriously debated whether the Vicomte had committed murder, for no one but the official executioner is authorised to take a life. In 1807, when a soldier was hanged for robbing a watch-maker, he seemed such a long time dying that the hangman, to hasten the process, swung on to his legs. This caused the rope to stretch, and the soldier's feet touched the ground, and he slipped the halter off with his own hands. He received the King's pardon.

The last execution on this spot was in 1829, when Philippe Jolin paid the penalty for the murder of his father. An immense crowd covered the hill. He made a speech from the scaffold: "You see to what a state I have been brought by drink. Yes, it is the drink that has been the cause of all my troubles. I recognise the justice of my sentence, etc., etc." Then a white bag was slipped over his head. The Burial Service was read; the bolt was drawn, and the trap-door on which he was standing fell, and he was left dangling. This was still considered an edifying spectacle. One local paper wrote: "Let us hope that the execution of this terrible sentence has touched the hearts of parents, and taught them a stern lesson that will lead them to control their children's actions with stricter vigilance. Pray God above all that the young people present may profit by it."

But Westmount has other memories. When the French took the town by surprise in 1781, five companies of the 78th Highlanders were billeted in the hospital. They at once marched out and took up a strong position on Gallows Hill. Here, as soon as the news was known in the country parishes, about 2,000 militiamen hurried up to join them, some in complete battalions, others singly.

When Major Peirson arrived from St Peter with five companies of the 95th Foot, he took command, arranged the guns, which some of the companies had brought, on the hill to cover his retreat, if one should become necessary. He marched across the sand-dunes into the town, which did not then extend beyond Charing Cross, and fought and won the Battle of Jersey.

In the early part of the 19th century, before the sea-wall was built or Victoria Avenue, Clark's large ship-building yards covered the ground where the Lower Park is now. In 1857, when Robert Pipon Marett, who later became Bailiff, was Constable of St Helier, he obtained permission from the seigneur of Mélèches, in whose fief the hill was, to plant the common with trees. Knowing how difficult it was to persuade the parish assembly to agree to any improvement, he did this entirely on his own responsibility without consulting them. This naturally roused resentment, but before long even his critics had to acknowledge that he had made a great addition to the amenities of the town. In 1865 the assembly bought the common and the hill for £4,000 to be converted into a public park. In 1883 the old name of Gallows Hill was discarded, and it was officially rechristened Westmount. To end on a note of gaiety, it is along Victoria Avenue at the foot of Westmount that the Battle of Flowers takes place each summer. With a somewhat misleading title this annual carnival has become famous, and attracts enormous crowds. The decorated floats are entered by parishes, societies, groups, or individuals, and incredible skill and ingenuity are shown in preparing these displays, which are entirely made of flowers, hydrangeas, gladioli, marigolds, asters, and many others. There are also usually some life-like animals modelled in hare's tail grass (*Lagurus ovatus*). It is a gay and colourful sight, and the highlight of the visitor season.

SOME UNFAMILIAR TERMS IN USE IN JERSEY

ASSIZE D'HÉRITAGE. A sitting of the Heritage division of the Royal Court at which certain seigneurs attend and answer in affirmation that they owe suit of court for their fiefs. Included among them is the Lieutenant-Governor who answers for the escheated ecclesiastical fiefs which became Crown property.

BAILIFF (*Bailli*). Chief Magistrate of the Island. President of the Royal Court and the States.

BAILIWICK. A district administered by a Bailiff. In the Channel Islands there are two, one being Jersey with the outlying dependencies of Les Ecréhous and Les Minquiers, and the second comprising Guernsey with the other islands.

BÉNITIER. A carved stone alcove found in some old Jersey houses, about 20 examples being recorded. Probably a piscina removed from a parish church or a small chapel at the Reformation.

CALVINISM. A form of Protestantism originated by John Calvin, a Frenchman, with a Presbyterian form of Church government, which laid great stress on moral discipline administered by the Church Courts.

CENTENIERS. The second rank in the honorary parochial police force, elected for three years to be the Constable's chief assistants. Originally in charge of 100 homesteads. A Centenier may represent his Constable in the States.

CHANTRY CHAPEL. A private mediaeval chapel, sometimes attached to a church and sometimes a separate building, built that Masses might be sung in it for the founder's family.

CIST. A prehistoric tomb built of small stone slabs in the form of a box.

CLAMEUR DE HARO. See page 5.

COLOMBIER. A large stone tower containing hundreds of nesting-holes for pigeons, which certain manors were allowed to erect in their grounds.

CONSTABLE (*Connétable*). The civic head of each parish, who represents it in the States, presides over the Parish Assembly, and is

196

head of the parish police. There is no similarity with the English word Constable.

CÔTIL. A steep hill-side, generally covered with gorse and heather, but sometimes cultivated, and when it is, providing early land in compensation for the difficulties of working small patches of steep sloping ground.

DOLMEN. A prehistoric tomb built of large stone slabs in the form of a table. Usually of Neolithic date.

EXTENTE. A list of the revenues due to the Crown, with many details. Those of 1274, 1331, 1528, 1607, 1668, and 1749 have been published. This is a local Doomsday book.

FIEF. An estate held from the Crown on condition that certain services were rendered.

GOVERNOR or LIEUTENANT-GOVERNOR. The King's Representative in the Island. The last Governor was Lord Beresford, who died in 1854, and since then the Crown has been represented by a Lieutenant-Governor only.

JURATS (*Jurés Justiciers*). Twelve honorary elected Judges, who with the Bailiff form the Royal Court. Before 1948 they also had seats in the States.

LIVRES, sols, deniers tournois. Money minted at Tours and current in Jersey until 1834. The livre tournois was worth only a few shillings.

MEGALITHS. A general term covering any form of prehistoric structure formed of large stones.

MENHIR. A single standing stone of prehistoric date, marking burials or some other sacred site, though sometimes they may have been boundary stones.

MILITIA. For 600 years service in this was compulsory for all able-bodied men and was unpaid. In 1924 this was made a volunteer force, which served in World War II. In 1954 an Act of the States repealed all the militia laws.

NEOLITHIC. Belonging to the New Stone Age, which lasted in Jersey from about 3000 to 1800 B.C., when ground or polished stone implements prevailed.

PALAEOLITHIC. Belonging to the Old Stone Age, about 100,000 to 50,000 B.C.

PASSAGE-GRAVE. A prehistoric tomb of the Neolithic period in which an entrance-passage leads to a burial chamber.

PERQUAGE. A Sanctuary Path from a church to the sea on which a fugitive from the law was safe from arrest, before the Reformation, and again during Mary Tudor's short reign. These paths always followed a stream but did not necessarily take a direct route.

PISCINA. A stone basin in a church wall near the altar at which the priest washed his hands and sometimes the sacred vessels.

RENTE. Interest payable on a loan, the security being real estate. The amount due was paid in kind, usually in wheat, in the past, and for a long time continued to be calculated according to the price of wheat each year.

ROYAL COURT. The Court of Justice composed of the Bailiff and the twelve Jurats.

SEIGNEURS. Lords of the manors.

STATES (*États*). The Island Parliament, consisting before 1948 of Jurats, Rectors, Constables, and Deputies; since 1948 of Senators, Constables, and Deputies.

TOURELLE. Circular stone newel staircase within a round or square tower, at the back of many local houses. Such stairs ceased to be built early in the 18th century and were gradually replaced by wooden staircases.

VERGÉE. A land-measure of about 2,150 English square yards: two and a quarter Jersey vergées are roughly an English acre.

VINGTAINE. A subdivision of a parish. St Saviour has six vingtaines, St Peter five, St Mary only two.

VINGTENIERS. The third rank in the honorary parochial police force. Also they assist the Constable in collecting the parish rates.

VRAIC. Local seaweed (*Fucus vesiculosus*, *Fucus serratus*, and *Fucus nodosus*, and most valuable of all, *Laminaria digitata*, *Laminaria bulbosa*, and *Laminaria saccharina*), gathered in large quantities and used for manure.

SOME MODERN BOOKS THAT WILL GIVE ADDITIONAL INFORMATION

A Chronology of Jersey. R. Mollet (Société Jersiaise).

A History of Jersey from the Cave Men to the German Occupation and After. G. R. Balleine (Staples).

A Biographical Dictionary of Jersey. G. R. Balleine (Staples).

Archaeology of the Channel Islands, Vol. II: *The Bailiwick of Jersey.* Jacquetta Hawkes (Société Jersiaise).

The Medieval Administration of the Channel Islands, 1199–1399. J. H. Le Patourel (Oxford University Press).

The Channel Islands under Tudor Government, 1485–1642. A. J. Eagleston (Cambridge University Press).

The Town of St. Helier. E. T. Nicolle (Société Jersiaise).

Mont Orgueil Castle: its History and Description. E. T. Nicolle (Société Jersiaise).

Gorey Castle: Official Guide. N. V. L. Rybot (States of Jersey).

The Islet of St. Helier and Elizabeth Castle. N. V. L. Rybot (States of Jersey).

Charles II in the Channel Islands. S. E. Hoskins (Bentley).

Surprise de Jersey en 1781. M. Perrot (Berger-Levrault, Paris).

Jersey Under the Swastika. R. Mollet (Hyperion Press).

The German Occupation of Jersey. L. P. Sinel ("Evening Post", Jersey).

Jersey Folk-lore. J. H. L'Amy (Bigwood, Jersey).

A Flora of the Island of Jersey. L. V. Lester Garland (Newman).

Islands in Danger (German Occupation). A. & M. Wood (Evans).

Jersey, Ile Agricole Anglo Normande. P. Dalido (Chaumerox, Vannes).

Jersey, Our Island. S. W. Bisson (The Batchworth Press).

Old Jersey Houses. Joan Stevens. (Commerical Art Company, Jersey).

Dictionnaire Jersiais-Français. F. Le Maistre. (Don Balleine Trust, Jersey).

Medieval Land Tenures. G. F. B. de Gruchy. (Bigwood, Jersey).

INDEX

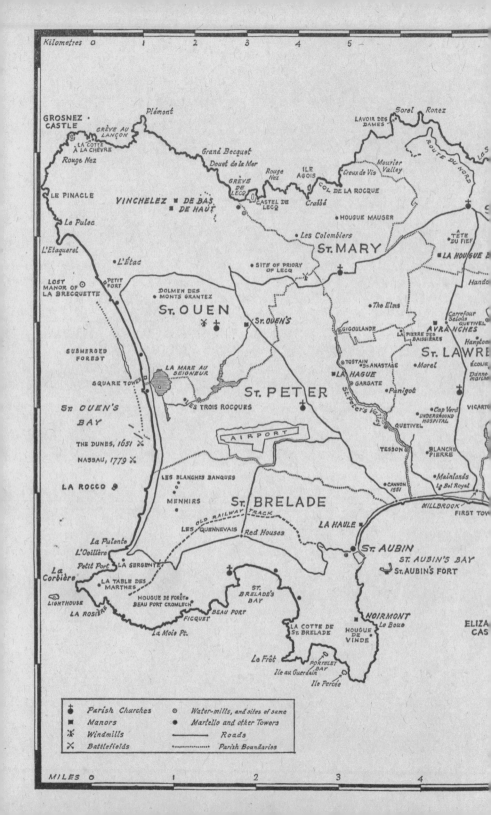